What I Have Learned

What I Have Learned

THINKING ABOUT THE FUTURE THEN AND NOW

EDITED BY **Michael Marien**
AND **Lane Jennings**

 Greenwood Press

NEW YORK · WESTPORT, CONNECTICUT · LONDON

Library of Congress Cataloging-in-Publication Data

What I have learned.

Bibliography: p.
Includes index.
1. Forecasting. I. Marien, Michael. II. Jennings,
Lane.
CB158.W52 1987 303.4'9 86–14958
ISBN 0–313–25071–5 (lib. bdg. : alk. paper)

Library of Congress Catalog Card Number: 86–14958
ISBN: 0–313–25071–5

First published in 1987

Greenwood Press, Inc.
88 Post Road West, Westport, Connecticut 06881

Printed in the United States of America

The paper used in this book complies with the
Permanent Paper Standard issued by the National
Information Standards Organization (Z39.48–1984).

10 9 8 7 6 5 4 3 2 1

Copyright Acknowledgments

The following have given permission to reprint previously
copyrighted essays:

Chapters 1, 2, 3, 4, and 13 appeared originally in the *World
Future Society Bulletin*. Copyright 1984 by the World Future
Society. Chapters 10 and 14 appeared originally in the *Futures
Research Quarterly*. Copyright 1985 by the World Future Society.
Reprinted, with changes, by permission of the publisher. Those
who wish to obtain further information on the World Future Society
may write to: 4916 St. Elmo Avenue, Bethesda, MD 20814–5089.

Chapter 7 has been adapted from an article in *Futures* (1985).
Copyright 1985 by Donald N. Michael. Reprinted by permission
of the author.

CONTENTS

PART III: REFLECTIONS ON LEARNING

Michael Marien and Lane Jennings

INTRODUCTION

Over the past twenty years, "futurist" has become a familiar term, suggesting someone who thinks about possible, probable, or preferable futures, and the assumptions that we make in imagining these varied futures for people, communities, institutions, technologies, and societies. Earlier in this century, a "futurist" was a member of an art movement that extolled the modern, and "futuristic" is still widely used to suggest that which is seemingly ahead of its time, especially as concerns awesome technology. But contrary to these older meanings, today's serious futurist is likely to take a balanced or neutral view of modernity and new technology or, if value judgments are expressed, is apt to be more critical than supportive.

The contemporary notion of the futurist grew out of a cultural vogue in the late 1960s and early 1970s, fueled by the Commission on the Year 2000, the formation of the World Future Society in the United States and Futuribles in France, and publication of *The Year 2000* (1967), *Future Shock* (1970), *The Limits to Growth* (1972), and many other books explicitly about futures themes.

In his introduction to a collection of readings entitled *The Futurists* (Random House, 1972), Alvin Toffler stated:

The word now denotes a growing school of social critics, scientists, philosophers, planners, and others who concern themselves with the alternatives facing man as the human race collides with an onrushing future ... today's futurists, for the most part, lay no claim to the ability to predict. Wary of dogmatic statements about what "will" happen, they focus, rather, on the array of alternatives open to decision-makers, stressing that the future is fluid, not fixed or frozen. . . . Some are driven by a passionate wish to induce social change ... others are more preoccupied by the methods with which we generate images. . . . Still others are intellectually fascinated by questions having to do with time and knowledge.

The variety in the interests and values of futurists still persists, as the essays in this book should make abundantly clear.

But what has changed since 1972 is the nature of the "futures movement." In introducing *The Futurists*, Toffler enthusiastically described the modern futurist movement as having "spread rapidly around the globe," with futures-oriented institutes, seminars, conferences, clubs, and classes "springing up everywhere." Toffler felt at that time that throughout the world of higher learning, "some of the new energies flowing into 'futuristic studies' are spilling over into and influencing the social sciences, the humanities, and other disciplines." Indeed, he went on to edit another volume, *Learning for Tomorrow* (1974), to serve as a "manifesto" for those who wish to see the future introduced into education at all levels—a book intended to help serious educators "smash the disciplinary conventions."

The activity and enthusiasm of the late 1960s and early 1970s have not continued into the 1980s to any substantial degree. The "disciplinary conventions" of academia, which inhibit most serious thinking about the future, are still alive and well. Membership in the World Future Society has declined since its peak in 1980. Futures-oriented institutes and conferences come and go but appear to be no greater in number, staffing, or attendance than in the 1970s, and their focus is more on matters of narrow and immediate policy. Futuristic studies, or futures studies, as an academic topic has not taken hold to any serious degree; although there is a scattering of successful courses and small programs, energies and interests have been dissipated into such concerns as policy studies, peace studies, environmental studies, and women's studies.

In the mid–1980s there are still thinkers who call themselves futurists, or who view themselves with multiple identities, including that of "futurist." Yet it is worth noting that even in our overly bureaucratized and credentialized society, there are no qualifications for being a futurist. A futurist is simply someone who calls himself or herself by that title, or who is seen as such. They may have wise insights into what is happening in today's society, what may happen, or how we can take more effective action. Or their views may be foolish or dangerous. A futurist has no monopoly on wisdom and foresight, but those who spend some time in this broad area of concern may be able to offer some guidance to those who have only recently begun to think about futures-related questions.

Of necessity, many people are thinking about the future or acting to shape it. Relatively few of these people identify themselves as futurists. For those who wish to do so, membership in the World Future Society, a nonprofit association for the study of alternative futures, is open to anyone for the modest fee of twenty-five dollars a year. The World Future Society also offers a Professional Membership, which includes a subscription to *Futures Research Quarterly*. Similar to the lack of any qualifications for being a "futurist," a "professional futurist" is also a matter of self-selection and is open to anyone. There are perhaps several hundred "professional" futurists in the United States and possibly twice that number in Europe and Japan, with a sprinkling in Second and Third World nations. The World Futures Studies Federation, which roughly approximates a global professional organization, had about 425 members as of late 1985.

There is an abundance of literature that can be called futures-relevant, but as a whole, it does not constitute a "field," let alone a "discipline," deserving the suffix of "-ology," as in "futurology." There is no futurology, only a disparate scattering of futurists, with little or no common background, who engage in a variety of activities.

The quantity and quality of futurists, professional futurists, and futures literature are thus ambiguous. It is clear, though, that the futures vogue of the late 1960s and early 1970s has passed. There is no longer the robust sense of a snowballing movement. Some may see the "movement" at middle age, or merely at a plateau. Others may acknowledge decline because of the rise of conservative thinkers, accompanied by the death of many leading figures of the futures movement, e.g., Herman Kahn, Buckminster Fuller, John McHale, Margaret Mead, Marshall McLuhan, E. F. Schumacher, Erich Jantsch, Geoffrey Vickers, Constantinos Doxiadis, Dennis Gabor, and Aurelio Peccei. A new futures vogue—not necessarily with "futures" in its titling—could very well take shape as the millennial year 2000 approaches. The new futurism might seek to cooperate with the conventional academic disciplines, rather than "smash" them in 1960s rage. Intelligent thinking about the complex and interrelated problems of the present moment, as well as the future, is needed today, more than ever. But for the moment there is a relative lull in futurist activity per se. It is a time for reflection.

Such is the background out of which the idea for this book was born. Michael Marien, who calls himself a social scientist and a futurist, is the founding editor of *Future Survey*, an abstract journal of futures-relevant literature published by the World Future Society since 1979. Lane Jennings, a journalist and poet, who views himself as a futurist "outsider," was editor of the *World Future Society Bulletin*, the predecessor professional publication to *Futures Research Quarterly*. Marien had made several contributions to the *Bulletin*, and Jennings continues to supervise the production of *Future Survey*. Both of us were concerned about the quantity and quality of contributions to the *Bulletin*.

The specific origin of this book can be precisely traced to the back seat of a Chevrolet in the middle of Minnesota. Michael Marien was in the front seat, being driven to an October 1983 meeting of the Itasca Seminar in Brainerd, Minnesota. Donald Michael was in the back seat. Marien had been thinking about a series of articles by well-seasoned futurists to enhance the *WFS Bulletin*. He turned to Don Michael and proposed that Michael would be an exemplary futurist to lead off a series on "What I Have Learned," in that Michael has frequently stressed the theme of learning.

With characteristic enthusiasm for shaping a better future, Michael responded (as recollection goes): "That's a marvelous idea; it should be a book." The logic was hard to resist.

The idea of a book, rather than a mere series of articles, rapidly took shape at this point. Lane Jennings agreed to collaborate in editorial duties. A key contributor, Kenneth Boulding, agreed to write an essay, adding that the notion of "a clouded crystal ball anthology" was intriguing. Other informal queries received similar enthusiastic responses.

Formal invitations were then sent to forty-four leading American futurists, selected from the World Future Society's directory, *The Future: A Guide to Information Sources*. We intentionally did not invite futurists from Canada, Europe, or elsewhere simply because of the large number of Americans who deserved to be invited. Perhaps this book might stimulate a European, Asian, or Third World book.

The invitation read as follows:

We want contributors who were prominent leaders of futures-oriented thinking during the "futures vogue" of the 1960s and early 1970s. How has the realized future of the 1980s differed from what you anticipated and/or advocated? What have you learned since the 1960s about social change and non-change, thought and action, ideals and realities, hopes and fears?

About a dozen invitees were never heard from. We received several polite "Thank you but I'm much too busy" notes. One well-known futurist responded that "I still stand by what I wrote a dozen or so years ago." Several others promised an essay but were unable to write anything, or anything that we found useful for this book.

From an initial list of forty-four invitees, we thus have ended with sixteen contributions by seventeen contributors. The essays are arranged in three groups.

Part I largely focuses on updates and revisions of previous thinking. W. Warren Wagar uses his own intellectual autobiography to illustrate the dependence of futures studies on present-day structures of belief, concluding that images of the future are sure to keep changing in rough synchronism with values of the societies of the image-makers. Based on his new understanding, Wagar discusses three long-term paths to the future: the final consolidation of the capitalist world-economy, to be followed by socialism and then by eco-decentralism.

A more problematic future is described by Kenneth E. Boulding, who reassesses three traps—the war trap, the population trap, and the entropy trap—that he first identified in *The Meaning of the Twentieth Century* (1964). To these continuing problems he adds several more: the one-world trap, the profit-minus-interest trap, the cost-maximizing trap, the political incompetence trap, and the fundamentalist trap.

Willis W. Harman describes his growing understanding of a society in transformation, possibly to a better world for all. He has found that to study futures is to change oneself and that there is no better pursuit than to be totally involved with both inner and outer transformation. The awakening or reperception, he argues, is real and spreading.

Reflecting themes in the first three essays, Victor Ferkiss acknowledges that predicting the future is harder than many once believed, and prescribing desirable futures is perhaps even harder. He has grown increasingly aware of the culture-bound nature of the futures movement, and of the ultimate mystery of human existence, which puts a whole new perspective on the psychological and philosophical basis of futurism. This is not seen as a counsel of despair, for we must still do the best we can.

In contrast to the broad social, cultural, and political perspectives of the essays already mentioned, Irene Taviss Thomson focuses on a single but fundamental aspect of individuals: the shift to a fluid identity from a relatively unified and fixed identity. We may thus be using a model of man, she argues, that is no longer accurate or appropriate.

Another specialized perspective, on the technology of reproductive biology, is offered by Robert T. Francoeur, who confesses that he was too conservative about our technological future—but too optimistic about our ability to adapt to accompanying radical social change.

In Part II the essays dwell on summarizing lessons learned, rather than on updating published thoughts of ten or twenty years ago. Donald N. Michael forthrightly acknowledges the epistemological limbo of futures studies resulting from the many possible constructions of the present and the past. Nevertheless, there are useful functions of futures studies similar to those of storytelling, and some methodological injunctions are offered for the would-be responsible teller of stories about futures.

Jim Dator relates the early formative influences on his thinking, and his experiences with Hawaii 2000 and the World Futures Studies Federation. He concludes with some especially salient lessons, for example: the future cannot be predicted but can be invented; many statements about the future may at first appear ridiculous; futures studies is more about the present than about the future; and the future is too important to be left to experts.

Amitai Etzioni emphasizes that we should approach the future with greater humility and less arrogance—as people who have much to learn and know relatively little. Among the rules he stresses for coping with "future angst" are knowing the relative predictability of the sector you are dealing with, allowing for a margin of error, hedging your bets, and using futures studies for nonpredictive purposes.

Reflecting on his extensive experiences in business and government, Walter A. Hahn distills twenty lessons. Among them are the importance of labels, the need for interdisciplinary teamwork and synthesis, and the continuing urge among nonfuturists to kill the bad-news messenger. He concludes that neither technology assessment nor futures studies is a discipline or a profession, but both can be pursued in a professional manner by members of many professions.

Joseph F. Coates, a "working futurist" who sells his specialized intellectual services, writes that exploring assumptions is the key to the game, that the study of the future is an art form, and that we can identify trends and foresee their implications to an extent that is useful in planning. But most people, he suggests, are not cut out to be futurists because they lack playfulness and toleration of enormous uncertainty.

Some of the lessons learned by Vary T. Coates: technology assessment is best seen as applied futures research; the temptation to moralize is an occupational hazard; the freedom of the university can sometimes lead to irrelevance; and there are dangers in rigorous quantification. She concludes that we are still learning how to ask questions and a long way from having easy answers; still, futures is fun and useful.

Joseph P. Martino utilizes a Kipling poem, "The Gods of the Copybook Headings," to warn that technological forecasters should not disregard the wisdom of seemingly trite sayings. Forecasters can be tempted to desert the trite and unexciting lessons that they should be applying, lured by the Gods of the Marketplace who promise results without effort or discipline.

Harold A. Linstone reflects on his experiences in technological forecasting and defense planning since the late 1950s. He now sees the critical need for the multiple perspectives concept, which encompasses the technical/analytical, the organizational/societal, and the personal/individual. Multiple perspectives bring to the surface vital core assumptions and minimize self-delusion, making one more at ease with complexity.

The two contributions in Part III are more personal and oriented more toward reflections on learning than toward reflections on the future. Bertram Gross and Kusum Singh have learned that learning together can be highly rewarding, and that learning means change in ideas and values. Individually and together, they reflect on what they have learned while growing up, respectively, in the West and the East, especially regarding the concept of freedom. They discuss freedom from illusion and liberation from one-dimensional political labeling, as well as the freedom/planning dichotomy.

Hazel Henderson, in her first attempt ever at poetic form, asks what high purpose gives deepest meaning to the lovers of learning. What deeply known roles can the players don to help reduce the strife and reweave the patterns that bind us all within the wheel of life? Lovers with high purposes can choose kingly roles, or flit as butterflies. All can bring messages of light and see the beauty in the strutting information age.

To summarize, what have we—the editors—learned from the "what I have learned" exercise? The lessons that we see, which we hope will be learned by a wide variety of readers, can be grouped in three clusters.

The Variety of Futurists and Futures. This is one of those trite maxims that can be easily overlooked or ignored—an example of "The Gods of the Copybook Headings" of which Joseph Martino reminds us. We did not seek to demonstrate the variety of futurists and their ideas, but these sixteen contributions serve to underscore differences in backgrounds and styles. The contributors include three political scientists (Jim Dator, Victor Ferkiss, Bertram Gross), two sociologists (Amitai Etzioni, Irene Taviss Thomson), two technology forecasters (Harold A. Linstone, Joseph P. Martino), two technology assessors (Vary T. Coates, Walter A. Hahn), a historian (W. Warren Wagar), an economist (Kenneth E. Boulding), a communications analyst (Kusum Singh), a biologist (Robert T. Francoeur), a social psychologist (Donald N. Michael), and three generalists (Joseph F. Coates with a background in technology assessment, Willis W. Harman with a background in engineering and educational policy, and Hazel Henderson with a background in economic criticism). The editors, incidentally, have backgrounds in interdisciplinary social science and educational policy (Marien) and poetry and literature (Jennings).

The uniting theme in this book is "thinking about the future," but this encompasses such themes as long-term socioeconomic systems (Wagar), the profit-minus-interest trap in capitalist societies (Boulding), the trend to fluid personal identities (Thomson), high-tech sex in the zoos (Francoeur), the psychological functions of futures studies (Michael), Hawaii 2000 (Dator), the International Society for Technology Assessment (Hahn), forecasting helicopter performance (Martino), and the limits of political labels (Gross/ Singh). Does this constitute an emerging discipline or even a "field"? We think not. The distinguishing trait of any discipline or field is not only a common focus, but also a common background. Even in disciplines as disparate as sociology and political science, the serious practictioners have the modest benefit of at least some shared educational experience and literature. Readers of this book may note that there is virtually no shared literature among the contributors and few instances in which one contributor cites the thinking of another.

Despite various futurists in search of respectability who wax enthusiastic about an emerging field or even a discipline—but never offer any supporting evidence—we have long harbored the suspicion that futures studies is not a field in any stage of development. The essays in this book give us strong encouragement to state this suspicion in print. Futures studies may only receive its proper nourishment when it is seen for what it is—an important cross-cutting of all fields of knowledge. Accordingly, generalizations about "what futurists think" (a frequent device of some journalists) should, in most instances, be dismissed as ignorant statements.

The Value of Thinking About the Future. Despite the great variety of futurists and thoughts about the future, one of the common themes in this book is that thinking about the future can be useful. If the lessons learned are followed, it can be useful not only in anticipating certain developments—

especially technologies—but also in asking better questions and learning more about one's self.

This is not to suggest that futurists are notably prescient, but who is? A popular fiction is that futurists hope to predict with high accuracy, as weather forecasters do. Some futurists do the best they can to forecast under conditions far more complex than those faced by weather forecasters (who themselves are frequently wrong). But contrary to popular notions, forecasting is only one of several futurist functions. Perhaps the most important function, as pointed out by Joseph Coates, is examining assumptions about the present.

In contrast to the futures-thinking of ten or twenty years ago, one might detect a new sobriety from the essays here: as Victor Ferkiss neatly states in his essay, "not quite so easy as it looked." But no one, at least no one in this book, suggests that futures thinking is without its rewards or that the costs outweigh the benefits. Despite the many imperfections and uncertainties in thinking about the future, the alternative of not thinking about the future has nothing to recommend it (except perhaps as a momentary escape from problems).

The Value of Mid-Career Reassessment. The activity of looking back at "what I have learned" is not unique to this book. Many professionals voluntarily write books and articles that update their worldview. Indeed, a series of "what I have learned" essays was published by *Saturday Review* in the 1965–1967 period, in which several dozen distinguished contemporaries were asked to write on the lessons they had learned from life—a summing up of personal experiences and ideas. Noteworthy in this series is "How Little I Know" by Buckminster Fuller, *Saturday Review*, November 12, 1966.

What is unique in this book is a somewhat more focused effort to bring together the wisdom of what was learned about a generally shared concern (the future) over a common period of time (the past two decades). This would seem to be a particularly valuable exercise for futurists because one's image of the future is—or ought to be—constantly in formation and reformation. Several contributors mentioned that the experience was painful but on the whole quite profitable. If others who seek to think about the future were to heed some of the lessons learned that have been stated here, we might hope for a new generation of wiser futurists who have learned their essential lessons at an earlier age. And we would no longer encounter any "frozen futurists," as we did in several instances while soliciting essays for this book.

We also hope that this "what I have learned" exercise might be applied to other professional groups. In an era of rapidly changing realities, the familiar "lifelong learning" slogan becomes more important than ever for all adults, especially for those employed in the "knowledge sector." If our identities are shifting from fixed to fluid, as pointed out by Irene Taviss

Thomson, our understanding of the world should also be constantly updated. This book could well serve as a prototype model for other groups
of professionals to assess what they have learned. As futurists who seek a
better world, we conclude with the hope that published mid-career re-
assessments might soon be widespread.

PART I
Updates and Revisions

W. Warren Wagar

THE NEXT THREE FUTURES

THE SIXTIES

The future may be defined as the part of history that men and women can change. It follows that the study of the future is—or should be—the science of transformation.[1] The works of its practitioners faithfully reflect the utopias of their own time and place. In this sense, futures inquiry and normative social philosophy are inseparable.

What a paradox! I refer not to the inseparability of futurism and idealism, since none of the social sciences or humanities is value-free, but to the dependence of futures inquiry on the values of an ever-eroding present. Futures inquiry centers on the understanding and shaping of things to come, and yet the goals that it proclaims belong to its own present, not to the future that it tries to unveil. Images of the future are therefore certain to keep changing, in rough synchronism with changes in the values of the societies of the image-makers.

This is not necessarily a great evil. Different stages in human development may require different values, just as they require different laws, politics, and economies. In fact, the most important thing I have learned in my own quarter century of future studies is to see the future not as a utopia, but as a process in which all the destinations of the major competing value systems of the modern era (as well as destinations still unimagined) can be reached. If I am right, they will not be attained simultaneously in some vast eclectic never-never land, but rather one at a time, according to the dynamics of world history.

I will return to this point near the end of my essay. Meanwhile, l want to stress the dependence of futures studies on present-day structures of belief.

An earlier version of this essay appeared in the *World Future Society Bulletin* (Nov.-Dec. 1984). Copyright 1984 by the World Future Society. Reprinted by permission of the publisher.

My own seedtime, for example, was the late 1950s and early 1960s. My first ventures in studying the future could not have been mounted in any other period.

It was the start, as we know now with the benefit of hindsight, of a long wave of reform, radicalism, and rebellion that lasted into the early 1970s. Few of us at the beginning anticipated that it would crest so high or veer so sharply to the left. At first it was a liberal initiative for a new world order along many fronts. My earliest published article, in *The Virginia Quarterly Review*, applauded its nuclear pacifism and called on peace activists to widen their horizons.[2] No such widening occurred, but the campaign for nuclear disarmament did well, especially in Great Britain. In the United States this was the heroic period of the civil rights movement. An outbreak of nation building took place, especially in sub-Saharan Africa. American reformers, at least, could hope that even government was on their side, as the Eisenhower years yielded to the cool charisma of Kennedy. The Peace Corps and the Nuclear Test Ban Treaty were visible signs of something new in the air—or so we chose to think.

In the mid–1960s everything changed. The liberals in their suits and ties and close-cropped hair were replaced by shaggy-headed radicals in work clothes. Civil rights were upstaged by black nationalism, sexual tolerance by militant feminism and the demand for full erotic independence, piecemeal legislative reform by neo-Marxist resistance and rebellion, and nuclear pacifism by a worldwide protest against American military intervention in Vietnam. For some, modern industrial civilization itself had become invalid, and a counterculture appeared, a loosely woven fabric of environmentalists, decentralizers, consciousness-expanders, seekers of new transcendental faith, natural foods enthusiasts, and others, many of whom shunned the political process altogether. I am reminded of the French Revolution, which got off to a modest start and grew progressively more radical before running its course. The Kennedy liberals were our Girondists, the radicals of the late 1960s our Jacobins.

In any case, my connection to the history of those times is obvious. I seldom saw what was coming, from one year to the next, and I thought of myself as a free-swimming intellectual who went his own way, but everything I published and everything I taught in my classrooms was closely tethered to the events, ideas, and utopias of the period.

THE CITY OF MAN

By profession I was, and remain, an intellectual historian of modern Europe, with a special interest in images of the future. I began my teaching career at Wellesley College in 1958. My doctoral dissertation, "The Open Conspirator: H. G. Wells as a Prophet of World Order," turned into my first book under the title *H. G. Wells and the World State* in 1961. In 1963

Houghton Mifflin published a second book of mine, based on another project of my graduate student days, *The City of Man: Prophecies of a World Civilization in Twentieth-Century Thought.* The new work was in effect a sequel to the dissertation, even though it had been sketched out earlier. It examined visions of cosmopolis in the generation after Wells, mostly thinkers of the middle decades of the century, such as Pierre Teilhard de Chardin, Arnold J. Toynbee, Pitirim A. Sorokin, F.S.C. Northrop, and Lewis Mumford.[3]

In *The City of Man*[4] I took the view that civilizations normally expand until they occupy all or most of the living space accessible to them. They become world orders, with a universal law and citizenship, a single polity and economy, and a syncretic culture fusing all the nations in the *ecumene.* My model, as for Toynbee before me,[5] was the Helleno-Roman civilization of classical antiquity, but I found parallel world orders in the histories of Egypt, Mesopotamia, the Islamic Middle Ages, the India of the Maurya and Gupta dynasties, and Confucian China.

Arguing partly from analogy and partly from an implicit cyclical theory of social change, I saw the likeliest future of modern civilization as a grand synthesis of the viable elements of all the traditional cultures of East and West. Just as the world orders of the past had been forged from diversity, so it would be with us. The only difference between them and our coming world civilization would be a matter of scale. Theirs had filled a river valley, a subcontinent, or the shores of two or three continents. Ours would fill a planet.

And why not? With the help of new technologies of transport and communications, we could accomplish for all humanity what earlier civilizations had accomplished in their own smaller worlds, and with no greater difficulty. History more or less decreed such an outcome. Centripetal forces, the "planetizing" forces described by Teilhard de Chardin,[6] were irresistibly at work, compelling cultures to interpenetrate, as trade, emigration, warfare, global networks of information exchange, the missionary exploits of the major world religions, and the logic of modern science and technology squeezed humanity into a single mass of flesh and mind.

I allowed—and even insisted on—the possibility that things could go tragically wrong en route to cosmopolis. The most serious danger was a nuclear world war, "the absolute certainty of almost total obliteration if we fail to create a world commonwealth."[7] Without some kind of world state, I wrote, the superweapons would sooner or later be used in a terminal battle of the nations. Another peril was ecological: disastrous shortfalls of the arable land and minerals needed to sustain human life. I later received credit from Richard A. Falk for being one of the first writers on world order to bring such issues out into the open; I was only passing along the cogent warnings of Aldous Huxley and Harrison Brown, delivered many years before the publication of *The City of Man.*[8]

All of this notwithstanding, it was a hopeful book. More to the point, it was a liberal book. I deplored the official Marxist and Roman Catholic formulas for world order as dated and doctrinaire and put my money instead on the eventual emergence of an ideology of world integration carpentered from the thoughts of my genial company of bourgeois men of good will, such as Toynbee and Mumford. Even certain theologians and philosophers of religion might contribute, if they were of the liberal, tolerant, ecumenical sort. I was especially drawn to William Ernest Hocking's program for a world confederacy of faiths in *The Coming World Civilization.*[9] At the end of *The City of Man* I preached an open-ended cosmic humanism free of the paralyzing grip of dogma, made possible by what I saw as a coming change of heart in the intelligentsia. The age of dissent and fierce contention, like the age of class warfare, was fading, and in its place would arise an age of consensus mediated by "the will to agree."[10] Or else.

Or else, more chaos and eventually Armageddon. The key to a peaceful world order, I argued, was neither a federation of the existing states nor a revolutionary overthrow of those states, but the growth of an organic and consensual world culture. From such a culture a lasting world state would flower. Without it no world political authority would be anything better than a precarious makeshift, a finger in the dike.

In effect, what I had done in *The City of Man* was to elevate the reigning doctrines of mid-century American liberalism into a global ideology. The magic word was "consensus." Kennedy and Johnson Democrats told us that their Great Society had abolished the old desperate conflict between workers and owners. The middle class had absorbed the other two classes, and a benevolent new order had come into being, free, color-blind, founded on compromise and mutual respect, which would serve as a model for all mankind. With seasonable loans and a little help from the Peace Corps, the struggling peoples of the Third World would soon follow Japan into quasi-American affluence. Even the spoilsports in the Kremlin would eventually climb off their Marxist high horses and start drinking Coca-Cola like the rest of us. It was only a matter of time.

The City of Man viewed the world less simplemindedly than the Democratic rhetoric of the 1960s, but they belonged to the same climate of opinion. Both, in turn, owed much to an earlier outbreak of liberal hopefulness in the 1940s, the decade of the United Nations and world federalism, and the brief euphoria that followed mankind's delivery from fascism.

But no sooner had the Great Society begun to desegregate schools and outlaw poverty than it dropped like a vast mythical bird of prey on Vietnam and tore that country to bloody bits.

TURNING LEFT

The assault on Vietnam broke something in me, as I think it did in thousands of others of my generation. For me, at least, no repairs were or are or ever will be possible.

In the first year of the war I had resisted the temptation to condemn American policy. Then, like many others, I blamed our involvement on errors of judgment committed by the Johnson administration. But by 1970 it finally became clear to me that the Vietnam war was no more than a particularly vicious example of a system of world domination in place and functioning according to its own logic. Although the war itself had got out of hand, thanks to the tenacity of the "enemy" and the corruption of the regime in Saigon, it made perfectly good sense as an effort to protect and extend traditional American interests: the interlocking interests of capital, the military-industrial complex, and the United States as a player in the lethal games of superpower rivalry.

How could the author of *The City of Man*, with his professed loathing for "doctrinaire" Marxism, start thinking like a doctrinaire Marxist himself? The answer is not as simple as it might seem. I had not converted, in the usual evangelical sense of the term, to a classic Marxist analysis of world history and politics. But exposure to the writings of various New Left spokesmen from the mid–1960s onward did leave its mark. In particular I was attracted to the philosophy of Herbert Marcuse, Angela Davis' mentor at the University of California, San Diego. One result of that attraction was *Good Tidings: The Belief in Progress from Darwin to Marcuse*, my longest, if not my best, book. Its curious mix of dry academic relativism and qualified hope for civilization earned an acerbic review in a Marxist journal, but *Good Tidings* also showed my growing awareness of socialist humanism.[11]

Yet I would be lying if I gave the impression that my leftward turn in the late 1960s was due entirely to reading books and articles by socialist pundits. For one thing, I had sampled a fair amount of such material long before my leftward turn, and I had not been impressed. Quite the contrary. Except for H. G. Wells, a technocrat as much as a socialist, no socialist thinker seriously influenced me until the late 1960s. What made the difference was the times, and the timing. The Vietnam war set alarm bells ringing in my head. My personal and family life was also changing, as the nascent counterculture challenged conventional middle-class morality. I left puritan Massachusetts for the fresher air of New Mexico. All at once, for many reasons, it became possible and even necessary to imagine a future in which not only the nation-state system, but also capitalism, patriarchy, and bourgeois consciousness were left far behind.

In the summer of 1970 all this came together for me and I wrote *Building the City of Man: Outlines of a World Civilization*.[12] Although the title suggested that the new book was a sequel to *The City of Man*, in many ways it was nothing of the kind. It pictured a utopian world republic of the middle of the twenty-first century, but no longer the liberal, consensual, Kennedyesque polity of its forerunner. The new City of Man was unambiguously socialist, built by revolution. I foresaw the creation of a world revolutionary party with its own ideology, committed to the integration of mankind by persuasion where possible and by force where necessary. The coming unitary world state would quash capitalism, outlaw war, protect the environment, automate industry, and equalize wealth. It would preside over a new planetary culture devoted chiefly to education, personal growth, and a secular faith that I dubbed "the service of being." In a chapter on men and women I looked forward to the near extinction of the nuclear family. I also expected the disappearance of cities. All in all, *Building the City of Man*—despite the arguably sexist title—was a compendium of the utopias of the late 1960s.

Throughout the 1970s the book found its way into many classrooms as a supplementary text for courses on peace, world order, and the future. Written at something like white heat in just a few months, it is probably the best work I have done, just because of its intensity.

But as a study on the future, *Building the City of Man* fell short in at least one crucial respect. It was a utopia: a still-life vision of future time rather than a moving picture. In spite of my leftward turn I had yet to develop a theory of historical change that advanced beyond the crude analogical thinking of Toynbee and *The City of Man*. In the earlier book I argued that a world state would arrive simply because past civilizations had given rise to world states. The whys and wherefores were not really addressed. I ignored the cumulative progress of science, technology, and industry, and I detected nothing of fundamental importance in the history of the social relations of production. The same blindness carried over into *Building the City of Man*. There would be a revolution, now, but it would happen because we radicals chose to make it happen. We would see what needed doing, we would do it, and then we would have our cosmopolis. Too easy! Some of the hard words aimed by Marx and Engels at the utopian socialists of the first half of the nineteenth century apply equally well to my *City of Man* books. I failed to see that global transformation is not just a matter of radical visions or even of radical politics. It will occur, if it does, only because it is in the cards: meaning, a futurible outcome of processes intrinsic to world history.

THREE PATHS TO THE FUTURE

The decade of the 1970s brought further changes. I was lured away from New Mexico to upstate New York by Norman F. Cantor, then chairman of the history department at the State University of New York, Binghamton. Cantor had set for himself the Sisyphean task of making the department one of the "top ten" in the nation. In this he failed, but he did encourage me to introduce a new course, "The History of the Future," which I have offered every year since 1974. Until recently, *Building the City of Man* was one of its required books.

As the futures movement expanded in the 1970s and the bibliography for my course grew accordingly, with the expert guidance of my upstate friend Michael Marien,[13] I came to see that futurists divide into three major camps. Each is readily subdivisible into several factions, but the big camps and their programs were not difficult to identify.

The first and largest camp is occupied by the insiders of the established order in the capitalist West and by their confederates and sympathizers worldwide: so-called conservatives, so-called liberals, and all those who believe that the future holds in store more capitalism, more middle-class democracy, and more solutions to problems as they arise through investment in capital-intensive technology. Within this camp, rows regularly break out between the advocates of open-throttle capitalism and the supporters of a restricted capitalism that would maintain public services at a high level while limiting capital growth to husband resources. But capitalists, whether they call themselves conservatives or liberals, are still capitalists. The differences between them, like those between the two major political parties in the United States and Canada, are not fundamental.[14]

In the second camp are found not only various insiders of the established order in the nominally socialist East, but also many authentic radicals everywhere who believe that the future holds in store the world victory of socialism. Perhaps the truest of these believers are, in fact, leftists in the West and in the Third World, together with what Rudolf Bahro has called "heretical Marxists" in the socialist countries.[15] More and more, spokesmen of the officially Marxist states speak and behave like capitalists.

The third camp houses the heirs of the counterculture of the 1960s. The old counterculture lost some of its romantic fervor and mass appeal in the more conservative atmosphere of the 1970s and 1980s, but it did not collapse as some had expected. Its more serious faction consists of eco-decentralists, followers of the late E. F. Schumacher and a few others like him, who argue that the wave of the future is local initiative, self-sufficiency, and a new moral balance between mankind and nature made possible by "appropriate" technology. Eco-decentralism foresees a transvaluation of human values that will render obsolete high-capital centralized systems in both government and the economy, and restore to individuals and communities full control of their own lives. Many of its adherents look forward to a recovery of mankind's sense of the sacred.[16]

The longer I taught my course and the more I steeped myself in the literature of these three camps, the clearer it became to me that all three visions were valid in one way or another, and that the fierce criticisms directed by each against its rivals deserved a careful hearing. I learned from all of them.

At the same time I tried to avoid the errors of *The City of Man*. I did not attempt to concoct a synthesis of the three visions that could only be, in the final analysis, a restatement of liberalism. In 1975, at the second General Assembly of the World Future Society, I chose to make a formal commitment to the radical camp, the camp of Marxist humanism.[17] Ten

years later that commitment remains firm. It was the direction in which I
had been moving steadily since the mid–1960s.

My continuing allegiance to a radical worldview and to radical futurism
rests on two considerations—the first pragmatic, the second theoretical.

Of the two the pragmatic weighed more heavily in my thoughts in the
mid–1970s. It was simply this: modern civilization may not have time to
invent a comprehensive system of social thought superior to Marxism.
Movements of ideas often need centuries to take root, mature, and gain
worldwide acceptance. Yet as I have thought all my life, the time available
to us is short. In the four irretrievable decades of opportunity that have
slipped away since the start of the nuclear age, no ideology of a just world
order remotely comparable to Marxism has emerged. The capitalist and
eco-decentralist alternatives have much to say about the future, but they
have not produced a coherent analysis of the process of world integration,
and many futurists in both camps do not view the process itself with favor
or sympathy.

Meanwhile, throughout most of the world, Marxism is a living force with
a long headstart over any new system of thought that might come forward
in the future. In the Soviet Union, Eastern Europe, and much of east Asia
it is the ideology—although too often ignored or debased—of the ruling
party apparatus, and it inspires many of the best independent and dissident
minds. The fervent search for a Marxism with a human face in the nominally
socialist countries gives the lie to bourgeois critics who hold up the fossilized
leadership of the Communist party of the Soviet Union as evidence that
Marxism is dead.[18]

Elsewhere Marxism thrives still more vigorously. It is one of the chief
agents of progressive social change and national liberation in the Third
World.[19] It plays a decisive part in the political and intellectual life of
Western Europe.[20] Even in darkest North America, Marxist humanism has
won a secure foothold, especially in the social sciences. As the countdown
to nuclear oblivion ticks on inexorably, it makes sense to rally around the
most rational, humane, and astute vision of world integration already available to us that has any chance of being able to command planetwide allegiance in time to make a difference.

But my second reason for embracing Marxist humanism is the superiority
of its analysis of world history, both for an understanding of the past and
for its predictive power. As I delved more deeply into Marxist literature in
the 1970s, I found fresh perspectives above all in the world-system theory
of such Marxist sociologists as Immanuel Wallerstein and André Gunder
Frank. Their work blends Marxist methods and values with the historiog-
raphy of modern capitalism of the *Annaliste* school in France.[21] The result
is a theoretical structure anchored in the concrete world of historical continuity and change that is quite unique in modern sociology. Indeed, Wallerstein's aim is to fuse history and the social sciences into a new discipline,

"historical social science," which—I suspect—could furnish a systematic unifying methodology for future studies, something they do not begin to have now.[22]

World-system theory not only helped to strengthen my commitment to Marxist analysis. It also furnished me with some of the insights I required to sort out the most likely future of mankind if we do manage, against the odds, to avoid an apocalyptic third world war. In particular, it suggested to me a strategy for bringing together into one synoptic view—without eclecticism or "synthesis"—what remains valid in all the strands of the futurist thought that I had up to now encountered: bourgeois political economy, the utopian and scientific elements of Marxism, and eco-decentralism.

THE PROSPECT FOR CAPITALISM

By the early 1980s, then, I was finally in a position to start putting the pieces together. I will need more time to digest what I have learned and flesh it out. The few articles on the human future that I have published recently do not, by any means, tell the whole story.[23] But in what follows I will do my best to outline my current thinking, as evidence of work in progress.

My starting point is Wallerstein's thesis that the human race lives in a capitalist world-economy, a global division of labor with a plurality of sovereign states but only one marketplace, from which no nation or economic system has been able to remain isolated for long. The Soviet Union, China, and the would-be socialist states of Eastern Europe belong to this world-economy too, no matter what the rhetoric of their ruling circles may claim. Their state corporations produce goods for profitable exchange in the global market, which is the essence of capitalism. The peoples of the Third World occupy a peripheral or semiperipheral relationship to the super-industrialized Western (and Japanese) core of the world-economy, supplying essential primary products, cheap labor, and markets for Western commodities and capital.

I would go a step further and suggest that in some respects, the state capitalism of the Soviet Union foreshadows the economic future of the Western countries. The collective control of capital in the Soviet system by a small oligarchy of party officials, bureaucrats, and managers roughly approximates what Marx foresaw as the highest stage of capitalism, the stage of monopoly, not yet fully attained in the West.

What we can expect next is the final consolidation of the existing world-economy, which is still quite resilient. The current economic downturn began in the late 1960s and will probably end in the early 1990s, to be followed (albeit belatedly) by Herman Kahn's "coming boom."[24] I would not be surprised if the next boom in the world business cycle lasted for thirty years, fueled by major breakthroughs in energy production, industrial automation, and biotechnology.[25] In this phase of the future, many of the forecasts of Kahn, Julian L. Simon, and a host of other prophets of the capitalist establishment will look shrewd indeed.

In fact, the capitalist world-economy is probably good for one, or even two, more Kondratieff "long waves" of forty to fifty years each after the coming boom has come and gone.[26] Radicals who foresee its imminent collapse are victims of wishful thinking, a bad habit of Marxists that can be traced back well into the nineteenth century. The capitalist system, after all, did not clinch victory in its long war with feudalism until that century, and it is not in the nature of great world-economies to fall apart as soon as they have won their laurels.

All this assumes that the pressures exerted on the carrying capacity of the environment by capitalist production do not lead to some kind of ecological doomsday. At one time I saw "ecocide" as a real possibility, but today I am not so sure. Corporate planners are often myopic, thanks to their obsession with quick profits, but enough of them keep tabs on long-term opportunities to prevent the collapse of the system. The big companies and the governments they infiltrate will not let the world-economy run out of energy and resources. With the help of relentless progress in technology, they will keep at least one step ahead of the problems they themselves create. The system will survive. Even if whole countries in the Third World, especially in central Africa and south Asia, do not survive, the system—and above all its superindustrialized core—will plow ahead. On this point, prophets of the Kahn and Simon persuasion are substantially right. Although they underestimate the price that the planet and its people will have to pay for such "progress," ecocide is unlikely.

But this is not to say that capitalism is immortal. In due course, and only in small measure because of its rapacious environmental policies, it will pass from robust maturity to calcified old age. A great array of problems will beset it that had been manageable before but will now get out of hand. The inequitable distribution of wealth within and among nations, the tendency of capitalism to overproduce, the high price of worker co-option (in other words, the "welfare state"), the not-so-hidden social and environmental costs of growth, the falling profit rate as dependence on expensive high technologies increases, and the unavailability of new peripheral regions to exploit will combine in various ways, both predictable and unpredictable, to shake the system to its foundations.

Nor will it any longer boast the resilience of its twentieth-century good old days. As I read late capitalism, it will be a time of corporate giantism that dwarfs anything we see today. A handful of richly diversified multinationals will run the global market, hand in glove with their counterparts in the centrally planned economies. With the disappearance of small business

and agriculture, all but a few men and women will have become workers—
not proletarians, in the classic sense, but workers all the same, dependent
on earned income for their livelihood.

In the sphere of politics, monopoly capitalism will give rise to worldwide
technocracy, the rule of the possessors of know-how. Their forerunners are
the Eurocrats of the Common Market, the magi of the Trilateral Commission, and the managers and engineers who govern in late twentieth-century
Soviet Russia.[27] Among them, they will build an informal corporate world
order, neither safe nor just, but probably less threatening to international
stability on a day-to-day basis than the present arrangements. Ironically,
they may do their job so well that the small and medium-sized wars that
now help to keep the world-economy afloat will not occur, further weakening demand and slashing profits. Should this become a problem, however,
they can always follow the example of the three superstates in George
Orwell's *Nineteen Eighty-Four* and stage-manage an endless series of limited
phony wars.

It goes without saying that I have looked forward to what will happen
if capitalism evolves in a pattern consistent with the trajectory of its growth
up to this time. Although I interpret the pattern in a Marxist sense, many
of the same points might be made, and have been made in other language,
by seers of the capitalist establishment. The wild card in the process is the
risk of a new total war. Even if an informal global directorate of technocrats,
accompanied by more or less permanent détente among the nuclear powers,
greatly diminishes that risk, it is high now and will remain high, or at least
measurable, for many years to come, perhaps for centuries. Only one short,
swift sequence of strategic blunders on a single day is required to blow
civilization to smithereens and consign the survivors to the icy clutches of
a nuclear winter.[28]

In the shadow of such a threat, the prospect of another hundred years
or more of the capitalist world-economy is particularly dismal. But if Marxist analysis has taught us anything, it has taught us that few tricks can be
played with world history. An economic world-system takes time to mature
and disintegrate and pass on. No stage can be skipped, and there is no
possibility of true socialism without the prior full development of true capitalism.[29] The fiasco of "socialism" in Soviet Russia and Eastern Europe
speaks eloquently to that!

Assuming, however, that civilization dodges all its doomsdays, one can
readily imagine the kind of sclerotic capitalism that will rule the world in
the final years of its ancien régime. Top-heavy, overcentralized, super-
bureaucratized, monopoly capital in the era of global technocracy will be
an easy target for all the ills and contradictions cited earlier. It will have
none of the gusto of its younger and middle years. Increasingly, it will be
forced to turn to neofascist or neo-Stalinist methods to remain in power

against the resistance of its profoundly alienated working class. But if the radical vision and consciousness have thrived, as they must do, these methods will be adopted too late to avail.

Here, then, is the first of my three futures: capitalism triumphant, and in due course rotten ripe and ready to fall.

THE FUTURES AFTER THE FUTURE

The seed within the capitalist fruit is obviously socialism.

At this point my game plan should no longer be, if it ever was, a mystery. Establishment futurists, unless they are rank pessimists, expect the glorious consummation of capitalism; radical futurists expect a victory for the workers; eco-decentralist futurists expect something like Ernest Callenbach's Ecotopia.[30] Well and good. They may all be right, if they are willing to wait their turn. Granted that the first future in store for mankind coincides with at least some of the hopes of the capitalist establishment, we may anticipate that the second future (still generations away) will meet the deepest aspirations of radicals. The third future (still more distant) will bring us at last to Ecotopia.

My thoughts on the shape of this second future—a socialist world republic—and the forms of political thought and action required to achieve it have not changed appreciably since I wrote *Building the City of Man*. I am still reluctant to believe that socialism is possible worldwide without revolutionary struggle, although in many countries, victory may come without violence. The best opportunities for making the transition to socialism and a socialist cosmopolis will probably arise in hard times, such as in the aftermath of a major (but not apocalyptic) war or in the throes of a severe economic depression. Because we are considering a future that is far away, it is pointless to try to anticipate the exact circumstances.

However long it takes, the result can only be a *world* polity. To quote Wallerstein: "Socialism involves the creation of a new kind of *world*-system, neither a redistributive world-empire nor a capitalist world-economy but a socialist world-government."[31] Now that humanity occupies a single contiguous living space integrated by the daily worldwide exchange of goods, people, images, and ideas, sharing the finite resources of the same earth and the common peril of wars of mass annihilation, the only solutions that make any sense are planetary solutions. There is only one atmosphere, one hydrosphere, one lithosphere. We share the same winds and the same sun. Our poisons travel everywhere. Keeping all the earth's soon-to-be 10 billion citizens alive and well in the next century or two will require the intelligent use of all levels of technology, from highest to lowest, and a democratically elected socialist polity in command of all armed forces and the distribution and development of all resources. The house of earth cannot stand divided.

At first the socialist cosmopolis will meet our material needs well and promote the great revolutionary values of liberty, equality, fraternity, and justice under a binding common law. It will put an end to the warfare system once and for all by disarming the nation-states. Unshackled from the capitalist world-economy, the formerly peripheral countries will be free to evolve in their own ways toward democratic socialism, with the help of modest loans and grants-in-aid from the republic.

A society without war or exploitation will also be a society that protects the civil autonomy of the individual man and woman. The principle that the individual is not a slab of living tissue to be manipulated as raison d'état prescribes was already well established in classic bourgeois legalism, if only because capitalist economies could not have originated without private initiative, but it lies at the very heart of socialist humanism, whose final goal is the liberation of every individual from the iron laws of the marketplace. In regimes of the capitalist era civil liberties are often suspended or ignored, as in time of war, or when they collide with vital class interests. In the socialist era they will take their rightful place at the top of the hierarchy of public values. At the same time all individuals will have the power as well as the freedom to develop themselves to the limit of their abilities, unfettered by discrimination, poverty, ignorance, or any other injury that human policy can prevent.

But the writings of the prophets of eco-decentralism and a second look at the humanistic wellsprings of Marxism itself persuade me that the socialist world republic could easily turn into a dead end for mankind. The republic will be needed to dismantle the engines of war and private capital. It will be needed to clean up the earth and help to close the gap between North and South. In the process it will inherit many of the technologies, business management systems, and bureaucratic labyrinths of the capitalist ancien régime. The chances are good that a socialist cosmopolis will eventually breed its own caste of elitist technocrats who will find ways of evading democratic controls and perpetuating their power. In effect, the ruling caste might even become hereditary.

At such a point, mankind will be ready for its third future. This one, too, may take a revolution to build. There are hints of such an age in classic Marxism, although Marx and Engels carefully refrained from painting pretty pictures of a hypothetical Paradise. In their day too much utopianizing had given socialism a bad name; what was needed was close analysis of hard realities. But everyone knows of Engels' hopes for the gradual dying out of state power and of Marx's notes on the transition from socialism to the still higher stage of pure communism.[32] What both of them had in mind, given their deep roots in the thought world of German romantic idealism, was not so very different from the essence of eco-decentralism, as I understand that essence. Let us not forget that the greatest of the eco-decentralists, E. F. Schumacher, was both a German and a legatee of romanticism too!

But we can perceive both dangers and opportunities in the late twentieth century that were unforeseeable in Marx's lifetime. Classic Marxism rejoiced in mankind's mastery of nature, criticizing only the way in which it had been used to benefit some men and women at the expense of the rest. Today, in view of the enormous damage suffered by mother earth at our hands, and in view of the far worse damage now in our power to inflict, terms such as "mastery" take on a different coloration. They unmask the hubris that too much power can spawn in any of us, profiteering capitalist or not.

We also have more evidence than was available in Marx's century of the danger to democratic values when power is lodged in complex, distant machineries of government and management, and we grow too reliant on capital-intensive high technology. The decisions of bureaucrats are often far stupider and the products of assembly line industry are often far poorer than what we could do for and by ourselves.

The next several generations are unlikely to witness the spread of eco-decentralism. We approach times of boom, bust, war, revolution, and suffering on a global scale that demand global planning and action. But in the further future, after the building of socialism, I anticipate the arrival of a powerful new counterculture. There will be cries for a world order "as if people really mattered," for the restoration of full self-government to communities, and for a simpler, more self-reliant economy. Perhaps not all the bureaucratic spider webs of the old socialist cosmopolis will be brushed away. Agencies in charge of interregional conflict resolution and the management of terrestrial (and extraterrestrial) trade may stay on.

But on the whole the third future of mankind will probably mark the end of the collectivist era in history and the beginning of what Engels termed "the kingdom of freedom."[33] Engels meant freedom from the harsh necessities of the marketplace after the overthrow of capitalism, with its compulsive grasping after profit and its fetishism of commodities. Our great-grandchildren may define it, also, as freedom from bureaucrats. Cheaper soft-energy sources, self-replicating technologies, falling birth rates, and new life-styles will reduce dependence on the centralized systems that bureaucrats are needed to manage. Having unified and saved the world, the socialist republic will some day become redundant, and the scaffolding it has erected can be allowed to crumble.

Such a vision chimes with Herbert Marcuse's prophecy of a society without repression, political or erotic. It summons up memories of William Morris' holy anarchy in News from Nowhere, a work for which I have a heartfelt fondness. It suggests the kind of society that many West German Greens would like to build here and now, without waiting for capitalism to finish decaying from within and without waiting for an interlude of global socialism. Rudolf Bahro voices their hopes when he says that it is possible for the Federal Republic to advance directly from "black" to "green," from Christian democracy to Green populism, without a "red" phase.[34]

One might ask, why not? Why not build our Ecotopia right away, at least in those selected favored countries where the visions are available and the spirit is willing?

The answer is the same one that might be given to those who expect the disappearance of the capitalist world-economy next week or to those who claim that the Soviet Union is a socialist country because its rulers mouth Marxist phrases. A world-system is both worldwide and systemic. Countries that try to extricate themselves from it prematurely, before it has run its course, do not succeed.

Modern history is littered with such failed acts of world-historical bravado. The Burma of Ne Win, the Cambodia of Pol Pot, and the China of Mao Tse-tung during the period of the "Great Proletarian Cultural Revolution" are obvious cases in point. Since 1979 Iran has transformed itself into a neomedieval theocracy that nonetheless is compelled to sell oil and buy arms on the capitalist world market, and it is no more likely to insulate itself permanently from the contamination of the infidel than Israel has restored the kingdom of David.

In the real world in which all peoples live now, there is no option except capitalism, whatever political and theological facades we may erect to disguise the fact. Someday, if the Marxist analysis of capitalism is sound, it will be possible to effect the transition to a socialist world commonwealth. At that point in history the world-economy will be fundamentally socialist, although much of the Third World will require time and latitude to repair the damage wrought by centuries of capitalist exploitation and the destabilizing effects of forced rapid conversion to Western modes of production. After mankind has been knit together into one family, with justice and equality for all its children, and after the wounds of war and environmental plunder have healed, then and not before then can we even hope to dispense with state power.

In the meantime it is essential to keep the Ecotopian vision alive, just as it is essential to carry on the struggle for democratic socialism. Good things take time, and patience, and love, to achieve. Like a child, who needs a quarter century of nurturing to grow from conception to hardy manhood or womanhood, a new world-system is long in the making.

I must resist the temptation to go on. You see at least the broad outlines of what I have learned. Some will object that I have learned nothing except a little more jargon to help me continue my old Wellsian game of daydreaming about El Dorado. I wonder myself if (as in the 1960s) I am once again laboring under the spell of currently fashionable utopias.

Well, if so, so be it. I make no apologies for believing that mankind has a future and that it can be bright, free, and golden. It can also be a future of ashes and ice. We all have choices to make.

NOTES

1. I use "science" here in the sense of the German *Wissenschaft*, systematized knowledge, not in the narrow usage of everyday modern English, which excludes everything but the empirical natural and social sciences.

2. W. Warren Wagar, "Beyond the Peace Movement: The Idea of a World Civilization," *The Virginia Quarterly Review*, Vol. 39, Summer 1963, pp. 353–368.

3. W. Warren Wagar, *H. G. Wells and the World State*, New Haven, Conn.: Yale University Press, 1961; W. Warren Wagar, *The City of Man: Prophecies of a World Civilization in Twentieth-Century Thought*, Boston: Houghton Mifflin, 1963; and Baltimore: Penguin Books, 1967.

4. The book was scheduled to bear the title *World Integration*. A dust jacket had already been designed and printed when Houghton Mifflin's sales staff demurred. The salesmen feared that many people, especially in the Deep South, would think that I meant world racial integration.

5. See Arnold J. Toynbee, *A Study of History*, New York: Oxford University Press, 1934–1961, especially Vol. 12 (1961), pp. 158–186.

6. See Pierre Teilhard de Chardin, *The Phenomenon of Man*, New York: Harper & Bros., 1959; and, in particular, Pierre Teilhard de Chardin, *The Future of Man*, New York: Harper & Row, 1964, pp. 129–144.

7. Wagar, *City of Man*, p. 235.

8. See Aldous Huxley, *Themes and Variations*, New York: Harper & Bros., 1950, pp. 235–272; and Harrison Brown, *The Challenge of Man's Future*, New York: Viking Press, 1954. Falk paid his compliment in *This Endangered Planet: Prospects and Proposals for Human Survival*, New York: Random House, 1971, p. 366.

9. William Ernest Hocking, *The Coming World Civilization*, New York: Harper & Bros., 1956; also William Ernest Hocking, *Living Religions and a World Faith*, New York: Macmillan, 1940.

10. Wagar, *City of Man*, pp. 246–257.

11. W. Warren Wagar, *Good Tidings: The Belief in Progress from Darwin to Marcuse*, Bloomington: Indiana University Press, 1972. The negative review was by John Moran in *Science and Society*, Vol. 38, Winter 1974–1975, pp. 499–503.

12. W. Warren Wagar, *Building the City of Man: Outlines of a World Civilization*, New York: Grossman, 1971; and San Francisco: Freeman, 1972. My proposed title for this book was *World Integration: Building the City of Man*, but once again the phrase "world integration" was vetoed at the last minute, although not for the same reason as before. My publisher, Richard Grossman, complained that *World Integration* sounded too dry and sociological.

13. I was especially influenced by Marien's article "The Two Visions of Post-Industrial Society," *Futures: The Journal of Planning and Forecasting*, Vol. 9, October 1977, pp. 415–431. See also Marien, "Touring Futures: An Incomplete Guide to the Literature," *The Futurist*, Vol. 17, April 1983, pp. 12–21; and the journal he founded and edits, *Future Survey*, published monthly since 1979 by the World Future Society, Washington, D.C.

14. Measure the distance, for example, between *The Global 2000 Report to the President: Entering the Twenty-First Century*, Elmsford, N.Y.: Pergamon, 1980;

and Julian L. Simon and Herman Kahn, eds., *The Resourceful Earth: A Response to Global 2000*, New York: Blackwell, 1984. The policies recommended in the two studies are usually quite different, but neither advocates systemic change.

15. Rudolf Bahro, *From Red to Green: Interviews with New Left Review*, London: Verso, 1984, p. 218.

16. See, for example, E. F. Schumacher, *Small Is Beautiful: Economics As If People Mattered*, New York: Harper & Row, 1973; Ernest Callenbach, *Ecotopia*, New York: Bantam Books, 1977; Theodore Roszak, *Person/Planet: The Creative Disintegration of Industrial Society*, Garden City, N.Y.: Anchor Press, 1978; Willis W. Harman, *An Incomplete Guide to the Future*, New York: W. W. Norton, 1979; Duane Elgin, *Voluntary Simplicity: Toward a Way of Life That Is Outwardly Simple, Inwardly Rich*, New York: William Morrow, 1981; and O. W. Markley and Willis W. Harman, eds., *Changing Images of Man*, Elmsford, N.Y.: Pergamon, 1982.

17. My paper was never published, but a prolegomenon to it may be found in Andrew A. Spekke, ed., *The Next 25 Years: Crisis and Opportunity*, Washington, D.C.: World Future Society, 1975, pp. 51–53, entitled "The World-View of the Coming World Civilization." Most of the argument of the paper appears in "Epilogue: The Next World View," in W. Warren Wagar, *World Views: A Study in Comparative History*, Hinsdale, Ill.: Dryden, 1977, pp. 185–191.

18. I first encountered this search for a Marxism with a human face in some of the books of Erich Fromm, especially *Marx's Concept of Man*, New York: Ungar, 1961; and a volume of essays edited by Fromm, *Socialist Humanism: An International Symposium*, Garden City, N.Y.: Doubleday, 1965, which features contributions from more than a dozen East German, Polish, Czech, and Yugoslav Marxists. Over the years many other testimonies to the still-revolutionary power of Marxist humanism in officially Marxist societies have been published. One example is Rudolf Bahro, *The Alternative in Eastern Europe*, New York: Times Books, 1978; see also Ulf Wolter, ed., *Rudolf Bahro: Critical Responses*, White Plains, N.Y.: M. E. Sharpe, 1980. More recently, in *From Red to Green*, cited earlier, Bahro has said that insofar as Marxism is a doctrine of class struggle pitting the traditional proletariat against the traditional bourgeoisie, he has "left Marxism behind." *From Red to Green*, p. 219. An émigré from East Germany, Bahro joined the West German Green party in 1980. But Marxism plays a major role in the thought of the Greens and clearly continues to play a major role in Bahro's, as well. Indeed, there is relatively little difference between Bahro's call for utopian socialism and the mature thought of Herbert Marcuse. See Marcuse, "Protosocialism and Late Capitalism: Toward a Theoretical Synthesis Based on Bahro's Analysis," in Wolter, ed., *Rudolf Bahro*, pp. 25–48.

19. Marxism has even deeply penetrated radical Catholic thought in Latin America, in the movement known as "liberation theology." A representative text is *Marx Against the Marxists: The Christian Humanism of Karl Marx*, by the Mexican scholar José Porfirio Miranda, Maryknoll, N.Y.: Orbis Books, 1980. In its original Spanish-language version, Miranda's book was entitled *El cristianismo de Marx*.

20. A good starting point for examining Marxism in Western Europe is Perry Anderson, *Considerations on Western Marxism*, London: Verso, 1979.

21. See, for example, Immanuel Wallerstein, *The Modern World-System*, New York: Academic Press, 1976–1980; Immanuel Wallerstein, *The Capitalist World-Economy*, New York: Cambridge University Press, 1979; André Gunder Frank,

World Accumulation, 1492–1789, New York: Monthly Review Press, 1978; and Samir Amin, Giovanni Arrighi, André Gunder Frank, and Immanuel Wallerstein, *Dynamics of Global Crisis,* New York: Monthly Review Press, 1982. Also valuable is the quarterly journal *Review,* 1977–, edited by Wallerstein for the Fernand Braudel Center for the Study of Economies, Historical Systems, and Civilizations, headquartered at the State University of New York, Binghamton.

22. See the editorial by Immanuel Wallerstein, "The Tasks of Historical Social Science," in the first issue of *Review,* Vol. 1, Summer 1977, pp. 3–7. During my recent tenure as chairperson of the history department, Wallerstein and I sponsored and participated in a lecture series at the State University of New York, Binghamton, on the theme "The Historical Social Sciences: Issues of Theory and Method."

23. I also published a book in these years, *Terminal Visions: The Literature of Last Things,* Bloomington: Indiana University Press, 1982, a history of eschatological fiction since Mary Shelley's *The Last Man.* I initially decided to write this book in a mood of almost postorgasmic melancholy, in 1972, when I had not yet settled into my new surroundings in upstate New York and was feeling a sense of letdown after all the tumult of the late 1960s. Those who lived through the period will remember how suddenly everything seemed to collapse. In 1970, the New Left and the counterculture were in high gear. Within a year both had lost momentum and stalled. But by the time I actually got around to writing *Terminal Visions,* I converted it from an exercise in bourgeois weltschmerz to a study of how fiction of the world's end furnishes metaphors for world transformation.

24. Herman Kahn, *The Coming Boom: Economic, Political, and Social,* New York: Simon & Schuster, 1982.

25. Wallerstein makes the same point in *Dynamics of Global Crisis,* p. 40.

26. See N. D. Kondratieff, "The Long Waves in Economic Life," *Review,* Vol. 2, Spring 1979, pp. 519–562.

27. I have developed my thoughts on technocracy in three articles: "The Steel-Gray Saviour: Technocracy as Utopia and Ideology," *Alternative Futures: The Journal of Utopian Studies,* Vol. 2, Spring 1979, pp. 38–54; "Technocracy as the Highest Stage of Capitalism," in Frank Feather, ed., *Through the '80s,* Washington, D.C.: World Future Society, 1980, pp. 210–215; and "Down with Little Brother!: Orwell and the Human Prospect," in Howard F. Didsbury, Jr., ed., *Creating a Global Agenda,* Washington, D.C.: World Future Society, 1984, pp. 325–334.

28. See Paul R. Ehrlich et al., *The Cold and the Dark: The World after Nuclear War,* New York: W. W. Norton, 1984.

29. See Wallerstein's discussion of the alleged skipping of stages in *Capitalist World-Economy,* pp. 3–5, 10–13, and 33–36.

30. See earlier, n. 16.

31. *Capitalist World-Economy,* p. 35. Emphasis Wallerstein's. But Wallerstein may not mean by "socialist world-government" what I mean by the coming socialist world republic. He is reluctant to speculate at any length, but he insists that because states must wither away under socialism, a socialist world-government "presumably will *not* be one of our contemporary forms of state government writ large" (emphasis Wallerstein's). Immanuel Wallerstein, *The Politics of the World-Economy,* New York: Cambridge University Press, 1984, p. 172. In other words, he assumes that we will be able to move more or less directly to a stateless future, corresponding in part to my "third future" in the discussion that follows.

32. A succinct review of Marx and Engels on the human future, with most of the appropriate textual references, is available in M. M. Bober, *Karl Marx's Interpretation of History*, New York: W. W. Norton, 1965, pp. 275–277.

33. Friedrich Engels, *Socialism: Utopian and Scientific*, New York: International Publishers, 1975, p. 73. First published in 1880. To quote more fully:

The extraneous objective forces that have hitherto governed history pass under the control of man himself. Only from that time will man himself, more and more consciously, make his own history—only from that time will the social causes set in movement by him have, in the main and in a constantly growing measure, the results intended by him. It is the ascent of man from the kingdom of necessity to the kingdom of freedom.

34. Bahro, *From Red to Green*, p. 233.

THE MEANING OF THE TWENTY-FIRST CENTURY: REEXAMINING THE GREAT TRANSITION

It is now twenty years since I published *The Meaning of the Twentieth Century: The Great Transition* (1964). It originated in a series of lectures I gave on a student ship from New York to LeHavre in June 1963. We were on our way to Japan to spend a year at the International Christian University outside of Tokyo, and it was there that I wrote up my lecture notes into this little volume. It is a curious coincidence that I am writing these notes in Tokyo also, where I am spending a month at the United Nations University. There is something peculiarly appropriate in this, as I have often described Japan as the first twenty-first-century country.

Going back to an old book is a curious mixture of nostalgia and slight embarrassment, rather like an alumni reunion. It is a certain combination of "Did I really write that? That is pretty good!" and "How on earth did I make that mistake?" On the whole, I must confess with a slight smirk, that it stands up well. It is not really a book about the future so much as an attempt to identify the time patterns of human development. As the subtitle suggests, a major thesis is that we are living in the middle of a profound transition from "merely civilized societies" to "postcivilization." The transition is based essentially on the rise of the subculture of science in the past 500 years and the transformation of scientific "know-what" into "know-how," which has resulted in an enormous proliferation of human artifacts, a tremendous expansion of the ecological niche of the human race, with the consequent result of a phenomenal rise in the human population, which is in danger of overshooting a possibly contracting niche. I cannot remember where I got the figure (on page 8 of my book) that "about 25 percent of the human beings who have ever lived are now alive." This is

This essay appeared originally in the *World Future Society Bulletin* (July-Aug. 1984). Copyright 1984 by the World Future Society. Reprinted, with changes, by permission of the publisher.

certainly much too high. More recent estimates suggest that it is more like six or seven percent, but even this is a striking consequence of the enormous uprush of the population curve.

There have been other transitions in the past. There was the one that produced the human race itself in paleolithic cultures. Then there was the transition from the paleolithic to the neolithic, and the invention of agriculture, perhaps as a result of the misery of the human race in the mesolithic and the last ice age. It was agriculture that first produced a surplus of food. What I did not stress in my book is that this surplus food was storable, which, on the whole, the fruit and meat of the paleolithic were not. This opened the way for civilization, resting on some system of threats from either priest or king, which extracted the food surplus from the farmer and used it to feed armies, architects, builders, metalworkers, potters, weavers, and so on.

The impact of the rising body of scientific knowledge on technology really only began about 1860, with the chemical industry. Then came the electrical industry after 1880; then the oil industry, skyscrapers, airplanes, and so on. This is the "superculture," or postcivilization, which is now worldwide. In the rich countries of the temperate zone, this has reached down to the bulk of the population. In the poor countries, mainly in the tropics, it does not extend much beyond the airports and the capital cities. The rest of the population in these societies is still in the state of civilization. Precivilized societies are now rare indeed. The potential outcome of the great transition is a world in which poverty has been abolished, ill health is uncommon, and most human beings have the opportunity to realize a significant part of their potential for knowledge and enjoyment.

I designated, however, certain "traps," which may prevent the realization of this potential and could even drive us down to a condition far worse than what we have now. The three traps I developed fairly fully are, first, the war trap, which even twenty years ago I perceived as potentially threatening the very existence of the human race and the evolutionary process. Second is the population trap; unrestricted population growth can produce enormous human misery before it is checked. The third, even at that time, I called the entropy trap, (long before the term entropy became fashionable). This involves the exhaustion of nonrenewable resources, and pollution. I mentioned a fourth trap rather briefly, which might be called the "boredom trap." This might develop as a result of too much success and could pose profound dangers to the continuance of the developmental process.

What, then, has happened in the past twenty years? In some ways surprisingly little. The streets are still full of automobiles, a little smaller and more expensive than they were. Airports are busier than ever. Skyscrapers are still going up. People all over the world are still busy shopping. The Portuguese empire, on which I was a little hard, has disbanded, with some rather tragic results in some of the old colonies, like Timor. The Soviet

Union has changed very little, apart from the disastrous excursion into Afghanistan. China has changed a good deal, although, like the Soviet Union, it remains one of the last of the nineteenth-century empires. There is a sense of incipient crisis, or at least a malaise, pretty much the world over, although it takes different forms in the different systems. The crisis of communism is felt certainly in China, Poland, Romania, and Hungary, but there is also a crisis of capitalism—perhaps too long drawn out to deserve the name of crisis, but, again, a serious malaise—with rising unemployment, higher rates of inflation, and a worrying international debt situation.

In biotechnology, especially genetic engineering, we are not quite as far along as I thought we might be, but certainly movement is under way. There is more self-consciousness among the poor countries as represented, for instance, by the "Group of Seventy-Seven." There are pressures for a new international economic order, a new international information order, and other things that do not seem to have a great deal of substance, although they are symbolically important. The rise of the Organization of Petroleum Exporting Countries (OPEC) is perhaps the most striking event economically. It resulted in a tax of some 60 billion dollars a year paid to the oil producers. This has been only a minor inconvenience to the rich countries, but it quite severely damaged the development of the poor countries that had no oil.

Looking now at the original three traps, it is clear that the war trap has become much more dangerous than it was twenty years ago. There has been a severe arms race, a world war industry that has about doubled in this period—to the great detriment of virtually everybody—slowing down economic development in both the rich and the poor countries, especially perhaps in the poorest countries. The present system prides itself on being a system of deterrence, but it is a fundamental principle that deterrence must break down eventually into war if the situation continues, simply because if the probability of its breaking down were zero, it would not deter anybody. Thus, we saw a breakdown of deterrence in the Falklands War—an absurdity if ever there was one—and in the war between Iraq and Iran, which could be interpreted as a war of the breakdown of deterrence, even though Iraq was clearly the aggressor.

It is now even more clear than it was twenty years ago that nuclear war could easily be an irretrievable disaster, not only on account of the destruction of the ozone layer, but also because of the development of a cloud from the innumerable fires, which could produce what Carl Sagan has called a "nuclear winter," in which nothing would grow for perhaps four years over most of the earth, including the tropics. Yet the United States still talks about "limited nuclear war" without any apparatus whatever for limiting it once it has begun. Even a limited nuclear war would probably make Europe uninhabitable. It is clear that unilateral national defense has become the greatest enemy not only of national security, but also of the human race.

The world system of unilateral national defense is not intended, of course, to produce the destruction of the human race. Neither are automobiles intended to kill several tens of thousands of persons a year; it just happens that they are designed to do so. Similarly, unilateral national defense is designed as a system to bring the evolutionary process on earth to a stop.

In regard to the population trap, things perhaps look a little better than they did in 1964, but not much. There has been a noticeable reduction in fertility around the world, but not enough to prevent what could be a catastrophic increase in world population in the next fifty years. I have long maintained that fertility is one of the least predictable of social parameters, and the past twenty years certainly bring this out. Nobody really expected the sharp decline in fertility in the United States and in many of the rich countries that occurred after about 1961, which I had not really noticed when I was writing this book. The distortion of age distributions is still going on around the world and presents a serious underlying problem. China seems to be almost the only country that is making a serious effort at population control, but even here it seems largely confined to the cities, which account for less than twenty percent of the population.

In regard to the entropy trap, I must confess to a little more optimism than I had twenty years ago. We are still a long way from the economic use of solar energy, but we have made real progress, especially in the photo-electric cell, although the electricty storage problem still remains largely unsolved. OPEC, the oil crisis, and the sharp rise in the price of oil have released an enormous potential for energy conservation. It is a fundamental principle that nobody will conserve anything that is cheap. But as soon as it becomes expensive, all sorts of conservation techniques come into play. Even in regard to materials entropy, which is perhaps the most serious in the long run (for the earth is, as I suggested, potentially a closed system in materials), things look a little better than they did, simply because of the tremendous development of substitutes. One does not have to go all the way with Julian Simon's outrageously optimistic book, *The Ultimate Resource*, to recognize that there is indeed an ultimate resource in the human mind that is a long way from being exhausted. Natural resources, the real price of which has been coming down for nearly 200 years because of the continued use of the ultimate resource in economizing them, may continue to represent a fairly mild problem for quite a long time to come, although exhaustion may eventually catch up with us. There does not seem to have been much progress in the genuine recycling of materials in this period.

I think, however, that I would add a few more traps to the three or four mentioned in *The Meaning of the Twentieth Century*. One might be called the "one-world trap." So far, evolution has persisted on earth for a long time, despite the many catastrophes that are suggested in the record. Part of this resiliency may result from the fact that the biosphere has not been a single ecosystem, but a great mosaic of relatively isolated ecosystems, isolated by continental drift, like Australia; by the rise in water levels as a result of ice melting, producing archipelagos like the Galapagos Islands; and so on. The human race, however, because of its artifacts, beginning perhaps with fire, has been able to adapt itself to all ecosystems, even that of outer space. We have been to the top of the highest mountain and the bottom of the deepest ocean. Even in my lifetime all the empty places on the maps of the earth have disappeared.

Until the Great Transition, human society was divided into a large number of relatively isolated cultures; even on the relatively small island of Papua New Guinea, there are some 700 languages. The American Indians had 200 or 300, suggesting that there were a large number of virtually isolated groups, with representatives seldom meeting for trade or even warfare. The Great Transition, however, is making the world a single social system and, in some respects, even a single ecosystem, as the human race transports species, both plant and animal, from their original habitat to different habitats all around the world, often with considerable extinction of older species. The trouble with one world is that if anything goes wrong, everything goes wrong. With many worlds we could have a catastrophe in one, like the destruction of the Mayan civilization or the extinction of the dinosaurs or the eruption of Krakatoa, and the rest would remain unscathed because of isolation.

At the cultural level the "one world" of the Great Transition is producing much local enrichment. We see this in the worldwide spread of religions and the sciences. Even by the end of the nineteenth century there were Christian churches of some kind in virtually every country on earth. The United States now has Black Muslims, Hari Krishnas, Soka Gakkai Buddhists, and Sikhs. My home in Boulder, Colorado, has become a world center of Tibetan Buddhism. Now, blue jeans are worn by young people everywhere, and rock and roll is almost universal, despite its being frowned on by the more puritan and fundamentalist societies of the Soviet Union and Iran. Colonel Sanders' Kentucky Fried Chicken is all over Japan, Benihana Japanese restaurants in the United States, and so on. In my lifetime I feel that I have witnessed almost the disappearance of the exotic because of the capacity for travel, not only of people but of cultures themselves. If we survive into the twenty-first century, one of the main problems may well be the preservation of cultural variety.

In the capitalist economies we have run into a trap that was little anticipated and of not much importance twenty years ago. This might be called the "profit-minus-interest" trap. Capitalism depends for its success on an active labor market and a high demand for labor on the part of employers, for a large proportion of employment is in the private sector. It is surprisingly little realized that when an employer hires a worker and spends money on wages, the employer sacrifices the interest that might have been gained if he had used his money to purchase bonds or other forms of debt. The employer does so in the hope of profit on the products of the work because the work produces things that are capable of upward revaluation and of being sold at a price that is above their average cost. Cost is what goes down in the balance sheet when something else goes up, either through exchange or production. For the cost accountant, the cost of a product is equal to the reduction in other assets that producing the product has entailed, such as the using up of raw materials, the using up of cash to pay wages, and the depreciation of fixed capital. Only if products are sold at a price above this cost is there profit. Government payrolls and the payrolls of nationalized industries are somewhat less subject to this phenomenon because of the existence of a public grants economy that can make up losses through taxes. Still, this problem underlies a lot of the trouble in socialist economies as well.

In the past twenty years we have seen a steady erosion of profit by interest. In the early 1960s interest was barely one percent of the U.S. national income, hardly a burden to anyone. Today it is close to eight percent, a severe burden on what might be called "productive capital." Part of this is a shift in financing away from equities into debt, but an important part of it is a rise in the real interest rates themselves. The real interest rate is roughly equal to the nominal interest rate in current dollars minus the rate of inflation plus the rate of deflation. If I borrow one hundred dollars at thirteen percent, I will repay one hundred thirteen dollars in a year's time; but if, in the meantime, all prices have risen eight percent, in terms of the purchasing power of what I have lent I am only getting one hundred five dollars. The real rate of interest is thus five percent. This is not quite mathematically accurate, but it is a good approximation.

Interest can be thought of as a tax that is levied on society by an unproductive owner of net worth in order to enable those who are good at controlling resources to control resources that they do not own. Successful borrowing occurs when what is done with the borrowed money creates an asset equal to or greater than the debt. If borrowed money is squandered for armaments or unproductive extravagance, there is no corresponding increase in assets. The net worth of the borrower must then go down, sometimes to the point of insolvency, at which point the value of the debt to the lender also goes down. An organization can be insolvent for a long time without being bankrupted, although the debt remains a burden on the borrower in the shape of interest. If the burden becomes too great, however, bankruptcy may be declared, in which case the loss of net worth is borne by the lender. This could easily set off a chain of bankruptcies, as the loss is distributed among those who lend to lenders, those who lend to lenders of lenders, and so on. The world is in great danger of something like that happening at present, for in the past twenty years a lot of unproductive borrowing has been done from unwise lenders.

A critical question, which has not received the attention that it deserves, is the extent to which profit declines in a mature capitalism as a result of a decline in investment. Total profit in a period is the gross increase in net worth of the aggregate balance sheets of profit-making institutions, like businesses. It is clear that this takes place if there is real investment—that is, addition to the total value of the stock of real assets held by businesses. If there is no real investment, profits shrink to zero, and here we could invoke a famous, but much neglected, theory that Keynes developed in his early book, *A Treatise on Money*, called the "widow's cruse" theory. A "widow's cruse," it may be recalled, was that jar of oil blessed by the prophet Elijah so that it never ran dry (1 Kings 17:14). Keynes supposes, then, that if profit-makers distribute all their profits to their owners in households, and if these people spend the money they have received, the money will come back to businesses in the form of purchased goods and profit will be re-created. I have been tempted to call this the "K theory" because it has been formulated, in one form or another, by Keynes, Kaldor, Kalecki, and Kenneth (Boulding), in my *Reconstruction of Economics* (1949). It still contains some unsolved problems, but we can see how it functions in rough form in the following oversimplified model: Suppose we have an economy in which all of the gross product is distributed to labor as wages or to capitalists as profit, neglecting interest for the time being. Suppose, now, that we have 1,000 units of gross product, of which 800 go to wages, 200 to profit. There is no saving or investment, so 1,000 units are spent; the value of the product therefore is 1,000, of which, again, 800 go to wages and 200 to profit. This will go on indefinitely as long as there is no saving or investment. This will be true no matter what the division of the gross product. And 300 to profit and 700 to wages will be just as stable as 200 and 800. So it suggests that we do not have to have investment in order to create profits, although investment certainly creates them.

The death of capitalism, therefore, in its latest stages with the disappearance of profit—which even Adam Smith and Ricardo worried about and Marx insisted on—does not have to happen. We can have profit in a stationary state, but in order to have it there must be no net saving. Just where the distribution lies between profit and wages depends on the history of the system. It is not an equilibrium division, but what might be called a "historical equilibrium," which could be very different if the history were different.

Another economic trap is particularly associated with government-owned and -run industries, especially the war industry in capitalist societies or a great deal of industry in Communist societies. This might be called the "cost-maximizing" trap, in which the price of the firm's product is determined not by consumers in the market, according to what they are willing to pay, but by a public authority financed by taxes. There is then little incentive toward cost minimization. We see this in capitalist countries in the cost overruns in the war industry and in publicly controlled electric power. It is almost universal in the Communist countries. In the private market sector of the economy there are strong motivations for cost minimization, for what an individual firm receives in revenue is relatively constant, and if it can reduce costs, this is reflected in its own profit. Whether this is reflected in aggregate profit, as we have seen, is another question, but there are certainly strong motivations for cost minimization in the private sector. In the public sector these motivations are small; where what the firm gets is cost-plus, the bigger the costs, the more plus there is! It is not surprising that cost overruns go to the point where they become too scandalous to be endured. Cost overruns are probably not fatal to any society, but they certainly have an effect in diminishing its enrichment.

Another example of the failure of cost-plus is the economics of the light-water reactor in the nuclear power industry, which now seems to be turning out to be a real economic disaster, partly because it came out of the war industry, which is essentially unsuited for civilian purposes, not only because it is engaged in producing the means of negative production—that is, weapons—but also because of the cost-plus effects noted elsewhere. The civilian nuclear industry has inherited a lot of this. Another factor is that the war industry is quite unused to any regulation because of its secrecy, and the regulation of the civilian nuclear power industry seems to have been remarkably incompetent.

Another trap, which is fairly widespread, might be called the "political incompetence" trap. Political competence has many dimensions. It involves creating an environment in which enrichment can proceed. It is concerned about the limits imposed by the entropy traps. It also has important aspects in terms of human rights and liberties. I have formulated a proposition that I call the "dismal theorem of political science," feeling that political science is really much more dismal than economics, despite Malthus. This is the theorem that most of the skills that lead to the rise to power unfit people to exercise it. Hence, there is a constant tendency for the political process to throw up powerful incompetents who do not have realistic views of the world around them, or who are perverted by a value system that appeals to the worst rather than the best of their followers.

The great virtue of democratic elections is that they introduce a certain random element in the selection of powerful people and create a strong atmosphere of taboo in society against political violence. Where political violence is common, as it is in Latin America and in some of the new African countries, it is clear that the skills of being successful in political violence are by no means the skills of being successful in governing. Even in democratic societies, of course, people get elected for reasons that have little to do with their skill in governing. Nevertheless, there is a certain system of checks and balances, as we saw in the Watergate debacle; at least it seemed possible for our political structure and culture to correct a mistake. The same thing happened in Australia in 1975, when the governor appointed by the prime minister actually fired him and called an election that defeated him because he seemed to be carrying the country toward unacceptable inflation. In Argentina, however, it has taken forty or fifty years to correct some disastrous political choices. They are still not corrected in Chile and Uruguay.

The "cult of personality" that has plagued the Communist countries, whether Stalin in the Soviet Union; Mao, especially in his later years, in China; Hoxha in Albania; Kim in North Korea; Castro in Cuba, has often had devastating consequences, like the first Collectivization in the Soviet Union, the Great Leap Forward (that turned out to be a great leap backward) in China, and, still more, the Cultural Revolution, the nightmare of isolation and repression that is Albania, and so on. Nevertheless, there are signs of hope, even in the Communist countries. The solidarity movement in Poland, although it did not succeed, certainly provided some checks and balances on government, and the remarkable situation in Hungary, perhaps now the freest of the Communist countries, suggests that even leaders who rise to power because of violence can become fairly competent in government.

A good example of government incompetence that has lasted for a long time is the strong tendency for governments, particularly the authoritarian governments, to go in for disastrous price controls. We see this, for instance, in Egypt. A fascinating article by Morris Silver, "Controlling Grain Prices and Decontrolling Bubonic Plague" in the *Journal of Social and Biological Structures* (April 1982), makes a convincing case that it was the government policies that tried to keep grain prices down in time of scarcity, which led not only to famine, but also extensive storage of grains in the households, which in turn led to rats, fleas, and the bubonic plague. Many of the Arab countries, like Egypt and Tunisia, are examples of policies that certainly hover in this direction and could well turn out to be disastrous.

Finally, there is something related to the above that might be called the "fundamentalist" trap, in which the powerful leader rises to power because of appeal to some earlier source of personal identity and security, as, in a sense, Hitler did in Germany, Stalin did in the Soviet Union, Khomeini did in Iran, and Jerry Falwell might do in the United States, if he is ever successful. This leads into such things as the destruction of genetics in the Soviet Union under Stalin, the destruction of the Baha'i religious community in Iran under Khomeini, the destruction of the Jews under Hitler, and so on.

What, then, of the twenty-first century? Where will we be in sixteen years? There seem to be two major categories of possible futures. One is the possible total catastrophe of nuclear war, the probability of which has certainly been rising in the past few years. The other is a whole series of scenarios involving relatively minor changes in what we have now. One such change that seems likely to continue is the change in the status of women. If I were writing *The Meaning of the Twentieth Century* today, I would not use the sexist language that it often employs, particularly using the term man for the human race. This may seem like a small thing, but it is a profound and important symbol. Another thing that has been happening (which one hopes will continue) is an increasingly sophisticated study of the nature of threat systems. This is the essence of a great deal that goes under the name of "peace research," of which I have long been a strong advocate. The problem here is how to widen the agendas of decision of those decision-makers in charge of national defense, getting them away from the existing system, in which national defense has become the principal enemy of national security, into a policy of genuine security, which involves a much more specific and moderate use of threat and a much wider use of integrative structures.

One of the great men of the century was undoubtedly Martin Luther King, who understood, in a sense, how to use the hypocrisy of American ideology as a fulcrum to create significant social change in race relations, with remarkably little violence and yet with remarkable success. Even game theory has created a different world of ideas and image of reality for those who are familiar with it, as applied to all sorts of the practical and political problems of the world.

There is, therefore, hope, and it lies precisely in Julian Simon's "ultimate resource," the extraordinary capacity of the human mind for learning, which we are a long way from having exhausted. It is often hard to project these learning processes into the future because they frequently occur rather suddenly, like the remarkable change in the Catholic Church under Pope John XXIII. It gave up being *"semper eadem"*—that is, always the same—and became remarkably adaptable to some needs, at least, in the modern world. In terms of the population trap, it still has a certain way to go.

It is by no means impossible that the Soviet Union could produce a leader like Pope John who would bring enormous changes for the better in a short time, simply by being more relaxed. The ultimate message, therefore, is "where there is life, there are brains, and where there are brains, there is hope."

Willis W. Harman   **3**

HOW I LEARNED TO LOVE
THE FUTURE

Futures research is one of those professions that it is hardly possible to
engage in without undergoing change. Cultural anthropology is another
such area; to really put yourself "inside the skin" of a person in another
culture is, forever after, to see your own society in a different way. To really
grapple with the question of what futures are accessible to human thought,
and what critical choices society faces, whether conscious of them or not,
is to confront internal issues of personal values and priorities that we might
otherwise be tempted to evade. Hence, to study futures is to change. Whether
or not this generalization holds for everyone, I know that personal change
has occurred in me over the seventeen years since I plunged into the study
of the future. I have divided my remarks into two parts: Intellectual Evolution and Specific Insights.

INTELLECTUAL EVOLUTION

My formal educational background was in physics and electrical engineering. After only a brief taste of engineering practice I chose to go into
engineering teaching. Starting in 1948, I taught electronic circuit and electronic tube design, statistical communication theory, and systems analysis,
mainly at Stanford University, with brief stints at the University of Florida
and the Royal Technical University in Copenhagen.

Meanwhile, another aspect of my life was unfolding. In 1954 I had an
"upending" experience in the form of a two-week intensive seminar that
combined discussion of value, ethical, and spiritual issues with such experiential adjuncts as painting with the left hand, music listening and quiet

This essay appeared originally in the *World Future Society Bulletin* (Nov.-Dec. 1984).
Copyright 1984 by the World Future Society. Reprinted, with changes, by permission of the
publisher.

meditation, and sharing with others recollections of moving and significant life experiences. I remember sobbing at the final meeting of the group, bewildered by the feelings that were intruding on my well-ordered rational thought processes. That experience led, by a succession of steps, to my initiating a graduate seminar entitled "The Human Potentiality" (which continued for fourteen years before the human potential movement swept up from Esalen and made it seem unnecessary, since so many even more experiential educational opportunities were easily available). In the early 1960s I became deeply involved with the newly formed Association for Humanistic Psychology.

These two life streams converged in the mid–1960s with the opportunity to combine concepts of systems analysis with values and cultural change in the new discipline of futures research. The U.S. Office of Education invited proposals, in 1966, to do research and policy analysis relating to long-term future prospects of the United States (ten- to 30-year projections) and their implications for educational policy. I moved part-time to Stanford Research Institute (later SRI International) to work on the proposal and within a few years had essentially completed the shift from engineering teaching to futures research.

The Early Years of Futures Research

The group I assembled at SRI to undertake this work included several individuals who saw great promise for using systems analysis and computer-based models of society, as well as the array of other systematic futures research techniques that were much talked about at the time. We did indeed embark on a two-year endeavor to systematically generate an exhaustive set of scenarios for the United States for the next thirty years, attempting to bracket all plausible major trend developments. (This turned out to be a sobering exercise. Among the forty-odd scenarios we looked at in some detail, only two or three portrayed "future histories" that anyone would be likely to voluntarily choose to live through; and even these few required, for their realization, more political foresight than the United States has habitually displayed.)

We were simultaneously pursuing a second track, that of analyzing cultural trends, value shifts, and similar "soft" indicators. This approach, when combined with insights from various historians, sociologists, cultural anthropologists, and other analysts who had adopted more whole-system approaches, turned out to be quite fruitful. It eventually spun off SRI's "Values and Lifestyles" (VALS) program, which went on to become commercially successful as a tool for corporate marketing and strategic planning.

We published several research notes during our first six months, one of which had to do with the relationship between basic cultural premises and educational policy. One insight in that report turned out to have a number of interesting applications, and I summarize it briefly here.

The Importance of Underlying Assumptions

We argued that policy inevitably reflects an underlying belief system, and that sometimes the apparent policy issues at stake are actually mere reflections of deeper belief system issues. We created a simply taxonomy of these underlying sets of basic assumptions by examining the answers that people seem to assume for the three questions:

1. *How do we acquire knowledge?* (Through our physical senses alone, through intuition, extrasensory perception, instinctual heredity, revelation?)
2. *What is the direction of ultimate "explanations" of phenomena?* (Do we think that we are moving closer to understanding a phenomenon when we relate it to elemental factors? Or when we experience it fully and existentially? Or when we attribute it to God's will?)
3. *What is the direction of understanding motivations, needs, goals, values?* (Through elemental biochemical tensions? Conscious decision? An unconscious conflict between the id and the superego? Some evolutionary cosmic force?)

We identified the following five major sets of assumptions, of which four at least had been around for many centuries:

1. *Positivist-behaviorist*, strongly influencing modern science
2. *Dynamic-psychological*, strongly represented in neo-Freudian psychotherapy
3. *Humanistic-existential*, a persistent mainstream in the humanities now making a bid for scientific recognition in humanistic psychology
4. *Creationist*, dominant in the Middle Ages and an important influence in education at virtually all times and places in Western civilization
5. *"Perennial wisdom,"* the esoteric core understandings common to most of the world's spiritual traditions

We pointed out that within the United States there exist entire educational systems predicated on each of these five outlooks, and argued that even though many other things seemed to be going on, in fact these many-dimensional policy discussions reflected a basic reassessment of the relative fruitfulness, not to say "truth," of these five bases.

It seems to me still, as it did seventeen years ago, that such basic assumptions, partly unconscious, play a far greater role in individual and collective behavior than do the ideologies, attitudes, and values to which we pay so much more attention, partly because they are easier to get at with survey research and other probes. I am also convinced of what was at that time much more tentative: that the most fundamental level of global change at the present time and the most crucial issues are at this subterranean level of tacitly held, relatively unspoken premises. But of that, more later.

The Importance of Subtle Factors

In a slightly later report, attempting to derive a unifying focus for educational policy research, I wrote some observations on the importance of "subtle factors."

We were addressing the question, What factors in the educational process really make a difference, and how can the U.S. educational system be changed to optimize the desired effects of these factors? Observing that the necessary research had by no means been accomplished, I ventured a guess as to how it would eventually come out. I suggested that the factors important to positive educational outcomes would tend to fall into two groups. One is a group of manifest factors that are the obvious sorts of things one would assess to describe an educational situation, e.g., cost per pupil, student-teacher ratio, use of visual aids, curricular organization, physical environment. The other group, of what might be termed "subtle factors," is difficult to get at in operational terms and is typically overlooked in describing an educational situation. The second list might include such items as the teacher's expectations of the students, the teacher's basic self-esteem, the student's perception of the relevance of the whole learning situation to his or her own goals, and the congruence of stated and nonverbal messages. My hunch was (and still is) that the manifest factors would turn out to be quite unimportant and the subtle factors, far more important than is presently thought. The implications of this conclusion, if correct, are profound.

In considering the second part of the questions regarding system change, again it seemed likely that manipulating such obvious variables as budgets, curricula, and organizational strategies would produce the appearance of change but not much real improvement in outcomes. On the other hand, some of the subtle factors would turn out to be critical. Thus, I wrote that real change would require changing the "cultural image" of the function of the schools, the role of the teachers, and the growth potentialities of the children. This may not seem very different from the many current proposals to upgrade education through improved curricula and more technology. What I am talking about is, in fact, radically different. It is different in precisely the way that a neurotic begins functioning differently when he or she acquires a new self rather than being split into warring factions. This crucial image difference makes it possible to recognize personal complicity in one's "problems" and proceed in an integrated way toward finding solutions. To attain this kind of change in a learning situation is difficult, subtle, and nonsuperficial in precisely the same way.

Similar observations could be made with regard to other social objectives and broader societal change. By the early 1970s it was increasingly apparent to me that profound societal change was under way, and that the forces bringing this about were to be discovered in deep changes in the collective psyche.

The Emerging Transformation Picture

One could identify three cultural currents, each of which was contributing to societal change, and hence to a high degree of uncertainty about the future. The three were as follows:

1. The *industrial/postindustrial* thrust, on the basis of which most forecasts were being made. This thrust, and its consequences if it remained dominant, was well described by Daniel Bell in his scholarly book on the postindustrial society. But I didn't believe that we would be traveling that path because of the growing strength of the other two forces.

2. The *reactionary* thrust, which one could see coming because of the fear generated as people looked ahead at a future, many features of which involved diminishment of qualities of life they had cherished. The emphasis in this group was on re-establishing (if possible) the conditions existing when things worked well and life was simpler, and when moral, quality-of-life, family, and community values were not threatened. (In fact, a segment of this group later adopted the name "The Moral Majority," a name that somewhat overstates their present or future influence in all probability.)

3. The *"new consciousness"* thrust, which lumped several superficially dissimilar things together with the argument that they were manifestations of a deeper unity. The three major components I saw in this thrust were (a) a consciousness and an affirmation of the self as unique, with unlimited potentiality, and a sense of a basic "right to personhood," as Theodore Roszak later described it; (b) a consciousness of being part of an interconnected whole, and hence affirming both a cooperative and an ecological ethic; and (c) an affirmation of one's own culture or subculture, gender, ethnic group, etc. These three components may be present in varying degrees in the different groups making up this thrust. For example, many are spiritual, with a sort of "neo-Transcendentalist" belief system, but some are not. For some, cultural identity is a crucial issue; for others, not.

In general, the overall thrust of "new consciousness" is life-affirming and relatively noninvolved with the issues of evil, sin, and guilt (which received much more attention in the reactionary group). This current tends to embody an image of a desirable future that entails a fundamental transformation of industrial society. (It was later described in detail by Marilyn Ferguson and dubbed *The Aquarian Conspiracy.*)

If these three thrusts do indeed correctly identify the three major currents of change, then several generic scenarios suggest themselves:

1. *Postindustrial*, in which the first thrust prevails and the other two peter out;

2. *Transformational*, in which the third thrust comes to predominate after a transition period that might involve a considerable degree of economic and social disruption; and

3. *Collapse into authoritarianism*, in which neither of the first two thrusts clearly prevails and the resulting conflicts essentially tear the society apart.

Something like these three scenarios, with embellishments and augmentations, remained in the background of our policy research and strategic-planning consulting from the early 1970s on. Typically, our clients (which were increasing in number and beginning to include corporations as well as public sector agencies) preferred that discussion of the transformational scenario be muted or eliminated. They apparently feared the prospect of being judged "flaky" or "far out" more than the "realistic pessimism" of the economic collapse scenario.

I will comment later on the conceptual assistance we were getting in these early years through various historians, sociologists, and anthropologists, but I want to mention at this point one particular giant on whose shoulders we stood. Some future historian, looking back at the intellectual achievements of the twentieth century, will single out for special honors the sociologist Pitirim Sorokin of Harvard University. We made great use of his work on the decline and transformation of societies and of his later work on the transformative potentialities of "creative altruism." He was decades ahead of his time and suffered ostracism by his social science colleagues for daring to do research on such a squishy subject as altruistic love. He was raising the crucial issues of survival of the planet at a time (the 1950s) when most of us were fast asleep.

Through the next dozen years, until our futures research group at SRI was disbanded in 1983, this image of a society in transformation strengthened and my understanding of it deepened. As it did I found it irksome to do routine work for those clients who preferred not to see the signs of a coming climacteric. I found myself drifting away from the standard strategic-planning studies and into individual contributions in the form of workshops and seminars. I saw myself as neither "establishment" nor "new age," but quite comfortable in the space between, concentrating on what, by then, seemed to me to be the critical issue—how to get through the transition period (which I have come to take as a given) with a minimum of social disruption and attendant human misery. There were no clients for this issue per se, but it became and remains a central focus for me.

In 1977 I joined ex-astronaut Edgar Mitchell's Institute of Noetic Sciences as president, dropping back to half-time at SRI. This decision was a reflection of the importance I had come to attach to research on consciousness and unconscious processes, and the relevance to individuals and to the planet of a clearer understanding of both the psychic origins of our problems and the underused inner resources to help with their solution. This interest intensified until concern with healing—of the individual and of the planet— became an obsession that leaves little room for anything else. This is my present state.

SPECIFIC INSIGHTS

A few specific insights came to me along the way and might possibly be of use to someone else. I won't attempt to argue their correctness, but just describe them as they appear to me.

Studying the future requires interpreting the present. It is of little use to imaginatively construct a gaggle of alternative scenarios of the future unless you seriously address the question of plausibility. Is it plausible that we could get there from here?

It may seem a simple thing to describe the here and now. Don't we have a good estimate of the population, gross national product, inflation rate, balance of trade, and other important indicators? Would those have told us where we were in history in, say, 1968? What was the real meaning of the assassinations, the ghetto riots, the anti-Vietnam demonstrations, the hippies, the growing dependence on Middle East oil?

The point is, we can understand the present better than we typically do. We can understand it in terms of history, particularly cultural history. We can understand the hopes and fears and dreams and frustrations, and the signs of attitude change and consciousness change—the forces that impel people to affect history. We can understand, to some extent at least, the indications of powerful forces arising in the collective mind, partly unconscious. And when we understand the present better, then we can better forecast the future, and create scenarios that embody the dynamic of change rather than merely the uninformative surface indicators of change.

Societal change takes place at various levels. The French historian Fernand Braudel puts us on to this. In his introduction to *The Mediterranean* he described why he was writing three separate histories of the region in the age of Philip II. One is the usual sort of history, an accounting of events and their supposed connections. The second is a history of institutional evolution. The third is at the level of slowly varying but fundamental shaping forces—climate, demographics, geography, deep cultural change. His point is that the common form of history is deceptive in its presumed causal understandings; changes at the deeper levels shape what is happening at the events level in ways that will not be discerned without a thorough analysis of the deeper levels. Futures research at the level of events (e.g., cross-impact matrices) is likewise superficial and deceptive.

It is important to understand the present in terms of different time scales. If we think in terms of years, we might come up with an understanding of certain social developments in 1984 as being influenced by characteristics of the Reagan administration, the recession, the ups and downs of oil prices, attitudes of Third World debtor nations, and so on. Understanding the same developments in terms of decades, we might see them as being influenced by such factors as the changes in values and attitudes that seem to have started in the mid–1960s, the growth of OPEC, the cold war mentality after World War II, and the spread of the mass consumption society. Now looking at the same developments with a time horizon of centuries, we might note the long-term trends since the industrial revolution, and how these inevitably encounter fundamental resource and environmental problems almost re-gardless of any conceivable governmental and international actions. Think-ing of the same developments in terms of millennia, one observes the fundamental transformation of Western Europe at the end of the Middle Ages, notes certain similarities, and wonders if we may now be approaching a similarly fundamental transformation—only far more rapidly.

All of these interpretations are important. All of them are essential to a fuller understanding of what the future may hold.

Extraordinary change sometimes happens. It was another historian who told us that ordinary historical change may seem to be caused by techno-logical, political, and economic developments; battles and treaties; elections and assassinations; legislation and government programs; and so on. But rarely in history there appears another kind of "extraordinary" change, such as the profound transformation in Europe at the end of the Roman Empire, or again at the end of the Middle Ages. When such a fundamental transformation occurs, said our historian friend, it is because "vast numbers of people change their minds a little bit." What "causes" them to change? The question may not be answerable. Is that what has been happening in the United States and, indeed, in much of the rest of the world since the mid–1960s? I believe it is.

Alternate perceptions of reality are real. (Here I quote from a method-ological comment in one of SRI's energy policy studies.) The Japanese movie *Rashomon* is based on the tale "In a Grove," by Ryunosuke Akutagawa. In this story a robber assaults a couple in a cedar grove, and the husband is stabbed to death. The incident is described by five eyewitnesses, each of whom has a distinctly different impression of what happened. All five di-vergent stories are "correct." The power of the story, as the author's intro-duction remarks, "undermines our prosaic confidence in distinguishing between subjective and objective, truth and fiction."

The American anthropologist Oscar Lewis used a "Rashomon technique" based on this concept in his attempts to understand the culture of poverty. Another anthropologist, Ruth Benedict, introduced the concept of patterns of perception in *Patterns of Culture*, as her basic analysis tool for under-standing and comparing societies. Graham Allison used a similar technique in his analysis of the Cuban missile crisis (see his book *Essence of Decision*).

The same basic idea is useful for making sense out of the extremely complex area of energy policy. We start from the assumption that different groups in society (e.g., the nuclear power industry, Middle Eastern oil suppliers, government bureaucrats, environmentalists) experience different perceptual realities. They literally see different worlds. If one aspires to help resolve the conflicts between them, it is important to recognize that none of these perceptual realities is "wrong."

Analysis of policy issues from this assumption may seem similar to the sort of stakeholder group analysis that one may find in a major technology assessment. There is, however, a significant difference. The function of stakeholder analysis is to help assess a proposed technological development by clarifying who wins and who loses, and how much. The analysis of perceptual patterns, on the other hand, is more concerned with how the different groups define winning, and what factors they consider of fundamental importance—to the eventual end of improving communications and facilitating the common seeking of solutions. I am convinced that this approach has far more to offer than has so far been recognized, in many controversial areas but especially with regard to the issues surrounding the nuclear weapons dilemma.

A Personal Choice

If you have concluded that beyond all reasonable doubt, this generation is living through one of the most fateful periods in history, what do you do? Continue with business as usual? It hardly fits. The times demand a more creative response.

The foregoing account will, I hope, convey some ideas of how I arrived at a number of interconnected conclusions:

First, that the awakening—the reperception—is real and spreading, and thus that the transformation to a better world is *possible*. (This means a better world for all, with peace and fairness and protection of human rights and caring for the earth—without throwing away humanity's technological gains, although we may have to curb our appetites a bit.)

Second, that none of the possible alternatives to this transformation look attractive or even safe.

Third, that because of the power of an attractive image of the future to transform the present, every time one person shifts over to affirming the possibility and necessity of a future that works for everybody, that ripples around the globe and increases the probability a little bit.

Fourth, that all this being so, I can think of no better thing to do with my life than to be totally involved, as best I know how, with the inner and outer transformation that I am now convinced is the only path toward a future that I would feel good about bequeathing to my grandchildren.

And that's how it is.

4

THE FUTURE: NOT QUITE SO
EASY AS IT LOOKED

As I look back over my writings of the past fifteen years, I am struck by two ideas. One is that predicting the future is harder than many of us were wont to believe, even simply on the descriptive level. The second idea is that prescribing futures on the normative level—deciding what kind of future we would like to achieve and how we would like to achieve it—is perhaps even harder.

In large measure the second conclusion stems from the first. Achieving desired goals necessarily involves choosing means toward ends, and if we are unsure about how particular means empirically relate to particular ends, then the ends themselves become more obscure as a practical matter. Historical examples of this principle abound, not simply the "noble experiment" of Prohibition, with its unintended consequence of increased criminality and disrespect for law, but more recently the vexing and all-important question of whether or not deterrence based on large nuclear weapons stockpiles is more or less likely to bring on the global Armageddon every sane person fears.

In *Technological Man: The Myth and the Reality* (1969) I argued for several propositions. On the level of description I held that technology was not yet fundamentally changing our political, social, or cultural structures as much as many futurists were claiming (or hoping) was so. My reason was that technology was still under the control of bourgeois man, with his traditional views of the nature of society and the universe.[1] On the level of normative prescription I held that it was necessary to create what I called "technological man," who would so understand technology that he could control it for human ends, in accordance with a view of the universe that

This essay appeared originally in the *World Future Society Bulletin* (May-June 1984). Copyright 1984 by the World Future Society. Reprinted, with changes, by permission of the publisher.

was naturalistic (acknowledging that "man is in fact part of nature rather than something apart from it"),[2] holistic (that everything is interconnected), and immanentist (that the world is "determined not from outside but from within").[3] Based on these principles, technological man could create a more humane society using technology not as an end in itself, but as a means to human growth and fulfillment.

In *The Future of Technological Civilization* (1974)[4] I attempted to outline a desirable future society based on what I called "ecological humanism," the belief that man "must live in a conscious ecological relationship with nature and with other men, and that the ecological perspective on the natural order provides a necessary analogue for the social order."[5] This new social order would be brought about by what I called an "immanent revolution," in which the converging activities of individual men and women throughout the world would, over time, bring about a basic change in the values and structures of our civilization.

Critical reaction to my ideas was mixed. Some readers welcomed *Technological Man* because they saw in it—correctly—an alternative to the perceived antitechnological doomsaying of critics such as Jacques Ellul and others. But too often these very readers—apparently unable to escape from the "either/or" thinking that plagues most social controversy—lumped me together with those who believe that advanced technology can do no wrong and should be uncritically embraced. Response to *The Future of Technological Civilization* was similar, except that some thoughtful critics took it as another example of "prophetic politics" in the utopian tradition—long on goals but short on explaining how one achieved them in the real world.[6] While the first book achieved some success as presenting an alternative to the various simplistic views that technology was all bad in its consequences, the second was largely lost in the shuffle of contention over the "limits to growth" and the largely parallel ideas of social change pushed by Charles Reich as "Consciousness III," in his book *The Greening of America*.[7]

How do I view my earlier ideas today, and the criticisms made of them? First of all (although this is not the most important point), I am far more aware today than I was when I wrote *Technological Man* of the issues raised by feminist criticism of the constant general use by society of the word *man* to describe all humankind. In *The Future of Technological Civilization* I tried to avoid sexist language as much as possible. But more recently still, I have become more aware of the possibly radical differences between male and female ways of looking at the world, and the possibility that contemporary technology, from its inception centuries ago, represents a particularly masculine reaction to the total natural environment. Were I writing either book today, I would certainly try to take into account the vast feminist literature on science, philosophy, and related subjects.[8]

More fundamentally, however, since writing these two books I have undergone a subtle but important change of mood, if not of basic conviction about the nature of the universe. Both books were designed to appeal to a general, educated Western readership on the level of reason and science, as understood by the dominant scientific paradigms, although I tried to integrate insights from the newer ones that have been emerging in many areas.[9] But at the explicit level, neither book dealt directly with the problems raised by religion, assuming, in the tradition of St. Thomas Aquinas, that the natural order was, at a certain level of analysis, an autonomous system of phenomena. In my writings God was only implicit in an almost deistic, ecumenical sense. Although my explicit convictions about the relation between the natural and the supernatural orders of reality have not changed since writing the books, and I would still hold that these two levels of reality are not really separate, but interpenetrate at reality's heart,[10] I have developed an increasing consciousness of the ultimate mystery that is at the heart of human existence on both the individual and the social level. This leads of necessity to a less rationalistic view of the world, and hence to a more skeptical view of the possibilities of prediction and ultimate analysis. As an epigram popular in some circles puts it: "Life is a mystery to be lived, not a problem to be solved." Accepting this dictum, as I now do, puts a whole new perspective on the psychological and philosophical basis of futurism—indeed of the whole human enterprise.

I turn now to particulars. Since writing *Technological Man* I have been impressed by the extent to which bourgeois man (gender intended) remains in firm control in the industrialized world, including the so-called Communist bloc. Although vast changes in technology—new energy sources, computers, genetic engineering, and so on—are shaking the roots of our civilization, the decisions as to how these are to be introduced and utilized remain under the control of the dominant traditional orders. Not only is bourgeois man still dominant today, as I argued, but he is even more firmly entrenched. I had not anticipated that this would be the case. Although right-wing governments have been coming to power generally throughout the world, it is especially in the United States (under the Reagan administration—one of the most ideological in our history) that old-fashioned capitalism more than ever calls the tune. The future now facing us in the short run appears increasingly Heinleinian.[11] Already, private enterprise is moving in on the U.S. space program, dominating energy generation (including solar, which is now essentially under the control of the old-line oil companies) and genetic engineering applications. Universities are becoming increasingly (and, if possible, even more openly) dominated by private industry through research consortia of various kinds. As a consequence, decisions about technology in the widest sense are being based on market considerations rather than on broader social ones. In the Soviet and Chinese spheres the interests of the traditional state party system—however one wishes to define these—still prevail. Technological man is not emerging in the control centers of either Western capitalist or socialist societies.

The general result is that technology remains, for practical purposes, an independent variable in society, subject only to the constraints of the market. Otherwise, whatever can be done will be done. Even the defeat a decade ago of the U.S. supersonic transport plane, the high point, in many ways, of the revolt against technological independence from society, was, it must be remembered, not a triumph over market forces, but simply a refusal by government to further subsidize one specific new technology.

What is true in the case of civilian technology is even more dramatically true in the case of military technology. Almost any new weapons system that can be envisioned is being pushed, subject only to economic competition among alternatives (and in recent years in the United States not even much of that). The belief that if the United States does not do something, the Soviets will (or might) is used to justify the B–1 bomber, the MX missile system, updating nerve gas stockpiles, and similar projects. Once-discarded systems and weapons are revived, new refinements of nuclear weaponry proceed apace, and space increasingly becomes an arena of military (as well as private corporate) hegemony. Since President Reagan's "Star Wars" speech of early 1983, this trend has increased dramatically.

It may be objected that countertrends or examples exist. But the Interior Department and the Environmental Protection Agency (EPA) have—to put it mildly—exerted much less of a check on technological change and unbridled gross economic growth than they once did. It is even doubtful whether the National Environmental Policy Act of 1969, or similar legislation, could be passed under present conditions. Ironically, while the environmental movement is fighting a rear guard action in the United States and in many other Western nations, there are indications that both the Soviet Union and China are encountering unexpectedly heavy pressures on their economies caused by environmental disasters.

The paradox and irony of all this is seen in the combination of increased consciousness of major problems accompanied by relative indifference to them. In the United States, studies by the EPA and the National Academy of Sciences indicate—although they disagree about how urgent the problem is—that human activity is actually making the earth warmer, with possible dire consequences. But these warnings have elicited little response beyond assertions that more study is needed, that nothing practical can be done to change the activity patterns in time to prevent disaster, or that people will adjust to a warmer earth through the normal slow social mechanisms. It will be interesting to see what, if any, effect on nuclear strategy results from the studies by American and Russian scientists suggesting that even a small nuclear exchange will make the earth catastrophically colder.[12] So far there has been virtually no response from governments. "Things" are firmly in the saddle.

None of this denies that changes in consciousness are in fact taking place among many people, as thinkers such as Marilyn Ferguson and others have pointed out.[13] New paradigms are emerging in realms as apparently far apart from one another as physics and psychology; millions of Americans embrace "voluntary simplicity";[14] more people every day reject the manipulative, exploitative ethics of industrial man. But these changes, on which so many hopes for "immanent revolution" were based, are not taking place fast enough, and there is a parallel increase in the number of Americans who consciously believe that it is necessary not only to remain in the old consciousness, but also to intensify it. Such beliefs have emerged not only in the United States, but elsewhere too, as American civilization has spread. Dramatic examples include the rising tide of extreme nationalism, militarism, and religious fundamentalism in America, as well as the increasing extent to which students—especially at the college level—are vocationally oriented in step with the traditional value system. What is actually taking place is a race between two trends: one toward bourgeois man and one toward technological man, and the first of these seems to be winning.

But something else is taking place as well. At the time I wrote the books under discussion, it was easy for me to assume—however naively—that what was taking place in the United States would necessarily take place in the future throughout the world as a whole. Like most futurists of the time, I took it as axiomatic that, as the world's greatest industrial nation, the United States represented the "wave of the future." This assumption is no longer valid. Americans today are confronted with "exogenous variables" of vast significance, most notably the assertion of self-consciousness on the part of "Third World" nations and the rise in economic power of Japan and Western Europe.

In the case of the Third World, one of the most fundamental tenets of futurists and of the whole modern development community is being challenged. It has largely been taken for granted—following an explicit or often simply implicit assumption of technological determinism—that the spread of Western technology to other parts of the world would be accompanied by secularization and social modernization generally. The Islamic world, however, seems to be moving in another direction, most dramatically exemplified by Iran. Only time will tell whether or not the resurgence of fundamentalism throughout Islam represents a long-range trend or simply a "blip" on the screen of history, but the idea that modern machines would immediately and inexorably bring about the end of traditional world views is no longer quite as certain as it once seemed to be.

Along with this trend in the Third World has come the loss of the complete economic dominance of the world once enjoyed by the United States (this despite remaining paradoxically the world's largest national economy by far). The United States is no longer as clearly supreme in new technology as it once seemed to be, and how to meet the challenge of new high-tech industries arising in other nations is a major—perhaps *the* major—issue in current U.S. economic policy.

Although the ramifications of these developments are vast and complex, one thing they make clear is that the question of where America is headed no longer simply depends on the outcome of competition among modes of consciousness or life-styles within the United States. What happens in the rest of the world, not simply what happens in the United States, will determine the planet's future. Indeed, what happens in the rest of the world will increasingly influence what happens in the United States.

One great problem of all utopias has always been their relation to the outside world. Plato and Thomas More sought isolation in different ways. America, too, it can be argued, has its own utopian tradition central to its sense of identity, the "city set upon the hill."[15] One may contend that Jefferson's dream of a pastoral America fell early prey to the need to industrialize and defend ourselves against foreign foes.[16] Often throughout history a civilization more advanced in terms of culture and human values has been defeated by one more adept in the use of brutal power. Implicit in many futurist utopian schemes—including in large measure my own normative aspirations in *The Future of Technological Civilization*—was the assumption of America's relative autonomy vis-à-vis the rest of the world, or at least of American leadership. This assumption now seems to me clearly part of America's whole paradoxically isolationist-messianic national tradition, and is of course no longer valid. The future world will be one in which powerful others—Europe, the Third World, the Soviet Union, Japan, and China—do not share U.S. visions of the future, and Americans will have to be prepared to alter their hopes and expectations accordingly. This central fact has vast implications for such movements as decentralization, voluntary simplicity, feminism, and almost any hopeful American trend one can name.

There is, of course, a significant literature that deals with the global future as such, but it is small in comparison with the volume of futurist writings as a whole, and culture-bound in the same sense that the whole futures movement has been.[17] Increasingly, U.S. futurists will need to take into account not only that other cultures may have substantively different views of the future, but also that they may actually conceive of time itself in a different way.

How do I view the future differently today than I did in earlier years? Basically, three new convictions have emerged to dominate my thinking. One I have just mentioned is the belief that the United States and other advanced industrial nations can not entirely control even their own futures—much less the future of the world. The second is that U.S. futurists have tended to unduly aggregate the future, speaking as if the "world" were the only possible unit of change. At some level, of course, it is—as in questions such as global nuclear war—but that does not rule out the possibility that different nations and cultures may experience radically different futures and perhaps move in different directions from one another at the same time, making generalizations about "the future" difficult. The future, whatever its precise outline, will be a disjunctive one, between nations and even within individual nations. There may well be no future for the "global village" as such, but different futures for different neighborhoods in the "global metropolis." This will be true even if major ecological forces, such as climatic changes, take place and affect the planet as a whole, for they will impact differently on different localities and be responded to in different fashions by particular groups and areas. The future will not be a single picture, but a mosaic, and it may not be a clearly patterned one.

Third, I view the future with increasing uncertainty. Most of the assumptions on which we futurists built up our pictures of the future—be they as optimistic as those of Herman Kahn or as pessimistic as those of the Club of Rome—are turning out to have been simplistic in various ways and at various levels. Along with greater complexity than we bargained for comes greater uncertainty, both as to general characteristics and to particulars.

Are these new convictions counsels of despair at either the descriptive or the normative level? I think not. Hard as it may be to foretell the future, we still have to do the best we can, both as individuals and as societies. Unless we abandon ourselves to a completely present-centered view of existence, we have no choice. I am still enough of a Westerner to believe that some coherent vision of the future is necessary for social health in any society.[18] But we must learn not to place too much credence on our own judgments about what is to come, and to prepare ourselves as fully as possible for unforeseen developments. As far as our values are concerned, we ought to act with judicious skepticism, yet recognize that we must do what we believe will make life better for those who come after us, even if (as is perhaps both necessary and desirable) the determination of the future is not entirely in our hands.

NOTES

1. Victor Ferkiss, *Technological Man: The Myth and the Reality*, New York: George Braziller, 1969, passim.

2. Ibid., p. 250.

3. Ibid., p. 251.

4. Victor Ferkiss, *The Future of Technological Civilization*, New York: George Braziller, 1974.

5. Ibid., p. 206.

6. Neil Riemer, "Prophetic Politics: On the Political Philosophy of Stavrianos, Ferkiss, and Falk," *Alternative Futures*, Vol. 2, Fall 1979, pp. 66–82.

7. Charles Reich, *The Greening of America*, New York: Random House, 1970.

8. See especially Carolyn Merchant, *The Death of Nature: Women, Ecology, and the Scientific Revolution*, San Francisco: Harper & Row, 1979.

9. For example, Fritjof Capra, *The Tao of Physics*, Boulder, Colo.: Shambala,

1975, and Gary Zukav, *The Dancing Wu Li Masters: An Overview of the New Physics*, New York: William Morrow, 1979.

10. For related ideas, see Matthew Fox, *Original Blessing*, Santa Fe, N.M.: Bear & Co., 1983.

11. Beginning in 1939, the noted science fiction writer Robert A. Heinlein began producing his "Future History" series of novels and short stories. Although extremely popular and critically acclaimed, the view of the world presented in the series appears decidedly militaristic, chauvinistic, and sexist by today's standards.

12. See R. P. Turco, O. B. Toon, T. P. Ackerman, J. B. Pollack, and Carl Sagan, "Nuclear Winter: Global Consequences of Multiple Nuclear Explosions," *Science*, Vol. 222, December 23, 1983, pp. 1283–1292.

13. Marilyn Ferguson, *The Aquarian Conspiracy: Personal and Social Transformation in the 1980s*, Los Angeles: J. P. Tarcher, 1980.

14. Duane Elgin and Arnold Mitchell, "Voluntary Simplicity (3)," *The Co-Evolution Quarterly*, No. 14, Summer 1977, pp. 4–19, and Richard Gregg, "Voluntary Simplicity (1)," *The CoEvolution Quarterly*, No. 14, Summer 1977, pp. 20–27.

15. Mircea Eleade, "Paradise and Utopia: Mythical Geography and Eschatology," in Frank E. Manuel (ed.), *Utopia*, Boston: Houghton Mifflin, 1966, pp. 160–180.

16. Ferkiss, *Future of Technological Civilization*, pp. 35–36.

17. Notable exceptions are such books as Ervin Laszlo et al., *Goals for Mankind: A Report to the Club of Rome on the New Horizons of Global Community*, New York: E. P. Dutton, 1977, and the work of the Center for the Study of Developing Societies, publishers of the journal *Alternatives: A Journal of World Policy*.

18. Fred L. Polak, *The Image of the Future*, translated and abridged by Elise Boulding, Amsterdam: Elsevier Scientific Publishing Co., 1973, pp. 19, 222, 300. Also see Polak, "Utopia and Cultural Renewal," in Manuel, *Utopia*, pp. 281–295.

FROM FIXED TO FLUID IDENTITY

In looking back at my past writings I was relieved to find that I had not made any predictions that might now be subject to verification. I soon found out, however, that this did not exempt me from the charge of lacking foresight. For as I reread my own prose of some fifteen years ago, I was struck by the strangely dated quality of some of it. I could not dismiss this as being due to topical references. Nor had the issues I discussed become irrelevant with the passage of time. Rather, much of what I had viewed as problems or "crises" to be overcome, I now see as being endemic to modern life.

Along with many of my contemporaries, I had then expressed concern about the pervasive sense of uncertainty surrounding both values and individual identity. It seemed that late-twentieth-century man was suffering from the absence of fixities. Since he had few, if any, taken-for-granted and stable values on which to pin his identity, his very sense of self seemed uncertain.

What I have come to recognize in the intervening years is that such concerns presuppose a model of man that may no longer be accurate or appropriate: they assume a relatively fixed identity. If a fluid identity has become the hallmark of modern society, as I now believe is the case, then instability and uncertainty are problems only from the perspective of those who yearn for the fixity of a simpler society.

VALUE UNCERTAINTIES AND INDIVIDUAL IDENTITIES

The cultural underpinnings that secure commitments to a given set of values seem to have become less firm. There is a sense of the relativity of all values, of the absence of any "eternal verities." Values are often adhered to in a flexible way, so that commitments to them are weak and traditional values are readily and frequently questioned. It is this dimension of value change that is at the root of the sense of "value crisis" in our age.[1]

The tolls that change, mobility, and differentiation take on the human psyche... have been the subject of commentary and analysis since the days of the Industrial Revolution. Because advanced technology exacerbates these phenomena, problems of psychic unity or identity appear to become more serious as well.[2]

Implicit in these excerpts from my earlier writing is a model of the human psyche that contains a unified and fixed identity, rooted in a set of enduring social values that have been internalized. For such a psyche, the need to adapt to rapid and constant change does produce difficulty. But while it may be true that "an advanced technological society...seems to make individual adjustment a more complex process" than in the past,[3] the adjustment process itself takes on a different meaning if human identity is perceived as fluid and open to individual construction and reconstruction. If I can decide who I am and who I want to be throughout my lifetime, then change is no longer an unusual external force to which I must adapt. Only those individuals whose identities are fixed experience social change as a matter of reconciling oneself to exogenous social forces.

I had earlier noted that "because the actions of individuals in a complex technological society have more and greater ramifications for...society,... greater social control seems to be needed. At the same time, increased individuation would seem to imply that there is less intrinsic or natural social control than earlier."[4] The assumption underlying this formulation is that the more "individuated" a person is—that is, the more separated from membership in well-defined social groups or categories—the more difficult it is to align personal behavior choices with societal needs. This presupposes that social control over individual behavior operates through the internalization of the fixed values and norms of one's social groups. But if integration into the society is more consciously and deliberately fashioned by the individual—so that each person chooses the groups to which he gives allegiance and the norms to which he conforms—then social control will operate differently too. It will be a matter of interpersonal sensitivities, or symbiotic needs, or of the demands of particular situations. The process of social control is thus different from what it had been, but not necessarily more difficult or less trustworthy.

While such changes in identity and social control are likely to alter individual decision making, they are unlikely to alter the difficulty that individuals face in satisfying their needs for both individualism and incorporation into the group. Thus it will probably remain true that people will experience some "malaise...traceable to the attempts at self-definition in apposition to others—the quest for uniqueness of identity—or conversely, to the attempt to find 'community' or 'rootedness' in relationships with others."[5] An overemphasis on one need or the other can easily produce such difficulty. But swings between the extremes of individualism and conformity will become less significant than the fluidity of identity that allows such alternations to occur with relative ease and frequency.

A fluid identity did not, of course, emerge all at once since the late 1960s or early 1970s. Indeed, a few perspicacious writers had begun to signal the emergence of a more flexible identity during the 1960s—Robert J. Lifton described a new "protean man" whose life-style hinged on continual experimentation,[6] and Bennett Berger suggested that the idea of an integrated and stable identity was a "myth."[7] Yet such arguments remained a minority view; it was not until the late 1970s that greater plausibility came to be attached to them. Because it wreaks havoc with both popular and social scientific images of man, the new character type has not been readily perceived or accepted. (Reviewing my own work, I find that I gave not only insufficient weight to the characterizations of Lifton and Berger, but I even suggested that "the greater degree of behavioral flexibility [had become] a new kind of burden in the mid-twentieth century."[8])

One of the earliest perceptions of a fundamental change in American character was David Riesman's analysis of "other-direction" in his famous book, *The Lonely Crowd*, published in 1950.[9] While most of the considerable attention paid to Riesman's work was devoted to understanding the extreme conformity of the other-directed person, the basic underpinnings of this character type lay in its extreme flexibility. As distinct from his "inner-directed" predecessor, the other-directed person does not internalize a set of values and norms early in life to which he then adheres fairly consistently throughout his life. Rather, he scans the environment for clues to appropriate behavior and learns to alter himself as necessary.

As Philp Slater has observed, this pattern is necessary because "internalized controls of a fixed kind rapidly become irrelevant to a changing social environment." Hence, we have developed "a system of internalized controls that incorporates moral relativism." Yet

this idea is offensive to many and has generated a whole tradition of angry nostalgia among postwar critics of American society. Riesman himself, while not in the least responsible for the gross distortions of his basic arguments, shares in this nostalgia to a certain degree. His use of the term "gyroscope" to describe the conformity mechanism of the inner-directed man betrays this sentiment. (A less flattering metaphor would be a wind-up toy.)[10]

And Philip Rieff, in a book that anticipated by a decade the characterization of contemporary narcissism, spoke similarly of a "modern cultural revolution ... being fought for a permanent disestablishment of any deeply internalized moral demands."[11]

Yet the lion's share of critical concern remained focused on the conformity of the other-directed society. The other-directed person was dependent on the judgment of his peers because having a pleasing personality and being well liked were major motivations for him. Hence, he looked to his peers for clues about how to behave; and the conformist, other-directed "organization man"[12] became the scourge of social critics of all stripes during the 1950s.

A scant twenty years later, however, the focus of critical concern shifted to the excesses of the "me decade,"[13] and best-selling books decried rampant "narcissism."[14] Social critics now portrayed a character that is highly self-absorbed and withdrawn from social institutions. Far from the conformity of the other-directed person, the narcissist pursues no goals other than his own gratification and finds meaning only in what relates to the self: a "true self" that is discovered by turning inward. He is concerned about being independent, "open" (to his own feelings and to the responses of others), and capable of change and "growth."

How could such radical change occur so quickly? Perhaps the portraits drawn by the analysts and social critics were inaccurate. Yet survey data seem to confirm their perception that the population of the 1970s was more introspective and concerned with self-fulfillment than the preceding generation had been and less concerned with duty and social status.[15]

I have argued elsewhere that we can account for the seeming rapidity of this change if we recognize that narcissism is in fact continuous with other-direction.[16] For despite the conformity of other-direction and the individualism attached to narcissism, both character types share an ability and a willingness to be flexible—the narcissist sometimes carries this to the extreme of rejecting all commitments that might limit his future choices. Also, both of these character types attach great importance to interpersonal relationships—the other-directed person because of his concern for being emotionally in tune with others; the narcissist because of his need for authenticity in relationships. And they both manifest a high degree of sensitivity to their own feelings, and the feelings of others.

In essence, then, the other-directed person responded to the demands of a changing society by becoming flexible and sensitive to others. For such an individual, a new situation led to the playing of new roles, even while one's sense of self remained uncertain. One experienced anxiety about one's identity, about the real self underneath all the role playing. The narcissist, on the other hand, has greater facility in role playing and more awareness of self, and thus comes to take change for granted. One can now alter both one's roles and one's sense of self and there is no longer a concern about finding a stable identity. Identity has become fluid.

Evidence of such a change in identity began to accumulate during the 1970s, when a shift toward "impulsive"[17] or "mutable"[18] selves was observed. In response to the "Twenty Statements Test" (which asks respondents to answer twenty times the question "Who am I?"), students during the 1950s gave a preponderance of "institutional" responses—that is, those that refer to the self in terms of statuses and roles, such as student, daughter, psychology major, Hispanic. By 1970 the dominant response had shifted to the "reflective" or "impulsive" mode, in which characteristic moods, opinions, preferences, and ways of thinking and behaving are described—for example, I am a happy person, I worry too much, I'm fun-loving.[19] And despite the reputed return to conservatism among students in the late 1970s, a replication using the Twenty Statements Test on a large sample of students between 1976 and 1979 continued to find high levels of "reflective" responses.[20]

Support for this change in identity is also found in a 1976 replication of a 1957 national survey. The authors conclude that "role and status anchors for the definitions of self have...become less critical in the 1976 population."[21] In a similar vein, a replication in 1975 of a 1965 study found that students in the later period judged the Twenty Statements Test to be the most accurate among a series of self-concept tests, whereas the earlier sample had favored fixed-response tests. Apparently, the earlier sample had accepted "the legitimacy of externally derived self-definitions," whereas the later one did not.[22]

Such evidence of a movement away from social definitions of the self should not be seen as signifying the death of society. The major theorists of the new identity view flexibility, not asocial attitudes, as its leading characteristic. Thus both Louis A. Zurcher's "mutable self"[23] and Lifton's "protean man"[24] are able to move freely along the continuum between individualism and social embeddedness, and Ralph H. Turner maintains that most people will seek both "institutional" and "impulsive" self-anchors at various points in their lives.[25] The point is that people will be free to choose their self-definitions and to alter them. Indeed, Marjorie Fiske's longitudinal study of adult transitions over a ten-year period finds support for this idea of flexible identities. Fiske notes that "the often dramatic shifts in their [the subjects'] hierarchies of commitment over relatively short periods of time suggest the possibility of recurring periods of identity diffusion over far shorter intervals than I had reason to expect."[26] By her choice of language—the use of the term identity diffusion—Fiske suggests that she finds such flexibility disfunctional or distasteful.

The intent here is not, by contrast, to offer a Panglossian view of the development of flexible identities. Clearly, such flexibility may entail anxiety, and the value relativism involved is not free of problems either (including the danger of nihilism). The intent is rather to show that all those speculations about the future, including my own, which assumed a relatively fixed identity were in error. For, as Zurcher has noted: "The balance of self has shifted to a sense of identity not linked with social structure, but linked with the existential phenomena experienced by the individual. Since those processes are always changing (with each new experience), the rate of socio-cultural change, now essentially external to him, has minimal impact."[27] Seen in this light, attempts to analyze the psychological difficulties attendant on rapid technological change may have been misguided. What is more, the very technology that had been seen as generating problems concerning human adaptability may itself be an aid in fostering flexibility.

COMPUTERS, COGNITION, AND CHARACTER

I have noted elsewhere that one can discern a series of social changes that have been conducive to the development of more flexible identities: "urbanization and increased population density, the growth of the mass media and communication and transportation technologies, increased occupational and geographical mobility, higher educational attainments for a larger proportion of the population, and an increasingly cognitive orientation in both public and private decision-making."[28] Surveying present and future developments that might affect identity, it appears likely to me that prolonged exposure to computer use might be of prime importance in altering the ways in which we think and learn. If human cognition is altered through computer use, how might such changes correspond to the change in character or identity outlined above?

Two major patterns may be discerned in the characteristic modes of thinking that accompany computer use: (1) procedural reasoning and thinking about thinking, and (2) increased flexibility and a different perception of error. While neither of these is new to human thinking, putting emphasis on such skills and attitudes may have significant effects on how we understand ourselves and our environment.

Procedural reasoning entails the ability to spell out precisely how one goes about accomplishing a task or arriving at a conclusion. To think in terms of giving instructions to a computer, it is necessary for us to abandon any shared meanings or sets of expectations that we might use in giving instructions to another person. This is often difficult, insofar as people tend to select and use information for purposes of interacting with or influencing other people. They may thus lack "a basic notion of information processing as distinct from the social processes that embodied it in their environment."[29] In working with the computer it is the information processing itself that is central.

Moreover, the procedural thinking that appears in everyday life—in playing a game or giving directions to a motorist, for example—is "lived and used" but "not necessarily reflected on."[30] Yet it is precisely in such reflexiveness, in thinking about thinking, that we may see one of the significant cognitive consequences of the computer.

In the LOGO system designed by Seymour Papert and others, children learned to instruct a movable cursor called a "turtle" to draw a square, a circle, a house, or a design. To do so, the child must first reflect on how he himself would accomplish this task and then specify precisely how to do each part of the whole job. "Teaching the turtle to act or to 'think' can lead one to reflect on one's own actions and thinking. And as children move on, they program the computer to make more complex decisions and find themselves engaged in reflecting on more complex aspects of their own thinking."[31] The use of computers for word processing also encourages a greater awareness of cognitive processes, as writers learn "to monitor their own writing process and to evaluate the product..., to reflect on their writing in inner dialogues about their texts."[32]

Whether in programming a LOGO turtle or in writing with a word processor, the computer user is encouraged to be more flexible, more playful with ideas. "For many students, seeing words dance around a screen... generates quite a different sense of the 'risk' involved in committing themselves to writing. They no longer feel their words to be 'carved in stone.' "[33] Not only can one alter one's words or one's program with relative ease, but the idea that one can easily fix one's mistakes may lead us into a new view of human error.

"The question to ask about the program," says Papert, "is not whether it is right or wrong, but if it is fixable. If this way of looking at intellectual products were generalized to how the larger culture thinks about knowledge and its acquisition, we all might be less intimidated by our fears of 'being wrong.' "[34] Ultimately our view of the concept of failure itself might be altered. Encouraged by the computational way of thinking, we might come to see that "so-called 'failure' is really mistake; and a mistake is a miss-taking of the procedural nature of the problem that can be explained and rectified."[35] Such a view would encourage self-correction and would imply that the learning process is not based on such fixed characteristics as innate abilities and talents.

Clearly, there is a close correspondence between the flexibility of thought induced by computer usage and the fluid identity that appears to be emerging in contemporary America. In our cognition, as in our character, commitment to a particular pattern of thought or behavior may be tentative and subject to correction. Fixed characteristics are of less importance than the ability to change.

The reflexiveness attendant on procedural reasoning is also convergent with the modern identity, since considerable introspection and self-consciousness are needed to define and redefine one's identity. The form of thinking that makes us question how we know what we know and how we do what we do is clearly helpful in this connection. Thus computer usage appears to foster modes of thinking that are highly congruent with emerging forms of social character.

CONCLUSION

It is impossible to conclude an appraisal of one's earlier work without wondering how accurate or cogent one's current arguments will appear in another ten or fifteen years. Such is the nature of social science knowledge: we have no critical experiments to resolve our uncertainties; and the course of social life seldom follows any logical progression.

Thus even while describing the new identity, one must take note of the persistence of older patterns of identity and values. Not only do older and newer patterns coexist, but sometimes "change intensifies fixities as men struggle to reaffirm the threatened."[36] Even if the flexible identity were to become the modal pattern, there would still be segments of the population that were different. How important such "deviants" might be would, of course, depend on the degree of influence they were able to exert. In any event, social life offers many examples of the simultaneous persistence of opposite trends—for instance, secularization and the growth of new religious movements, the persistence and the waning of the Protestant Ethic.

Moreover, perceptions of social reality, even if inaccurate, may themselves have significant consequences. This becomes apparent if one considers those segments of the population—such as the Moral Majority and their sympathizers—for whom what has been described here as a new identity is defined as the death of morality or the destruction of human character. Their efforts to overcome such problems through public policy alterations have had real social consequences in recent years.

Nor can we assume that the promise of computers for improving our ways of thinking and learning will be fulfilled. This promise, after all, coexists with the prospect of using computers to institutionalize and rigidify those sterile and unhelpful pedagogical tools that already abound in institutions of education.

If we set aside the uncertainties of present and future to ask what can be learned from the recent past, we find some obvious morals—although, as always, these are easier to state than to use. First of all, it is clear that we should never assume that human character at any given time constitutes the end point or final stage of development. To varying degrees, analysts of both other-direction and narcissism explained these phenomena as if they were the outcome of long-term historical trends, and hence somehow immutable. Second, we must learn to avoid the traps inherent in our use of language, since the same words often continue to be used when their meaning has changed dramatically. Thus, as fluid identities emerge, the very terms identity, commitment, and values will take on different meanings. Finally, we must be alert to the fact that in studying social change, we are charting not only changes in technology, social structure, and human character, but also changes in the very models that we use in our analysis. Using older models to deal with newer realities may generate faulty perceptions of our problems.

NOTES

1. Irene Taviss, *Our Tool-Making Society*, Englewood Cliffs, N.J.: Prentice-Hall, 1972, p. 55.

2. Ibid., p. 66.

3. Ibid., p. 61.

4. Ibid., p. 52–53.

5. Ibid., p. 66.

6. Robert Jay Lifton, "Protean Man," *Partisan Review*, Vol. 35, Winter 1968, pp. 13–27.

7. Bennett Berger, "The Identity Myth," in *Looking for America*, Englewood Cliffs, N.J.: Prentice-Hall, 1974. (This paper was originally delivered as a lecture at Forest Hospital, Des Plaines, Illinois, in January 1968.)

8. Irene Taviss, "Changes in the Form of Alienation: The 1900's vs. The 1950's," *American Sociological Review*, Vol. 34, February 1969, p. 56.

9. David Riesman, *The Lonely Crowd*, New Haven, Conn.: Yale University Press, 1950.

10. Philip E. Slater, "Some Social Consequences of Temporary Systems," in Warren G. Bennis and Philip E. Slater, *The Temporary Society*, New York: Harper & Row, 1968, p. 87.

11. Philip Rieff, *The Triumph of the Therapeutic*, New York: Harper & Row, 1966. (I must acknowledge that although I had read this work previously, I did not at the time accept Rieff's vision of a new character.)

12. William H. Whyte, Jr., *The Organization Man*, Garden City, N.Y.: Doubleday, 1956.

13. Tom Wolfe, "The Me Decade and the Third Great Awakening," in *Mauve Gloves and Madmen, Clutter and Vine*, New York: Farrar, Straus, & Giroux, 1976, pp. 126–167.

14. Christopher Lasch, *The Culture of Narcissism*, New York: W. W. Norton, 1978. See also Richard Sennett, *The Fall of Public Man*, New York: Alfred A. Knopf, 1977.

15. See Joseph Veroff, Elizabeth Douvan, and Richard A. Kulka, *The Inner American. A Self-Portrait from 1957 to 1976*, New York: Basic Books, 1981; Daniel Yankelovich, *New Rules: Searching for Self-Fulfillment in a World Turned Upside Down*, New York: Random House, 1981.

16. Irene Taviss Thomson, "From Other-Direction to the Me Decade: The Development of Fluid Identities and Personal Role Definitions," *Sociological Inquiry*, Vol. 55, Summer 1985, pp. 274–290. The argument in this and the following paragraph is taken from that article.

17. Ralph H. Turner, "The Real Self: From Institution to Impulse," *American Journal of Sociology*, Vol. 81, March 1976, pp. 989–1016.

18. Louis A. Zurcher, *The Mutable Self*, Beverly Hills, Calif.: Sage Publications, 1977.

19. Louis A. Zurcher, "The Mutable Self: An Adaptation to Accelerated Socio-Cultural Change," *et al.*, Vol. 3, 1972, pp. 3–15.

20. David A. Snow and Cynthia L. Phillips, "The Changing Self-Orientations of College Students: From Institution to Impulse," *Social Science Quarterly*, Vol. 63, September 1982, pp. 462–476.

21. Veroff, Douvan, and Kulka, *Inner American*, p. 534.

22. Stephan P. Spitzer and Jerry Parker, "Perceived Validity and Assessment of the Self: A Decade Later," *Sociological Quarterly*, Vol. 17, Spring 1976, p. 242.

23. Zurcher, *The Mutable Self*.

24. Lifton, "Protean Man."

25. Turner, "The Real Self: From Institution to Impulse."

26. Marjorie Fiske, "Changing Hierarchies of Commitment in Adulthood," in Neil J. Smelser and Erik H. Erikson, eds., *Themes of Work and Love in Adulthood*, Cambridge, Mass.: Harvard University Press, 1980, p. 240.

27. Zurcher, "The Mutable Self," p. 11.

28. Taviss, "Changes in the Form of Alienation," p. 54.

29. B. A. Sheil, "Coping with Complexity," in Richard A. Kasschau, Roy Lachman, and Kenneth R. Laughery, eds., *Information Technology and Psychology*, New York: Praeger, 1982, p. 83.

30. Seymour Papert, *Mindstorms*, New York: Basic Books, 1980, p. 154.

31. Taviss, *Our Tool-Making Society*, p. 28.

32. Colette A. Daiute, "The Computer as Stylus and Audience," *College Composition and Communication*, Vol. 34, 1983, p. 142.

33. Stephen Marcus, "Real-Time Gadgets with Feedback: Special Effects in Computer-Assisted Instruction," *The Writing Instructor*, 1983, pp. 157–158.

34. Papert, *Mindstorms*, p. 23.

35. Margaret A. Boden, *Artificial Intelligence and Natural Man*, New York: Basic Books, 1977, p. 460.

36. Daniel T. Rodgers, *The Work Ethic in Industrial America 1850–1920*, Chicago: University of Chicago Press, 1974, p. 241.

Robert T. Francoeur   **6**

REPRODUCTIVE FUTURES: 1964, 1984, AND BEYOND

MY ARIADNE'S THREAD FROM THE CLASSICS TO THE FUTURE

No one starts off life as a futurist except in the general sense that we are always struggling to survive and enjoy another day, another month or year. Some of us are drawn to anticipate the future in a more structured, conscious way. And, while many people prefer to hide their heads in the present or past, I believe that the awareness of time and the attraction of the future can make us more fully human.

My own path to futures studies involved a traditional and classical education, with a six-year immersion in Latin, four years in classical Greek, two years of French, and a year of Hebrew. Add to this, undergraduate studies in scholastic philosophy and four years of Catholic theology in a 100-year-old Benedictine monastery while I was preparing for the priesthood. Ultimately, this deep taproot into classical and medieval cultures proved to be my bridge to the future.

In my mid-twenties this taproot was enriched by afternoons with a genial Benedictine monk, Edward Wenstrup, a biologist out of Columbia University with the scars of a veteran who insisted, in the dark ages of the 1930s and 1940s, that there was no conflict or contradiction between Darwinian evolution and the Catholic faith. Many pleasant hours were spent listening to Father Ed's recollections of intellectual jousts between enlightened scientific knights and dogmatic Vatican theologians. Those knights were as romantic and inspiring to me as any hero of biblical or Arthurian legends. In the Transvaal, where the bones of our australopithecine ancestors were discovered in the 1920s, Jan Christian Smuts, the philosopher prime minister of South Africa, had woven Einstein's relativity, Darwin's natural selection, and Christian theology into a theory of "evolutionary holism." In Belgium a brave Canon Dorlodot twitted the defenders of the faith with his 1922 pioneering reconciliation of Darwinism and Catholic thought. In the 1930s and 1940s the gauntlet was carried by an English monsignor, one Ernest Messenger, who led me deep into literary criticism and exegesis of the writings of Greek philosophers and the ancient Fathers of the Christian era, Jerome, Augustine, the three Cappadocians, and others.

For my master's thesis in theology a classmate suggested that I examine a more contemporary knight. Pierre Lecomte du Nouy worked on wound regeneration at the Rockefeller Institute and helped to develop an early artificial heart with Charles Lindbergh, but in the public eye he was known for his attempted synthesis of evolution and faith in the 1945 best-seller *Human Destiny*. My study of his synthesis of evolution and theology was mixed with a strong dose of the latest biblical interpretations from l'Ecole biblique in Jerusalem, thanks to two young Benedictine professors at St. Vincent's.

In 1956 my Ariadne's thread began to twist like an ascending spiral as Lecomte du Nouy led me to the writings of Pierre Teilhard de Chardin. Teilhard became my absolute obsession. We shared a French ancestry, and more. Teilhard was a scientist, a paleontologist, a Jesuit priest, a mystic, and a visionary with warm, riveting eyes. Exiled by Vatican authorities to the wilderness of Chou Kou Tien in China, Teilhard countered by joining the team that, in 1927, discovered the Peking Man. This chance twist of fate, coupled with his vision and faith, made Teilhard an international figure in paleontology and human evolution.

Unfortunately, I never met Teilhard personally—he died in 1955, a year before I first heard about him. Still I soon knew him well. I wrote to his friends in France and persuaded them to share with me their typewritten copies of his many unpublished essays. Dictionary in hand, I labored to translate his poetic visions. Despite being banned by the Vatican, Teilhard's masterwork, *The Phenomenon of Man*, was published in French months after he died in 1955, followed by a dozen volumes of his essays with titles like *The Future of Man*, *The Divine Milieu*, *Man's Place in Nature*, and *The Appearance of Man*. Soon I was writing about Teilhard's vision of the past and the future in a variety of magazines and journals whose readers were thirsty for the latest translations and interpretations of this visionary scientist.

In 1963 I launched into doctoral studies at Fordham University just as the Jesuits there were beginning to acknowledge their exiled pioneering brother. Although I was only a naive graduate student, some buried bit of chutzpah prompted me to organize an American branch of the French Teilhard Association. This effort brought me into challenging contacts with geneticist Theodosius Dobzhansky, anthropologist Loren Eiseley, whose enthralling writings on human evolution are still classics, and, eventually, L. S. B. Leakey, whose discoveries of fossil man in Africa are legendary. Imperceptibly, my eyes shifted from the past to the future.

In 1965 a visiting professorship at Loyola University in Chicago finally set my mission on the future. As a bioanthropologist, I was asked to do a series of lectures, focusing first on the past of human evolution and then creating scenarios for the future of human reproduction and psychic development. As these lectures found their way into *Perspectives in Evolution* (1965) and *Evolving World Converging Man* (1970), I found a real challenge emerging in experimental embryology and the reproductive technologies, my professional specialization.

By 1967, when I finished the doctorate in experimental embryology, I was teaching at Fairleigh Dickinson University in Madison, New Jersey. The gentle green knolls of that campus, with its gardens, fountains, and mansions modeled on Henry VIII's Hampton Court, have since nourished my studies of the future. Whereas in a more staid, tradition-bound public institution my metadisciplinary pursuits would have been frowned on, if not outright discouraged, here my efforts to branch out in different, although complementary, directions found relatively smooth paths.

MY FOGGY, VINTAGE 1960S MICROSCOPE

So where did I go wrong with my forecasts for the future of human reproductive technologies and their social consequences twenty years ago, when I was a neophyte in future studies? Frankly, I must confess that I was both too conservative about our technological future and too optimistic about our ability to adapt to the radical social changes I was convinced would inevitably accompany these technological innovations.

I was fairly accurate in my forecast of what specific new developments we could expect in artificial insemination, infertility control, test tube fertilization, embryo transplants, and artificial wombs. The problem was I lacked imagination in anticipating how quickly these advances would move from forecast to reality. Innovations materialized far faster in the research laboratories and in experimental medicine than I had projected.

As an example, in a book on new trends in reproduction with the horrid title of *Utopian Motherhood* (1970), I suggested that artificial insemination and the embryo transplants then used in the breeding of domesticated animals might also provide a practical solution in the breeding of endangered animal species. Several popular science magazines like the *Bulletin of the Atomic Scientists* asked for more details, which I happily provided from my fertile imagination. Encouraged by my fantasies of high-tech sex in the zoos, and in need of some hard data for these articles, I contacted William Conway, at the New York Zoological Park and John Perry, assistant director at the National Zoo in Washington. Instead of condescending smiles, these professionals seemed intrigued by my advocating embryo transplants and the use of common marmosets as surrogate mothers to preserve the less than fifty golden lion marmosets then in captivity. By 1972 my occasional excursions to zoos around the country and correspondence with key people left me with the feeling that I had a good idea but one so radical that unless the threat of extinction became immediate for particular endangered species, the zoo managers would not be likely to call on experimental embryologists for help. Still, I thought, it would happen eventually, probably in the 1990s.

Then, in May 1972, John Perry presented my ideas at the First International Conference on the Planned Breeding of Endangered Animmals in Captivity on the Isle of Jersey. In the proceedings of that conference my paper on the uses of experimental embryology appeared almost as a post-script after practical discussions of the problems of breeding Galapagos tortoises, Congo peacocks, whooping cranes, eagle owls, prairie falcons, wallabies, lemurs, and Arabian oryxs. I appreciated the recognition given my proposals but still believed that any real use of reproductive technologies in the zoos was a long way off.

By 1985 high-tech sex in the zoos was grabbing headlines with fair regularity. At the San Antonio Zoo the first nonhuman primate to be born after embryo transplant, a female black baboon, was appropriately named "E.T.," while Pepito, a fascicularis monkey, was carried and birthed by a surrogate mother rhesus monkey. In Louisville a quarter horse gave birth to a zebra. A Holstein cow birthed a rare gaur calf, a giant wild ox from India, at the Bronx Zoo. In Cambridge, England, a horse gave birth to a donkey and embryos of a sheep and a goat were fused into the world's first "gheep." Pink pigeons from Madagascar were artificially inseminated. Tiny embryos of African bongos in a glass vial were warmed in the armpit of a veterinarian on their way to embryo transplant and a surrogate mother 2,000 miles away. Recombinant DNA specialists were even reporting some success in replicating chromosome fragments from the 100-year-old dessicated hide of an extinct African guagga.

It all happened much faster in the zoos than I expected twenty years ago. On the human level I had a similar lapse—what Arthur C. Clarke calls a "failure of imagination." Simply stated, I was naive about how simple the technological problems we faced actually were.

In the 1960s there seemed to be many serious obstacles that had to be overcome before we could collect human eggs for test tube fertilization and embryo transplant, flush human embryos before they implanted in the womb for transfer to surrogate mothers, freeze embryos for later pregnancy, or create functional artificial wombs. When asked for timetables, I thought we would need thirty to forty years to make these possibilities realities.

As with my zoo forecasts, I was not prepared for the real world taking over with a vengeance. Edwards and Steptoe succeeded with the first human embryo transplant, Louise Joy Brown, in 1978. Within three years *Life* magazine was running a cover story on the first twin, triplet, interracial, Chinese, black, Australian, French, German, and American embryo transplants. Noel Keane, a pioneering lawyer, advertised in local papers across the country for women to serve as surrogate mothers for a fee. A wealthy California couple created a novel legal dilemma when they died in a plane crash after returning from an Australian fertility clinic where they had arranged an embryo transplant to remedy their childless state. They left behind several frozen embryos, which at the couple's death, it would seem, became heirs apparent to their estate. The Australian court finally decided to allow the frozen embryos to be implanted in surrogate mothers, but the final disposition of the estate was not published. Then there was the widow of a Frenchman who died of testicular cancer shortly after his wedding. He had not had time to change his will or make arrangements for his frozen sperm. When his widow wanted to be artificially inseminated with his semen, the court at first said no, until the dead man's family rallied in support of his widow. Also, "Mr. and Mrs. A.," whom the British media reported to be an anonymous wealthy American couple, agreed to pay a British house-wife $7,474 to be artificially inseminated with Mr. A's semen and carry his baby for them. After considerable public uproar in early 1985 over wealthy Americans buying a British infant, the British court allowed the arrangement because it was in the best interests of the baby.

It almost seems today that the more outrageous my scenario was in 1964, the closer it came to the reality of 1984. Take my 1960s speculation about genetic, biological, and social parents and the reality of two California lesbians. In the 1970s Mary Jo had persuaded her brother to donate semen so she could inseminate her lesbian lover with the aid of a turkey baster. When the child was born, Mary Jo was listed on the birth certificate as the father, possibly because of her role as active impregnator of the genetic and biological mother. In 1983 Mary Jo won paternal visiting rights from the court when she broke up with her lover.

In *Utopian Motherhood* I had created some intriguing scenarios about changes in human reproductive technology, but my vision was not sharp enough to see these turning into realities as quickly as they did. Almost all the advances in reproductive technology I forecast in the 1960s are now a reality. Only in the area of artificial wombs and cloning have my predictions not reached reality as yet. In these two areas I suspect my timetables may prove more accurate. You will only know if the media carries an announce-ment of the decantation of the world's first human to spend its first nine months in an artificial placentation system, or genetic engineers replicate the DNA of a frozen woolly mammoth, as anticipated in a 1984 "report" in *Technology Review* that was accepted by many as a factual report, even though it was clearly dated April 1, 1984.

SOCIAL DIS-EASE AND THE REPRODUCTIVE TECHNOLOGIES

Like other futurists twenty years ago, I focused my explorations, projec-tions, and scenarios almost exclusively on accelerating linear projections of what was going on in experimental embryology, animal husbandry, and clinical work around the world. Analyzing the currents in medical progress is relatively safe, I thought, and certainly much easier than grappling with the personal emotions and changes in grass roots values that these technological changes are likely to provoke.

Despite this temptation, my training in the biological sciences came to my rescue. As a student of animal and human evolution, I knew that the human applications of experimental embryology would soon force some radical social adaptations on all of us. Biologists know that as an environment changes, individual animals and whole species have to adapt their behavior and life-styles to survive in the new ecosystem. The human species, as Teilhard de Chardin repeatedly pointed out, is radically modifying and creating its own environment. The technologies of machines, computers, television, space travel, and nuclear power have altered our environment and forced us to change our life-styles and behavior. One has only to recall the many accounts of peoples in stone age cultures suddenly being confronted with the twentieth century. Some adapt and survive; others cannot adapt and disappear.

The "nonpersonal" machinery technologies, however, do not directly impact on our understandings and images of human nature, of male and female relations, and on our sexuality the way that the reproductive technologies can and do alter these realities as we experience them. Because our reproductive technologies reach into the very core of our human experience, they are uniquely disturbing for almost everyone. I recall only recently the obvious *dis-ease* my discussion of alternative life-styles and sexual values created in a workshop at the Tenth World Congress of Sociology in Mexico City. Social scientists from Russia, Poland, Lithuania, and Yugoslavia were diplomatic in pointing out that our future collaboration depended on finding the right language to express our research team's interest in exploring the impact of human relations on economic planning and social research. Mario Kamenetzky, a social engineer, was able to suggest the nebulous but suficiently scientific sounding label of "gratuitous libidinal activities." This label was quite acceptable because it avoided implying a direct threat to the social status quo of cultures and political structures that are ill at ease with the central human consequence of the contraceptive and reproductive technologies: the total separation of human sexual relations and reproductive technologies.

In predicting how society might adapt to the advances of reproductive technology I was a gross optimist. In the past decade we have been repeatedly confronted with different reproductive technologies being used on the human level. Instead of trying to analyze the broad perspectives of this revolution created by the separation of sex and reproduction, we seem incapable of anything beyond a conditioned, fragmented response to this or that event. We reacted to the world's first test tube baby with shock, but as the reports continued we were numbed and lulled. It hadn't happened in our family or next door so why worry?

The legal apparatus continues to respond to challenges by tort, instead of trying to anticipate the trends. Mary Jo sues for paternal visiting rights, a French widow sues to have a child by her deceased husband, and potential heirs challenge the rights of frozen embryonic offspring. Still few are willing to go beyond these individual challenges "out there" to examine what these technological revolutions are and will do to our personal and social images of male and female, of family, and marriages. The realities of millions of single-parent families are finally penetrating our minds, but we are not yet ready to deal with how this reality will necessarily alter our views of family and impact on society.

Ten years after the U.S. Supreme Court legalized abortion, the lines between pro-choice and anti-abortion forces are more violently marked out than ever before. Dialogue is nearly impossible. Despite the distracting emotions, few, especially on the anti-abortion side, ever ask what we can do to reduce the number of unwanted pregnancies that lead to the demand for abortion. We do have some effective and inexpensive contraceptives, but for society to openly endorse and promote their use in and outside marriage would, in the minds of many, recognize pleasure and intimacy as the main rationale for modern sexual relations and promote an immoral amount of nonmarital sexual relations, which would almost be worse than the immorality of the millions of abortions that they oppose. Our society is not yet ready to deal with the fact that little of the sexual activity in America today is reproductive, either in motivation or outcome. Still we struggle to maintain the myth of a sexual behavior ethic based on marriage and reproduction as its sole justification. We might be able to cope with this behavioral/value change if, as Michael Marien suggests, we considered a "sunset law" that would set a fixed date, say January 1, 1995, after which abortion would be illegal except when medically required. Setting a fixed date a decade or so from now could force us to face and integrate on the changing sexual behaviors and new values.

In avoiding any discussion of the real social consequences of separating human sexual relations from reproduction and the preventive social measures that could reduce the need for abortion, our legal and social institutions are playing the same game that the Vatican and Pope John Paul II play as they desperately try to enforce a strict marital/reproductive sexual ethic. The ultimate social impact of today's contraceptive and reproductive technologies is much more radical than I saw in the 1960s or than most people see today. The Vatican instinctively fights any deviation from the male-established marital/reproductive ethic, with its double moral standard for males and females, because it threatens to undermine its male hierarchical power structure. So our civil institutions are unwilling to grapple with the consequences of medical technologies. We prefer to accept this or that new development piecemeal because it solves a particular need of the moment. As individuals and as a society, we seem myopically incapable of looking beyond the need of the moment. In the 1960s I wrote about this consequence, but I was not aware of how much personal and social resistance would emerge to avoid dealing with it or its ramifications on a conscious holistic level.

In the 1960s I gave far too much weight to the prophetic role of the Judeo-Christian religious institutions. Religious communities have traditionally prided themselves on their responsibilities as prophetic communities, calling the people to challenge inhumane conditions and move into the future with faith.

In the midst of the refreshing air of the Second Vatican Council and the humaneness of Pope John XXIII, it seemed as though the Catholic Church might lead the way in facing the realities of a radically reoriented human sexuality. Strong majorities favored the acceptance of contraception, married priests, and a communications and pleasure morality of sexual relations. Advocacy groups began to press for the inclusion of women in the church's hierarchy and the acceptance of divorce. But that prophetic current has been steadily smothered, starting with Pope Paul VI's rejection of the majority committee report favoring the moral acceptability of contraception in 1963 and continuing through a Vatican condemnation of the 1977 Catholic Theological Society of America report that attempted to open the door to new perspectives in sexuality. Pope John Paul II slammed the door in 1985 with his pleas for sexual abstinence in marriage and an attempt to expel twenty-four American nuns who joined other Catholics in stating that a variety of opinions are held by dedicated Catholics on the issue of abortion.

In 1970 a workstudy document on Sexuality and the Human Community from the United Presbyterian Church created a positive attitude toward the evolution of a new sexual morality, even though it was commonly ignored. The Episcopal Church made some clear efforts, mainly in the ordination of women and of gay ministers of both sexes. In the 1980s the United Church of Christ (Congregationalist) began a serious study of the whole issue of human sexuality, including ministries to and among gays. However, the efforts of the churches, in this area, have unfortunately proved to be sporadic and painfully slow.

When the contraceptive technologies of the 1960s liberated women, it became proper for women to be (almost) as sexually active as men. At least women were encouraged to be more sexual than their Victorian grandmothers, to enjoy sex, and even to initiate it. Then, starting with Masters and Johnson, specialists in the newly emerged field of sexology began documenting the sexual uniqueness of females, their superior potential for and ability to integrate sensual pleasure, and their much greater sexual capacity. Career women and the singles revolution burst on our society with little warning. At the same time, males began to exhibit a strong dis-ease with the new female they saw emerging from the sexual revolution.

In the midst of this maelstrom, sociologists and demographers suddenly, in the 1980s, began documenting a heretofore unidentified key factor, a devastating shift in the gender ratio. The post–World War II baby boom did not remedy the shortage of males. In fact, for unknown reasons, we now face an incredible long-term shortage of marriageable males for women over age 25. Among white Americans the shortfall in men now runs from 85 male mates for every 100 single women aged 25 to 29 to only 33 marriageable men for every 100 women aged 55 to 59. This imbalance of the sexes did not happen overnight. It was there in the 1960s but no one noticed it, not until hordes of sexually liberated women continually complained that they could find few eligible men.

We also did not anticipate, although it was perfectly logical, the negative impact in the 1980s of an explosion of sexually transmitted diseases, herpes and AIDS in particular, in limiting sexual relations in the 1980s. Nor did we anticipate, as we should have, the dramatic increase in male and female infertility. We should have forecast the consequences of sperm-inhibiting environmental toxins accumulating in the testes of young males. We should have anticipated an increase in female sterility owing to fallopian tubes that are blocked by subclinical pelvic infections picked up as young women experience sex with a variety of partners, or as the aftermath of an abortion. Women who have sex with a variety of partners also risk infertility as their immune systems respond to a variety of seminal proteins by building antibodies against all sperm. The biological principles were there in the 1960s and 1970s, only we lacked vision and creativity in applying them in our scenarios of sexual liberation.

SHIFTING SEXUAL VALUES: FROM HOT TO COOL

Twenty years ago I believed that by breaking the connection between sex, reproduction, and marriage, the contraceptive and reproductive technologies would radically alter our monolithic style of monogamy. I believed that our society was experiencing a combination of social ecosystem changes unique in human history. A doubled life expectancy, more leisure, more mobility, the legitimating effect of television talk shows focusing on the sexual revolution and new life-styles, Kinsey with Masters and Johnson, smaller families, later marriage, gay liberation, the economic liberation of women, earlier puberty, and the contraceptive and reproductive technologies—these changes, I believed, would force American men and women to openly accept a pluralism of sexual relations, life-styles, and marriage patterns. That kind of open acceptance and endorsement has not happened, nor does it seem likely in the near future.

In the 1970s it was easy enough for me to expand a seminal model of sexual values proposed in 1967 by Marshall McLuhan and George B. Leonard. McLuhan and Leonard had suggested that traditional sexual values, what they called "hot sex," consisted of highly defined concepts of male and female, clearly defined sex roles, a genital and performance-oriented obsession with sex, a double moral standard, a fear of nudity and emotions, an unwillingness to accept any adult life-style except heterosexual monogamy with premarital female virginity, and a patriarchal view of women as sex objects to be conquered and possessed. The new sexual values I saw emerging, McLuhan and Leonard's "cool sex," were person-oriented. They emphasized a diffused sensual and emotional sexuality, an egalitarianism in male-female relations, flexibility in sex roles, openness to alternative lifestyles, and a single moral standard for both genders.

As I wrote *Eve's New Rib: Twenty Faces of Sex, Marriage and Family* (1972), *Hot and Cool Sex: Cultures in Conflict* (1974), and *The Future of Sexual Relations* (1974) I was encouraged by the widespread agreement on the new value system I found among college students across the nation. What I was not prepared for and did not anticipate was the conservative reaction of the new religious right in the late 1970s and 1980s. I am still convinced that the social changes I predicted in the 1970s will come about, but not as painlessly, nor as quickly, as I had originally hoped.

What seems apparent is that we are holding on tenaciously to values and attitudes that worked well in the Victorian society of the industrial revolution. They do not function nearly as well today, but we persist in hanging on to them. As an older and, I hope, a more perceptive futurist, I am coming to realize that society does not live from day to day as a logical organism, but as a reluctant denizen of a world we have created with our technologies but are not comfortable with. Divorce and remarriage, serial monogamy, and single-parent families are as far as we are willing to consciously go. We are not about to resolve the male shortage in any logical or humane conscious adaptation by allowing within our legal and religious institutions a variety of marital and comarital relationships, such as sexually open marriages, nonpatriarchal polygamy, multilateral relations, intimate networks, extramarital polygamy, man-sharing, and gay, lesbian, and bisexual relationships.

Finally, beyond my naive social optimism, I must confess to a deep lack of appreciation of the wide varieties of ethnic and racial attitudinal systems that lead to very different responses to these reproductive technologies in the United States. Until recently, psychologists, family counselors, and sex therapists have approached human sexuality, male-female relations, family roles, and infertility/reproduction with a middle-class, white urban mentality, as if society were a homogeneous melting pot. Fortunately, in the early 1980s this distortion was challenged by a new awareness and appreciation among professionals in many disciplines of the ethnic flavors in the

American salad bowl. The impact of these ethnic variations on our social, legal, economic, religious, and political responses to the consequences of our reproductive technologies is only beginning to be studied. Still this ethnic pluralism will help to accelerate the shift from monolithic patriarchal monogamy to the flexible pluralism of life-styles and male-female relations that I projected in the 1960s and 1970s.

As a futurist, I am a generalist, a synthesizer, and a visionary, with roots deep in the evolutionary past and transcendent future. For me, that perspective creates a constant challenge that makes life more than worth living. It also makes it interesting to speculate about what I may write in retrospect of this essay ten or twenty years from now. But as the artist Paul Klee once remarked, "There is more reality in becoming than in being."

SELECTED READINGS

Francoeur, R. T. 1970; 1974; 1977. *Utopian Motherhood: New Trends in Human Reproduction.* New York: Doubleday; Cranbury, N.J.: A. S. Barnes.

Francoeur, R. T. 1972. *Eve's New Rib: Twenty Faces of Sex, Marriage and Family.* New York: Harcourt Brace Jovanovich.

Francoeur, R. T. 1976. "The Pleasure Bond: Reversing the Antisex Ethic." *The Futurist* 10(4):176–180.

Francoeur, R. T. 1980. "The Sexual Revolution: Will Hard Times Turn Back the Clock?" *The Futurist* 134(2):3–12.

Francoeur, R. T. 1983. "Is There a Sperm Bank in Your Future?" *Forum Magazine* 13(3):77–81.

Francoeur, R. T. 1987 (in press). "Changes in the Human Sex Ratio and What They Mean for the Future," *The Futurist*.

Francoeur, R. T., and Francoeur, A. K. 1974. *Hot and Cool Sex: Cultures in Conflict.* New York: Harcourt Brace Jovanovich.

Francoeur, R. T., and Francoeur, A. K., eds. 1974. *The Future of Sexual Relations.* Englewood Cliffs, N.J.: Prentice-Hall.

Guttentag, M., and Secord, P. F. 1983. *Too Many Women? The Sex Ratio Question.* Beverly Hills, Calif.: Sage Publications.

Kirkendall, L. A., and Gravatt, A. E., eds. 1984. *Marriage and the Family in the Year 2020.* Buffalo, N.Y.: Prometheus Press. Chapter 5, Transformations in Human Reproduction, and Chapter 10, Moral Concepts in the Year 2020: The Individual, the Family, and Society, by R. T. Francoeur.

Novack, W. 1984. *The Great American Man Shortage and What You Can Do About It.* New York: Bantam Books.

PART II
Lessons Learned

THE FUTURIST TELLS STORIES

How is it that, when I reflect on twenty-three years of sharing thoughts about the future, I really cannot convince myself that I know why my forecasts were right sometimes and wrong other times? Indeed, often I cannot clearly decide whether I have been right or wrong or both! Inadequate documentation contributes to this, but there are other far more profound reasons for my retrospective malaise. What follows recounts some of what I have learned about thinking about the future and about the appropriate use of such thoughts.

THE EPISTEMOLOGICAL LIMBO WHEREIN DWELLS THINKING ABOUT THE FUTURE

In 1963 I wrote:

[Thinking about the future] is not a scientific exercise based on consistent theory and heavily documented by field studies and laboratory research. No such theory exists for describing our society accurately—much less for predicting changes in it. ...Data are by no means trivial but in themselves they are seldom uniquely inter-pretable in terms of the range of conditions explored.[1]

Today as then, all we have are endless fragments of theory that "account" for bits and pieces of individual, organizational, and economic behavior. But we have no overarching or truly interconnecting theories, especially none that account for human behavior in its many personal and institutional manifestations in turbulent times.[2] Economic theory is an acknowledged shambles.[3,4,5,6] Social and behavioral theories are so inept that their

This essay has been adapted from an article in *Futures* 17 (April 1985). Copyright 1985 by Donald N. Michael. Reprinted by permission of the author.

formal status in political rhetoric is nil, and with a few notable exceptions, their uses in the planning and governance processes are more relegated to appendices than to basic designs and programs.[7,8] Most dismaying, even when we think we know the "true" explanation and have an ideal program for overcoming or attaining a state of affairs, we do not have formal theory instructing us in how to implement it.[2,9] That we are unable to correctly predict birthrates embarrassingly epitomizes our ignorance about the inter-connectedness of micro and macro processes in the human realm.

It has become increasingly clear to me that overcoming the footless status of futures studies—any detailed statement purporting to show where we are headed or will arrive in the future—is a far deeper problem than that of closing the gap between data and theory about changing human behavior in turbulent times. At root the problem is epistemological, even ontological.[10,11]

To begin with, we simply have no way of resolving through cause-effect concepts the place of significant persons and events. Do great persons or events make history, or does history make them significant? All future studies embody this epistemological fog wherein stumble ghostly images about the "momentum" of social "forces" and about the timing and magnitude of shifts in "direction" introduced by persons or events. To argue that each "causes" the other simply begs the question of how history—including future history—"happens."

Experience leads me to subscribe to M. Polanyi's arguments that creative human activities have an emergent quality: the "whole" is unpredictably "greater" than the sum of the parts.[12] This seems obvious in the conduct of art, science, and politics and in interpersonal relations. One cannot predict a new theory or art form or new political and personal developments from what has gone before. Nor can one predict the consequences of predictions about consequences.[13] *After* the new state of affairs has emerged, inter-pretations arise that purport to relate causes and effects so as to connect the new condition to what preceded it. But *not* before.

What is more, events are given meaning by treating them as causes or effects. But events are discrete only if we do not examine them too closely. We choose to identify the beginnings and endings of events (even events like assassinations and earthquakes) by one or another habitual, mythical, or professional convention that defines the event's boundaries. But every-thing we experience, especially in an information-dense world, tells us that, individually and collectively, the human condition is overdetermined: every-thing causes, affects, and is part of everything else, smeared, as it were, over time. In turbulent, systemic situations, sensitivity analysis can only refer to a *fragment* of a moot reality that is likely to have already changed.[14] If evidence is needed that it is beyond our conceptual capabilities to cohere all into anything remotely resembling a unified picture from which rational encompassing interpretations and decisions can be made, peruse any issue

of *Future Survey*. Whatever their separate limitations, the endless proliferation of contending fragments of explanation and the multiple levels of
analysis and synthesis that they imply amply attest to an overdetermination
of "causes" and "effects" in the conduct of the human enterprise.

In this regard a fundamental insight for me has been, there are *many*
pasts. No other mode of cognitive exposure has so informed me of my
ignorance about past, present, and future and my epistemological footlessness as has exposure to histories of ideas and societal change. This continues
to be a source of dismaying and exciting shocks to my emotions as well as
to my intellect.[15,16,17,18]

Alternative choices of events, time periods, interpretations, and intentions
provide unnumbered ways to link past events to a present. And there are
unnumbered ways of putting together the present: what is "really" happening and what is "really" important. Because the present is always "constructed" out of a presumed past, whether or not the past is consciously
acknowledged, I have learned that thoughts about the future derive from
preferred constructions of the present and the past. These constructions are
preferred because they are deemed "fitting" in that they seem, according to
the prevailing social construction of reality and its cultural norms, to be
sensible, familiar, logical, authoritative, or acceptable simply because one
has participated in their creation. To be sure, wild cards are included in
some thinking about the future, but it is no accident that such events are
suffused with the unacceptability that accompanies the semantics of "wild":
for the most part they tend to be ignored or evaded.

Less abstractly, from my own experience here are examples of three kinds
of unfittingness: (1) The then-president of the Brookings Instituton was
unhappy with the futures-oriented report I prepared under its auspices for
NASA (National Aeronautics and Space Administration)[19] because I dis-
coursed on the implications of discovering intelligent extraterrestrial life.
Most unfitting, by Brookings standards of respectability. (2) Some criticized
my book *The Next Generation* because I did not predict *the* future, but
instead suggested that things could go in different ways. A futures approach
was not as fitting then as it is now. (3) In the 1960s it was fitting to speculate
on the longer run implications of automation and computers, especially the
impacts on the work force and privacy—and I did, provoking international
attention.[20] In the 1970s there were fitting ways to deprecate the issue
and it essentially disappeared from future speculations. Now, of course, the
topic is real and it is hot...but as if the thinking of the 1960s never
happened.

Because multiple pasts and presents make it impossible to bound events
definitively as the "containers" of causes and effects, futures forecasts become questionable with regard to what is becoming what out of what. Fuzzy
realities, however, elicit psychological and ideological discomfort: few will
create or respond to such future descriptions. Instead, we arbitrarily and

habitually (i.e., fittingly) perceive the world as strings of discrete events—trends—delineated by anticipatory and retrospective expectations about what "is" an event. We construct (not necessarily consciously) our reality, and then construct our response to that construction—and so on into the future.[21,22,23,24] This is an aesthetic enterprise more than a logical one, even though some of the techniques used to further the aesthetic endeavor use logic, words, etc.[25]

I have learned that the pronouncements of experts are useful, when thinking about the future, not because their information is based on esoteric and valid knowledge about social change, although that occasionally could be so (but how is one to know?), but because by virtue of the authority with which they are endowed as *experts*, they are able to influence the definition of social reality others hold. Their expertness resides not in a prescience implicit in their modes of logical reasoning, but in the "psychologic" that logic activates: the *authority* of logical reasoning, and therefore of the expert as a practitioner of logical reasoning, is what carries weight. This source of authority legitimates the stories they tell. But the source also tends to subvert the storytellers' own recognition that they are telling stories. Their own belief in their authority—the authority of logic—leads them to believe that they are doing something very different from "merely" telling stories.

I complete this section of my review of what I have learned about the epistemological limbo in which thoughts about the future dwell with one more observation.

Look closely at an idea, a sentence, the components of a description or a definition and each gradually evaporates into metaphors and metametaphors. Words, whether about self or the "real" world, are unavoidably murky, sloppy, and incomplete. Meanings branch interminably and disappear into the gloom. Nevertheless, we act—and I believe it is beneficial to so act *some* of the time—as if words really do describe, as if we know what we are talking about: both presenter and recipient collude in this pretense.

That what I write reads as if I know what I am talking about is a consequence of both my habits of writing and of your expectations as reader. But for me, in the words of onetime futurist Karl Marx, "All that is solid melts into air." (This is so whether I write "I have learned" or "I believe." More accurately, all such assertions mean "I am learning a mood, a style, an approach to life, a sensation, a way of being in the world that is in part influenced by thinking about the future.")

SOME FUNCTIONS PERFORMED BY FUTURES STUDIES

Over the years these insights and learnings have led me more and more to questions and understandings regarding the *functions* futures studies perform, or could perform, and less and less to the *doing* of futures studies.

As I describe what I have observed about some functions served by futures studies and why are they used or not used, I must first acknowledge that the categories and processes on which I will focus imply a theory of social change and stasis, only some of whose characteristics are apparent to me. My comments about the epistemological and theoretical footlessness of futures studies apply as well to my own observations and interpretations.

I will emphasize some less well-recognized, nevertheless crucial ways in which thinking about the future affects individuals as individuals, and as members of groups, as participants in organizations and in society. Futures studies serve other functions too, but they are better understood, or at least more acknowledged, than those served at the all-important individual level.

All who create and use thinking about the future do so on the bases of values and myths about what is real, valuable, and meaningful. Whether a futures study is used, misused, or ignored depends on the producers' and consumers', or anticonsumers', values and beliefs, as these express themselves both consciously and through unconscious psychodynamic processes. I have come to believe that self-consciousness about these extrarational—and sometimes irrational—contributions is fundamental for more effective creation and use of futures studies that are intended to encourage a humane world. How these extrarational and irrational factors affect the creation and use of futures studies is a current preoccupation.

In the face of imposing intimations of a turbulent and problematic future, the existence of a futures study, the very fact that one can be done, provides for some, a kind of comforting talisman, a protection against the unknown. The study comforts by carrying into the future meaning based on what is supposedly happening *now* by using words and concepts that reinforce fitting images in today's society, words such as economic, age distribution, growth rate, corporation, national security, self-interest, profit, technology. These ideas, these *words*, just because they are familiar, offer a comforting sense that, indeed, the map *is* the territory—that behind all the current turbulence there are real, enduring processes and circumstances at work that can be counted on into the future. For those so moved, it can then seem plausible that the future *can* be shaped, manipulated, and its salient aspects controlled. Consequently, this anticipation bolsters a sense of self-confidence.

This sense is further reinforced through the "fitting" methodologies often used to create futures studies: logical processes involving mathematics, such as economic and global models, data, numbers, and graphs. And, too, there is "expert" input, which implies control over the subject matter, which, in keeping with the dominant Western mythology of the past 300 years, implies the promise of control over events. That the consumer of future studies is able to command, or at least draw on, the combined resources of logic and expertise itself engenders a comforting sense of being in control, thereby reducing anxiety about the unknown future.

Commissioners of futures studies are also comforted and reinforced in their sense of competence because they see themselves doing what *rational* persons *ought* to do—use logic and expertise to solve a problem. Of course, this implied rationality also comforts some of those who depend on the "good sense" and actions of the futures studies' sponsors. (In other times, even as today, leaders and their followers were comforted and confirmed in their sense of competence when preparing for the future by doing such fitting things as consulting oracles, praying, giving valuables to their "church," and doing good deeds. Faith, rather than rational procedures, provided protection from the unknown of tomorrow, and for that matter, still does for many people today.[26])

These satisfactions provided by futures studies are typical of those that accompany ritual affirmations of a culture's mythology. This does not make these ritual acts and their satisfactions bad, or wrong. Rituals contribute essential stabilities to society. Of exceeding importance: to the extent that rituals comfort and affirm, they encourage conduct compatible with them. Thus we have a situation in which extrarational norms and sometimes irrational needs encourage rational behavior.

All of the above pertains as well to the functions that futures studies perform for those who create them. In addition to these satisfactions there are other rewards for people who create futures studies. Doing so encourages the belief that one is influential, making a difference, being socially potent and powerful. These beliefs may be justified, or they may very well be demolished when nothing happens to the product, or if it is misused. But while his or her work is under way, I have yet to meet a "futurist" who didn't feel socially significant and personally vitalized by visions of potential effect amplified by the perceived status of the study commissioners. Often enough these beliefs and visions are inflated by the promotional exertions of authors, organizations, and publishers competing for the rewards of profit and status bestowed by consumers of thoughts about the future.[27]

I have also learned that, much more often than not, futures studies increase discomfort because they expose the recipient to the problematical ramifications of the future. Ambiguity and uncertainty more typically result in anxiety and feelings of role impotency or loss of control. In turn, this state of mind can activate psychodynamic responses that are not socially constructive.[28] One such response is to fix on or promulgate one or another future that reduces anxiety by gratuitously avoiding or deprecating the ambiguity, uncertainty, or other threats to favored beliefs about reality. This response is called "denial" in the psychodynamic realm.

To be sure, other motives, not all of them unconscious, contribute to these responses. Seldom are they exclusively the consequences of denial: earlier I depicted human behavior as overdetermined. But many experiences, discussions, and probings convince me that futures studies often elicit such unconscious psychodynamic processes. When confronted with the ambiguity and uncertainty that is the message of many futures studies, these processes serve to protect one's image of oneself as a capable person able to control the events for which one is responsible.

Thus we now have some futurists and their followers proclaiming that we are at a stage where, whether it be the result of evolution or Ilya Prigogene's dissipative structures, or whatever, we will inevitably emerge into a transformed, better world. That not all turbulence reconstitutes as higher-order systems; that, according to paleontological evidence, there are far more dead species than live ones; that denial is a frequent psychodynamic response to anxiety-provoking information—all are overlooked by believers who are unable to live with more problematic and threatening futures.

Thus, too, we have futurists and their followers who deny that there is anything seriously wrong with the world, and insist that technology, good mangement, and the operation of immutable laws of economics will straighten out present kinks and reward present purposes, and that those who claim otherwise are gloom-and-doomers whose outlook smacks of sin (and, in the United States, might even be unpatriotic).

Of course, these two groups of futurists do not begin to exhaust the class.[29] Many are able to steer a course between these extremes or navigate in different waters, making less threat-denying contributions to their clients' and audience's perspectives, anxieties, and enthusiasms.

I have also learned that future studies often elicit defensive psychodynamic processes because they frequently challenge the status quo regarding what is being done, how it is being done, and thereby imply that it might be necessary to discontinue a course of action, even if it is now rewarding. In 1973 I began emphasizing that one of the chief contributions of futures studies is to temper our satisfaction with how far we have come by exposing how far we have yet to go, thereby drawing attention to questions of the ethical and operational sufficiency of present actions and policies.[30]

However, each of us harbors conflicting values, which our unconscious mind and our culture help us to avoid recognizing most of the time. Therefore, a communication that, on the one hand, may well heighten one's anxiety over uncertainty about which future will eventuate and, on the other, heightens anxiety about where one stands ethically with regard to those futures is likely to elicit strong emotional responses. Although a futures study can enlarge the sense of the variety of win-win opportunities that perhaps reside in futures, for many they threaten to raise acutely discomforting issues about "What am I entitled to?" In response come anger, fear, denial—rejection of the study.

FUTURES STUDIES AS STORIES

The complex and unavoidable interplay of rewards and threats with which future studies confront their creators and consumers leads me to see the

functions that they serve for the individual and the responses that they elicit
as those accomplished by *storytelling*, that age-old device by which humans
have inspired, influenced, and engaged one another.

In what follows I recognize that futures studies styled as scenarios embody,
at their best, much of what I shall urge.[31,35] But even scenarios, much
less other modes of expressing thoughts about futures, seldom take all the
advantages of storytelling that are available to them. In the remainder of
this essay I intend to tell a story within a story, so to speak, not to establish
the logic and norms for doing so.

I do not intend to demean the usefulness or appropriateness of telling
some stories about the future in the style of a technical report, with its
logical and normative constraints. These are not necessarily cynical devices
used to mislead anyone about the future, any more than is a story about
human reality told in the form of a sonnet or painted impressionistically.
These are chosen methodological constraints within which the artist creates
realities. The same holds for thinking about the future presented in the form
of a story expressed within the constraints of a technical, logical study. But
what is being *told* is still a story, and it could be a richer story—eliciting
more responses—if it were recognized and accepted as such.[25] Answers
to the question "What does the future hold?" that are couched exclusively
in rational terms or legitimated in such terms are, at best, only partially
satisfying because even the most logical person has emotions as well. Herein
lies a large current limitation in the appeal of serious futures studies in
contrast to journalistic exercises. These, while substantively questionable,
appeal because they are emotionally satisfying. For this reason *their* limitations are seldom recognized by enthusiastic readers.

All worthy stories are, first and foremost, occasions, mirrors, and contexts
for learning about self by drawing one both inward and outward, by expanding one's sense of the plausible. By learning about self one learns about
others, for one always sees others through oneself. Thoughts about the
future, by the very expansion of context they provide, offer their audience
a larger mirror for viewing themselves, a larger mirror for viewing the world
and their part in it. Accepted as a story, the range of what is "fitting" can
be enlarged because a story need not be constrained by the canons of pro-
priety that apply when a communication is treated *as if* it were exclusively
an objective report undergirded with well-tested theory and bolstered by
data.

Three methodological injunctions emerge from this vision of the competent and responsible teller of stories about futures. How these are accomplished in a particular story will depend on the skill of the teller.

First, shared thoughts about the future ought to include acknowledgment
of both the multiple and the problematic nature of the futures explored,
and of the descriptions and interpretations of the putative past and present
from which the futures derive.

Second, shared thoughts about the future ought to be accompanied by an explicit theory about the processes of social change sufficiently detailed so the futures described can be derived from it. If there is no such explicit speculative or tested history, this ought to be acknowledged. Then both producer and consumer of the story can be more alert to the nature of the tacit and possibly questionable assumptions that they hold regarding social change and human nature.

In urging these alternative explicit stances I do not depreciate the contribution of those talented storytellers about futures who sometimes know without knowing how they know—a state of mind the renowned physical scientist and philosopher Michael Polanyi used as the basis for elaborating his ideas concerning emergence.[11] I would argue only that the creator of such a futures story is obligated to share the fact of this mind state with the consumer so that both can make the most imaginative use of a story built in part or wholly on intuitions.

Third, all involved should be vigorously aware that thoughts about the future unavoidably engage both constructive and destructive unconscious needs and images that influence conscious evaluations of purpose and pragmatics. Thereby, these unconscious contributions critically affect the destiny of futures study. Collusion in the dangerous illusion that one's beliefs and choices can be determined exclusively by rational considerations will gratuitously defeat admirable intentions.[32]

A worthy and well-told story implies a moral, and stories about the future are especially well suited to convey some crucial morals. One moral meriting emphasis is, that the nature of the future world will be an expression of emotions at least as much as rational deliberations, programs, and practices. Emotions are critical to what happens, both those emotions driving creativity and reasoning, aspiration, power seeking, greed, and the will to control; and those emotions responding to the existential questions of being human, which Seymour Sarason summarizes as: "How to dilute the individual's sense of aloneness in the world; how to engender and maintain a sense of community; and how to justify living even though one will die."[33]

Another moral would have it that the future is this splintered civilization's most available and useful context in which to face the personal question: "What is it worthwhile to be and to do?" It is not enough to share thoughts about the future that are restricted to a description of the costs and benefits of introducing one or another new technology, policy, or procedure to better realize the intentions of a public or private organization. Somewhere in the process the recipients of the study should be inspired to ask themselves, "What is it all for? Why give thought to the future? Surely not just for profits, or jobs, or the next election, or budget hearing. These are important, of course, but, really, what is it all for? Why am I doing what I am?" If stories about possible futures do not elicit such questions and reflections, where will they come from?[25] And who better to ponder deeply on these questions than those who commission or must respond to thoughts about the future?

Yet another moral: in an uncertain turbulent world, beset with such heavy burdens and challenges as we face, a precondition for a humane future— perhaps for any future at all—is that those who create and use futures studies become compassionate learners. By compassion I mean recognizing that

1. in the face of crucial issues nobody, including oneself, really knows what they are doing, certainly not in terms of the *consequences* of their acts;

2. everyone is, to some profound degree, living illusions, believing in the "factness" of what constitutes their world instead of recognizing that we live in an arbitrarily, although usually not consciously, *constructed* social reality; and

3. everyone is in one way or another struggling to cope with the three existential circumstances that Sarason emphasizes. This means, then, that everyone needs all the clarity they can muster, regarding their ignorance and finiteness, and all the support they can obtain in order to face the upsetting implications of what their clarity reveals to them. A compassionate person is one who, by virtue of accepting this situation, can provide others as well as self with such support.[34]

Well-told stories about futures can hardly avoid emphasizing the moral that resilient participation will require persons and organizations always to be seeking to *learn what* are the appropriate questions to ask about a changing and turbulent world and to *learn how* to discover and evaluate temporary "answers."[30] Acknowledging and experiencing the personal and organizational life of the learner depends on being open to unfamiliar ideas and experiences and on being increasingly interdependent. Both requirements demand exceptional vulnerability. But being vulnerable can lead to a humane world only if the norms of compassion are practiced. Otherwise, those willing to risk a learning stance will be destroyed by the power-hungry and hostile. That the human implications for the users of future thinking are still too seldom appreciated is easily evidenced by the number of organizations that apply some thinking about the future to their planning and strategy activities, but then go on to perform in the same managerial style as before. I began writing about this interconnection in the late 1960s,[27,30] but it is only recently that multiple circumstances (in their overdetermined way) have begun to encourage some efforts to humanize management that truly respond to the story told in some futures thinking. Learning how to establish such norms will be as difficult as it is unavoidable, and this, too, becomes a moral of futures stories.

There is one more moral to the story I am telling here and to the stories I propose be told by futures studies. I have learned that all these morals hold as well for the *authors* of future stories. We are not outside the story we tell: each of us is part of the story. Each must be a quester after existential meaning, vulnerable, uncertain, and ethically concerned about what happens to our thoughts about the future, since, if they are used, they will affect the futures we are telling stories about.

The Delphic injunction "Know thyself" is the most essential of all conditions for meaningful and responsible engagement when thinking about the future, for finding one's way among the claims, distortions, feelings, and fantasies that each of us harbors in our unconscious. Constructive and destructive unconscious needs drive "futurists"—myself included—as well as the consumers of futures studies. To be ignorant about or indifferent to the fact or impact of these individual characteristics is to forego crucial insights into our functions and responsibilities as the creators of futures studies.

What I've learned about thinking about the future is, of course, not the whole story. There are always stories within stories that, if told in the words of another storyteller, could emerge and take over. And there are stories that surround any given story that, when told, change the meaning of the story within. This is life, and it is precisely the value of a story, acknowledged as such, that it draws much more out of the audience and out of the world than does a story presented as something else—as a "logical," "scientific," "value free" report, for example.

Therefore, I don't doubt that telling this story about what I have learned about the storytelling we call thinking about the future will change the story I tell . . . some time in the future.

REFERENCES

I am grateful to Thomas C. Greening, Rollo May, and Pierre Wack, who have been most helpful with editorial and substantive suggestions, for whose use I am solely responsible.

1. Michael, D. *The Next Generation: Prospects Ahead for the Youth of Today and Tomorrow*, New York: Random House, 1965.
2. Crowe, B. "The Tragedy of the Commons Revisited." *Science* 166, November 28, 1969, pp. 1103–1107.
3. *The Public Interest*, special issue on "The Crisis in Economic Theory," 1980.
4. Georgescu-Roegen, N. *The Entropy Law and the Economic Process*. Cambridge, Mass.: Harvard University Press, 1971.
5. Leontief, V. "Academic Economics." *Science* 217, July 1982, pp. 104–107.
6. Striner, H. *Regaining the Lead*. New York: Praeger, 1984.
7. MacIntyre, A. *After Virtue*. Notre Dame, Ind.: U. of Notre Dame Press, 1984, chap. 8.
8. Koch, S. "The Nature and Limits of Psychological Knowledge." *American Psychologist* 36 (3), March 1981, pp. 257–269.
9. Rittel, H., and Webber, M. "Dilemmas in a General Theory of Planning." *Policy Sciences* 4, 1973, pp. 155–169.
10. Unger, R. *Knowledge and Politics*. New York: Free Press, 1975.

11. Mitroff, I., and Killman, R. *Methodological Approaches to Social Science.* San Francisco: Jossey-Bass, 1978.
12. Polanyi, M. *The Tacit Dimension.* New York: Doubleday, 1966.
13. Cochran, N. "Society as Emergent and More Than Rational: An Essay on the Inappropriateness of Program Evaluation." *Policy Sciences* 12, 1980, pp. 113–129.
14. Bauer, R., et al. *Second Order Consequences: A Methodological Essay on the Impact of Technology.* Cambridge, Mass.: MIT Press, 1969.
15. Arendt, H. *The Human Condition.* Garden City, N.Y.: Doubleday, 1958.
16. David, H. "Assumptions about Man and Society and Historical Constructs in Futures Research." *Futures* 2 (3), 1970, pp. 222–230.
17. Toynbee, A. *A Study of History.* New York: McGraw-Hill, 1972.
18. Wyatt, F. "The Reconstruction of the Individual and of the Collective Past." In R. White, ed., *The Study of Lives.* New York: Atherton Press, 1963.
19. Michael, D. *Proposed Studies on the Implications of Peaceful Space Activities for Human Affairs.* Washington, D.C.: Brookings Institution, 1961.
20. Michael, D. *Cybernation: The Silent Conquest.* Santa Barbara, Calif.: Center for the Study of Democratic Institutions, 1962.
21. Mannheim, K. *Man and Society in an Age of Reconstruction.* Trans. Edward Shills. London: Kegan Paul, 1940.
22. Novak, M. *The Experience of Nothingness.* New York: Harper & Row, 1970.
23. Berger, P., and Luckmann, T. *The Social Construction of Reality.* Garden City, N.Y.: Doubleday, 1964.
24. Vickers, G. *The Art of Judgment.* New York: Basic Books, 1965.
25. Michael, D. "Technology Assessment in an Emerging World." *Technological Forecasting and Social Change* 11, February 1978, pp. 189–195.
26. Churchman, C. West. *The Systems Approach and Its Enemies.* New York: Basic Books, 1979.
27. Michael, D. *The Unprepared Society: Planning for a Precarious Future.* New York: Basic Books, 1968.
28. Michael, D. "Reason's Shadow: Notes on the Psychodynamics of Obstruction." *Technological Forecasting and Social Change* 26, September 1984, pp. 149–153.
29. Marien, M. "Toward a New Futures Research: Insights from Twelve Types of Futurists." *Futures Research Quarterly*, Spring 1985, pp. 13–35.
30. Michael, D. *On Learning to Plan—and Planning to Learn.* San Francisco: Jossey-Bass, 1973.
31. Hawkins, P., Ogilvy, J., and Schwartz, P. *Seven Tomorrows.* New York: Bantam Books, 1982.
32. Michael, D. "Ritualized Rationality and Arms Control." *Bulletin of the Atomic Scientists* 17, February 1961, pp. 71–73.
33. Sarason, S. "The Nature of Problem Solving in Social Action." *American Psychologist*, April 1978, pp. 370–380.
34. Michael, D. "Learning from the Future." *World Future Society Bulletin* XII, July-August 1979, pp. 1–5.
35. Wick, P. "Scenarios: Uncharted Waters Ahead," and "Scenarios: Shooting the Rapids." *Harvard Business Review*, Sept.-Oct. and Nov.-Dec., 1985.

HAWAII 2000, THE WORLD FUTURES STUDIES FEDERATION, AND ME: THINKING LOCALLY AND ACTING GLOBALLY

I cannot remember when I was not interested in ideas about macro social change. At both Christ School in Arden, North Carolina, and Stetson University in DeLand, Florida, I was early drawn to the philosophies of St. Augustine and St. Thomas Aquinas, and later to the grand ideas of history presented by thinkers such as Karl Marx, Oswald Spengler, and Arnold Toynbee. In graduate school, at The American University in Washington, D.C., theories of economic and political development that were popular during the 1950s left their mark on me. But it was really the six years I spent teaching at a Japanese university in Tokyo (Rikkyo Daigaku) in the 1960s that led me into what I would subsequently understand to be "futures studies."

I went to Japan, fresh out of graduate school, with a Ph.D. and several months of intensive Japanese language training, for many reasons. One was to try to understand why that country had so quickly transformed itself from a closed feudal backwater into a globally aggressive industrial power. What was its secret? What was unique? Were there lessons—good or bad— to be learned from Japan? At that time Japan was wholly out of the public eye and of little concern to most academicians. But as a humanistically oriented social scientist, I was inclined to want to understand the relationships between values, attitudes, institutions, and technologies. Japan seemed to be a great place to try to do this. Indeed, from my study and experiences in Japan I concluded that a certain set of values and attitudes (toward work, nature, self, and others) are "necessary" for the creation of an industrial society, and that these values are found in abundance in successful industrial societies or regions, but not in unsuccessful or nonindustrial areas.

This conclusion enabled me to make some assumptions about the future of nonindustrial societies, but none about my own. This disparity really did not worry me much until I happened upon two articles that had a profound influence on me.

One I suspect is still largely unknown. It is an article that was published in *Japan Quarterly*, January-March 1964, by John Randolph, who had been head of Associated Press in Japan during the 1950s. It is entitled "The Senior Partner." Adopting Spengler's theory of the life cycles of civilizations, and assuming that Japan was a separate civilization and not part of a larger Chinese-Korean civilization, Randolph showed that Japan had gone through cycles of birth and growth in exactly the sequence that Spengler's theory would predict. Moreover, if Japanese civilization were placed beside Western civilization, Randolph argued, then it could be seen that Japan and the West had gone through exactly the same cycles, in the same sequence, and for about the same number of years' duration. But—Japan had experienced these sequences about *200 years ahead of the West*! I was dumbfounded. I could "see" the future of the West in the present of Japan! Specifically, the period from 1751 to 1945 in Japan should presumably tell me something about the period from 1960 to 2200 in the West.

My notions of Western superiority—of Japan and other "developing" nations somehow catching up with the West—were completely shattered and have never returned, even though it is likely that Randolph's specific theory is basically wrong. Nonetheless, that article, more than any other single thing, led me to devote my life to seeking answers to the questions "What are the causes of social change? What is the future of my, or any other, society, or part of it? If it is possible to consider grand theories that help to explain social change in the past, isn't it possible to use them, or to develop others, to help understand change toward the future?"

I was in the early stages of contemplating these questions when I ran across the "Manifesto of the Ad Hoc Committee on the Triple Revolution" (in *Liberation*, April 1964). Here was a possible answer to my questions regarding the United States: three massive changes were under way that would transform America. One was in warfare, as a consequence of the atomic bomb. A second was in human relations, as a consequence of the civil rights movement, and a third was in economics and jobs—or rather, in the very focus and meaning of life in industrial societies—as a consequence of "the cybernetic revolution."

I have never recovered from the one-two punch of those articles. Instead of continuing to devote my life to teaching and research in Japan, as I had initially intended, I returned to the United States at the first opportunity I had. That opportunity was to join the newly formed department of political science at Virginia Polytechnic Institute. While spending the summer of 1966 at the country home of a friend near Culpeper, Virginia, before going to VPI, I happened to read an article that finally sealed my fate. It was entitled "The Future as a Way of Life" (in *Horizon*, 1965) and was by some obscure journalist named Alvin Toffler. When I finally arrived at Virginia Tech in September 1966, I began to teach and study "futuristics" seriously and eagerly.

Indeed, it is possible that I taught the first college course in futures studies, which was regularly offered with formal approval through normal university channels, from 1967 at Virginia Tech. My thanks to the administrators and faculty who made this possible. After listening to the sad tales of other university professors, I have come to appreciate how rare that permission was!

In conjunction with the course, I developed a lengthy bibliography in futuristics that gained some attention in the United States and, especially, in Europe. It also happened that my duplex housemate in Blacksburg, Virginia, was David Greene, a member of the rambunctious group of British architects called "Archigram." Several others of that group were also at Virginia Tech, and they egged on my intense interests. One day David Greene, on reading a manuscript of mine called "Oh, We Belong to a Cybernetic, Post-Money, Situational Ethics Society, My Baby and Me," said that I sounded like "Marshall McLuhan." I did not know who McLuhan was. David also suggested that I get in touch with the World Future Society, which had recently formed in Washington, D.C. I did, and an excerpt of that article was published in the August 1967 issue of *The Futurist* as "Valuelessness and the Plastic Personality." While there are some things I might say differently now, I still stand by that excerpt, and especially by the longer piece, as a valid forecast of the future and a partial explanation of the present. I suspect it will read even better ten years from now, and better still during the early twenty-first century. Read it and see.

As pleasant as life and my colleagues and students were, a former military school, only recently turned coeducational, deep in the mountains of Virginia, was not the best place for me during the exciting and turbulent days of the later 1960s. So, when the chance came for me to join the faculty of the University of Hawaii, I grabbed it. Not only did the department specifically want me to develop futures studies further, but I knew that a Hawaii State Commission on the Year 2000 was being formed. Glenn Paige, a fellow political scientist on the organizing group, asked that I be made an advisor to it. That experience—the opportunity to try out my ideas about futuristics in an interactive community situation—was absolutely invaluable. I learned a great deal from it. Such an opportunity for praxis should be a major part of every intellectual's life.

George Chaplin, editor of the Honolulu *Advertiser* and chairman of the Commission, and Keiji Kawakami, a member of the Commission and owner of a local clothing manufacturing factory, along with several thousand citizens of Hawaii, have been my most important teachers since 1969. I am grateful to them all. The book *Hawaii 2000* (1971) edited by George Chaplin and Glenn Paige, which documents the Commission's initial activities, is one of the most important early books about futures studies.

The Hawaii 2000 experience, and my continuing involvements with futuristics in Hawaii; with Ran Ide and The Ontario Educational Communications Authority (TV Ontario) in Canada in the mid–1970s; and with various state and national attempts to involve the public in futures-oriented activities have led me to some conclusions about these processes. I believe they need to be guided by "the five senses."

1. *A Sense of Optimism or a Sense of Crisis.* Most successful citizen-based futures programs have been held at a time when the public (and its leaders) were either very optimistic about the future—and thus eager to see the wonders that lay ahead—or very pessimistic, with a sure feeling that nothing was working and that only creative and new ideas could get them out of the mess or malaise they were in.[1] Hawaii 2000 began during a period of tremendous optimism. The "Democratic Revolution" that had created the "New Hawaii" of the 1960s had achieved almost all it had set out to achieve, and the leaders and their publics were willing to look ahead boldly with confidence and creativity for wonders yet to come. Unfortunately, this optimism and confidence did not survive the "Ecology Movement," the "Oil Crisis," and the global economic restructuring that followed them both. Many of the far-sighted visionaries of the early Hawaii 2000 days became quite reactionary, or at best "caretakers of the dream," during the late 1970s. But a new generation of leaders, many of them children of the early Hawaii 2000 participants, are now creating a new "New Hawaii."

In other places with which I am familiar, leaders and the public have sought to look to the future as a way of getting out of current problems. Because nothing seems to be working now, they hope that solutions might be brought back to the present from the future. I would judge that this sense of crisis, or at least urgency, animates most futures-oriented programs today. Yet if one is completely demoralized about the present, then one is not likely to engage in *any* form of futuristics. Such appears to be the case for most Americans at present. Underlying the phenomenon of Reaganism is the pessimistic outlook: "Eat, drink, and be merry, and hope tomorrow never comes. In the meantime pretend you are very conservative and happy." An ostrich faces the future more appropriately than this!

2. *A Sense of Leadership—and of True Participation.* One of the most crucial variables needed for a successful community-based futures program is that one or more completely respected and widely influential persons head the project. In Hawaii the fact that the editor in chief of the morning newspaper not only headed Hawaii 2000, but also initially conceived it, secured active support and participation from business, governmental, labor, civic, and other leaders, and actively promoted it as a legitimate and important activity in his newspaper, went a long way in making it the tremendous success it was. At the same time it was equally the case that Hawaii 2000 was as truly "popular" an activity as *any* public project I am aware of. Many more than "a thousand flowers" bloomed. Every possible group, well respected or not, participated in some significant way.

The 2000 Committee itself was composed of a variety of task forces that looked into specific aspects of the future. Each used the expert and lay opinion of many people in Hawaii, and secured the guidance of an expert "futurist" from the Mainland, with whom they regularly corresponded.

Virtually every organized professional, business, religious, ethnic, or civic group held some kind of futures-oriented program for its members. There was a series of well-attended public lectures. There were programs on television and radio. Each county (on separate islands in Hawaii) had its own 2000 commission and activities, both for itself and to feed into the statewide program. There was even a youth congress, where, among other things, resolutions were passed urging the legalization of marijuana and that Hawaii secede from the Union.

Representatives of all of these preliminary activities attended a final three-day conference in the fall of 1970. Not only local people were there. A number of futurists from foreign countries were invited to attend—not as speakers, but as observers of the process. They were asked to write reports on their observations subsequently for Commission evaluation and guidance.

A combination of "respected" and official leadership, with genuine and broad participation by *all* of the diverse groups and people in the community, is absolutely essential for a true exercise in community futures-building. Without the established leadership the activities will be ineffectual. Without the participation of as many kinds of citizens as possible, including the "crazies" and other marginals, the program will be sterile and unimaginative—and thus unrelated to "the future." You can't have one without the other.

3. *A Sense of Alternatives*. The essence of futures studies, as I will reiterate below, is that there is no single "future" "out there" to be predicted, but a number of "alternative futures" "in here" to be invented. The organization and activities of a successful futures program must reflect this. While one of the alternatives might be a linear projection from the present, it should not be displayed as the "official" or "most likely" future. In my experience "official" linear forecasts are *unlikely* futures, no matter how commonplace they may be. It is the "ridiculous" alternative of the present that often ends up being the "real" future. This possibility—probability really—must be accepted and stressed by project organizers, and a wide variety of forecasts generated and discussed. Discussing the various implications of these alternative futures should be one of the most important activities shared by the expert and lay participants in the process. The invention and creation of various "preferred futures" should be another.

4. *A Sense of Continuity*. It is important that something "happen" to the futures project. This "something" might be ongoing activities; the creation of one or more futures-oriented bodies in governmental, educational, private, or other organizations; legislation specifically requested, or suggested, by the process, or the like. The creation of a book, such as *Hawaii 2000*,

is not enough by itself. Some such quality product is also desirable as a point of reference in the future; but the beat should go on.

In the case of Hawaii, the state legislature created a Commission on the Year 2000, which engaged in several important citizen-based activities in the early 1970s. One such was a major focus on "Alternative Economic Futures for Hawaii," which brought together business, labor, and other groups. In the late 1970s, under the inspired leadership of its executive secretary, Doreen Leland, the Commission sponsored an extensive series of meetings, workshops, dramatizations, contests, and the like around four alternative futures for Hawaii.

Since 1978 the state legislature has not continued funding for the Commission, and thus commissioners have not been appointed by the governor, but because of the way various other groups in Hawaii have taken up futures activities, there has been no sense of regret over this. On the contrary, the feeling in Hawaii has been that the Commission, in its original form, had done its work, and that it is time for a transition to other phases.

At the University of Hawaii a graduate program in alternative futures was established in the department of political science, and the university also agreed to host the secretariat of the World Futures Studies Federation for a period of time. Probably the most impressive acceptance of futures studies, however, was found in the Hawaii state judiciary. Lester Cingcade, the court administrator, saw that a chapter of the new court plan was devoted entirely to the relation of futures studies to judicial planning and administration in Hawaii. Interns from the university's alternative futures program regularly work in the Hawaii judiciary, routinely writing reports on "emerging issues" (long-range) and "trend reports" (short-range factors). They also issue a "Newsletter of Issues, Trends and Research Findings" entitled "Nu Hou Kanawai," which is Hawaiian for "Justice Horizons."

Conferences, seminars, courses, professional development workshops, radio and television programs, and the like on a futures theme—which refer specifically and seriously to the literature, theories, and methods of futures studies—have now become almost commonplace throughout the state. The IXth World Conference of the World Futures Studies Federation was also held in Hawaii in May 1986. This is the first time a World Conference of the Federation has been held on American territory.

The initiative toward the future, begun by Hawaii 2000, has certainly been continued by these and other activities. The future is alive and well.

5. *A Sense of Humor.* Seriously. One of the most important things to remember throughout all of these activities is that they should be fun, exciting, compelling, creative. Although some people may believe that anything "serious" (important) must be "serious" (solemn), my experience convinces me that things that are comical, satirical, fun, and otherwise humorous are even more valuable. One way to kill public participation—or to render it only formalistic—is to make it boring: "We held public

meetings, but no one showed up." Why should they? Would you willingly attend a boring formal public meeting in your spare time? Generally speaking, of course not! But when the activity is exciting—like a football game, a circus, or a religious revival, then the public does go out and participate.

But why should it have to "go out" to participate, in this day of the "electronic revolution"? Bring the future into their homes and into the bars, or wherever TV is watched. But bring it in a way that is competitive with people's normal viewing preferences. A live broadcast of a boring meeting is still a boring meeting. Be sure you spend as much time, effort, creativity, and money on the TV program as the Army does to attract young people to join it. Otherwise, the attempt at citizen participation by means of television will clearly be a sham and a delusion.

Programs such as Hawaii 2000 are acts of public education, and of self-education for all participants. They are not methods for finding out what "the future" *will be* so that each citizen (or, more likely, the ruling elite) can "get with the program" and succeed. They are iterative activities in an educational process that starts wherever appropriate with whatever resources are available, always changes, and never ends. The future never is what it used to be.

The first meeting of what would become the World Futures Studies Federation (WFSF) was held in Oslo, Norway, in 1967. The second was held in Kyoto, Japan, in 1970. Several of us from Hawaii attended the Kyoto meeting to learn, and to share our experiences. As a consequence, yet another important facet of my maturing interest in the future was revealed.

In contrast to the similarly named, privately run, America-focused, and popular-membership-oriented World Future Society (of which I have long been a member, and whose contributions to futures studies I very much appreciate), the WFSF began as a group of more or less "professional" futures researchers from various parts of the world. It was especially important to the first organizers (such as Johan Galtung from Norway, Robert Jungk from Austria, Igor Bestzhuzev-Lada from the Soviet Union, and John McHale from the United States) that the Federation be a place where persons from socialist and nonsocialist, developing as well as developed, parts of the world could meet and freely exchange their ideas about the future and futures studies.

I became deeply involved with the WFSF from 1970 onward, and this has certainly served to challenge, if not check, my otherwise American ethnocentric view of futures studies. While almost all futurists talk and write about the emergence of a global community and the value of cultural diversity, unless one spends a great deal of time in the company of people from different cultures in different places around the world, the limitations (and strengths) of one's own view of the future are almost certain to be inadequately perceived.

The WFSF is both a frustrating and an exciting organization to be affiliated with. Ever since the earliest discussions about organization of which I am aware—starting from the Kyoto meeting in 1970—the most active persons in the Federation have wanted to have an organization that was minimally bureaucratic and maximally responsive to the cultural and behavioral preferences of futurists from various parts of the world. While they wished to be open in the manner of a UN-affiliated nongovernmental organization, they definitely wanted to avoid the superbureaucratization too often characteristic of such entities. These persons were, and remain, fearful as well of the restrictions that come from receiving financial aid from governmental or private sources. Thus the organization is chronically underfunded. It operates on low membership fees (which are often not paid by some members who wish to participate but who, for a variety of reasons, find it difficult to pay). Many of the costs are absorbed by the individual or the institution that happens to house the secretariat for a while. As a consequence, almost nothing is done very well, very promptly, or very professionally. But almost everything is done with commitment and enthusiasm.

The office of the secretary-general, as well as that of president, is purposely passed around from region to region. Since its formal organization in 1972, these offices have been held by persons from France, West Germany, Italy, Morocco, Sweden, and Hawaii. Vice-presidents and members of the executive council are reasonably representative of all regions of the globe. Members of the Federation come from more than seventy nations.

The WFSF tries hard to see that no single culture, region, or country dominates the membership and the activities of the Federation. This is not easy to do and results in some problems. Futures studies originally began as, and in many ways still remains, a First World concern. Thus it would be easy for persons from Europe and, especially, the United States to overwhelm the futures studies activities emerging elsewhere. Yet the initial raison d'être for the Federation was to be a place where especially socialist and nonsocialist futurists could meet. The concern for full Third World participation immediately followed.

There was also a desire to see that the participants were "real" futurists, and not merely formal representatives of their governments (not a problem with American and some European participants, but definitely a possibility in some other places). Moreover, while the Federation wished to keep close ties with the various UN organizations, it did not want to mimic the extremely bureaucratic, nationalistic, and formalistic qualities of the UN.

At the same time it could not be a general open membership organization, or it would likely suffer the fate of so many other "international" bodies: it would be swamped by persons from certain cultures, nations, or social systems (e.g., the United States, France, the USSR, Africa), and thus drive out members from other areas. But to be selective was to open the organization to the charge—and fact—of a kind of elitism, which it also desired to avoid.

Finally, the determination to hold the major meetings of the Federation in different places around the world has had both good and bad consequences. The intention was to ensure that the members of the Federation would be forced to mingle with large numbers of persons from the host nation and to experience firsthand different images of the future. This has certainly been the case for the Federation, which has met in Norway, Japan, Romania, Italy, Yugoslavia, Egypt, Sweden, Costa Rica, and Hawaii in global conferences (and in many other places for regional meetings), and contrasts with the assemblies of the World Future Society, for example, which have always been in Washington, D.C., except for one meeting in Toronto, Canada, and another in New York City (compared with the conference sites of the WFSF, not places likely to result in images of the future that are strikingly different from those found along the Potomac!).

Holding major futures conferences in various spots around the globe also results in the generation of greater research, education, and awareness of futures studies worldwide. This has been one of the major positive features of the Federation's work. But it also means that getting to a WFSF global conference is difficult for everyone but the hosting country. The membership thus must either be personally rich, institutionally supported, or otherwise able to gain access to travel funds. Various international organizations, such as UNESCO (United Nations Educational, Scientific, and Cultural Organization), and the hosting nation have usually made the participation of specifically desired (especially socialist and Third World) persons possible. But many other "poor" but important persons in the First World have not been able to attend. I have been fortunate in that respect, and thus feel that I have a special obligation to perform the tasks of the secretary-general of the WFSF for a few years in appreciation to the tremendous education I have received from so many people in different parts of the world.

My involvement with the members of the WFSF has been a good counterbalance to my association with the people of Hawaii. For while I have had the opportunity of being influenced by images of the future from persons in various parts of Asia, South America, and, especially, Europe for moderately extended periods several times each year, I have also been able to retain close contact with students and a wide variety of members of the community in Hawaii as well.

In addition to teaching undergraduate and graduate courses in futures studies regularly at the University of Hawaii (and since 1978 administering a master's degree option in alternative futures through the department of political science), I have met on an average of two to three times a week with members of various community groups throughout the state. Thus, reversing a popular slogan among futurists, I feel that I "Think Locally and Act Globally." It is a deviation-amplifying experience.

So what have I learned from the experiences recounted above? Many things, and I am certainly still learning, I hope. Here are seven lessons that seem especially salient to me now.

1. *The future cannot be predicted, but it is possible to forecast alternative*

futures. One of the things that I learned first and have held most dear is that the impulse driving us all to study the future—the desire to predict things to come—is a mirage. The deep-seated desire to *know* the future—so deep-seated that it must have a profound biological/environmental basis—is impossible to fulfill. Futurists must resist the temptation to satisfy this desire in others by saying sooths and reducing anxieties by foretelling events. There is no such thing as "*the* future" that can be foretold if one only has the correct theory and the correct data. If it once were so, in an earlier time of real or perceived social stability, it is certainly not so now. The best, the only thing, we can do is to forecast (not predict) a range of alternative futures (not the future). While one can perhaps become rich and famous by pretending to predict the future, and by using the verb "will" in one's writing and speeches, one must be either a bigot, or a charlatan, or very hungry, to do so.

But the forecasting of alternative futures is difficult and demanding enough. Capturing the possibilities in the cone of time extending into the future—and into the past—is sufficiently difficult and rewarding to command our attention. My image of time does not resemble a telephone pole, with a single past buried below us underground and a single future stretching rigidly above us. Rather, time is like a tree—especially like the banyan trees that are common in Hawaii and other tropical areas: a vast complex of roots, some hidden below the ground, others stretching down from branches above. And the branches themselves—so rich and multivaried—are not linear and certain at all. Still all possibilities *are* caught in that canopy, and one of those twigs will become "*the* future": "the present at a later time."

If, as futurists, we can bound the possibilities, and, most important, learn for ourselves and help others to understand that it is the alternatives that are real and the image of a single future that is the mirage—and thus that our individual and collective plans and decisions must be made in the light of these constantly shifting alternative futures—then we will have done our best and most valuable job as futurists.

2. *The future cannot be predicted, but the future can be invented.* At least this is a corollary I derive from the previous lesson. If we cannot predict what *the* future will be, then perhaps we can become more active in envisioning, and working toward the creation of, futures we prefer. I do not pretend that we can in fact (individually or collectively) fully construct the world we may prefer, but I am convinced from years of teaching and community participation that this assumption is vital, rare, frustrating, and necessary.

We must come to understand that society itself is a social invention, and that, individually and collectively, we each have the responsibility and possibility of constantly inventing it anew, and improving on past inventions. Learning how to "reinvent" society must be the educational goal of "professional" futurists and the function of community-focused futures programs.

3. "*It is the business of the future to be dangerous.*" Alfred North White-head said that and I agree with him. But I also believe that it is the business of the futurist to speak (and live) dangerously. I might put it this way: "*Many presently helpful statements about the future appear, on first en-counter, to be ridiculous.*" It is the job of the futurist to speak about the future, which does not exist in the present, and therefore is not part of our common sense and understanding. If the general reaction to a futurist's statement is "yes, that makes sense. I've thought of that," then it is likely that the statement is not really about the future at all, but about the present. But if the reaction is "that is the dumbest thing I've ever heard! That is ridiculous," then there is at least a chance that the statement might be about the future. Of course, it really *might* be ridiculous, or worse. But that is a different matter.

After the first wave of reaction a futurist should be able to convince others that a stated occurrence is indeed plausible by showing its seeds, or perhaps early sprouts, in the present, or by constructing a convincing scenario of development into the future.

In my opinion the main work of the futurist, in contrast to that of the planner or short-term decision-maker, is to point out and help individuals— and society—to prepare for these "emerging issues." *When* in the future these emerging issues ultimately blossom as "problems" or "opportunities" is not the point—their growth curve may be steep and short, or long and slow. Rather, it is their presently "hidden" nature and potential for emerg-ence that make them important to the futurist, and hence to others.

4. *There is no such thing as "the present."* One of the things futurists hear most frequently from others is some variation on the theme "I don't have any time to think about the future. I'm up to my armpits in alligators now." Practical matters and present emergencies alone are considered reason enough to discount the future consistently and perpetually.

But just when is "the present?" Is it now? Or now? Or now? Or now? No! It does not exist or rather, it is so excruciatingly thin that it whizzes by before we can grasp it. In fact, *we* are the present—our conscious selves. And of what are we usually conscious? Not the present, for the most part. Rather, we are dreaming or daydreaming; remembering, regretting, recall-ing—or planning, scheming, plotting, anticipating. We live in the past and in the future far more than in the present.

But if the practical person still resists, then let us at least see if we can thicken and broaden the present. Let's stretch it, as the Danish futurist Arne Sorensen used to say, so that we have more room to maneuver. Let's stretch the present out so that it includes the next, say, thirty years. If we do that, we won't need to talk about the future because we will have finally made the present broad enough so that we have some breathing room.

5. Yet, *futures studies is in fact more about the present than the future* anyway. "The future" does not, and never will, exist. What does exist are

our *images of the future* in the present. Thus futures studies explore our *images* of the future, and not "the future" itself. In addition, one thing I most certainly have learned is that if you don't like the future now, wait a minute. That is to say, societal images of the future are extremely flexible and changeable.

For example, when I first began teaching futuristics, my students (and society generally) were optimistic, technology-oriented, eager to be creative and innovative. During the mid–1970s they tended to be more pessimistic, pro-ecology (and antitechnology), and interested in restoring older values and ways. By the late 1970s it was difficult to teach a class on "the future" because it all seemed so bleak to young people that they decided it was foolish to assume anyone could forestall disaster. Live for the moment, they seemed to say.

More recently, students have become concerned about the future again, and often from a pro-technology, yet concerned, stance. But wait a minute. Nothing is forever. This, too, will pass.

6. The following are the *basic components of futures studies* in my opinion. It is around these five concepts that I orient the classes I teach and the entire program in alternative futures at the University of Hawaii:

$$
\begin{array}{c}
\text{Theory} \\
\diagup \qquad \diagdown \\
\text{Trends} \!-\! \text{Images} \!-\! \text{Events} \\
\diagdown \qquad \diagup \\
\text{Methods}
\end{array}
$$

What are the *dominant images of the future*, now and historically? How are they distributed within and among social groups? What are their bases? What are their consequences?

My own "dominant image of the future" can be found in much of my writing, speaking, and teaching, and it changes as the images of the future found among different people in the world change. The image of my preferred future, which I call that of a "transformational society" can also be found in several of my articles. But it is the understanding of the importance of images of the future as guides to present action, and hence the individual and societal necessity of clarifying one's own image, that I stress in my writing and teaching—not the "validity" of my own preference.

What is your *theory of social change*? What is "society" and how is it structured? What keeps it from changing; what causes it to change? What do terms like "change" and "permanence" mean in a world where birth, maturation, and death are inescapable? What theories of social change exist? On what intellectual bases are they founded? What differences do they make? How should they be formulated?

A theory of social change should be at the heart of serious futures studies, but in fact this is often neglected. Among the many useful theories available,

I have tended to rely on my understanding of a statement by Marshall McLuhan: "We shape our tools, and thereafter our tools shape us" to guide my teaching and research in futures studies.

What *methods are appropriate for forecasting and designing the future?* What specifically "futuristic" methods are there? What is the theoretical and cosmological basis, and justification, for using some methods rather than others?

There are two categories of methods: those appropriate for forecasting and those helpful in designing the future. Methods in futures studies too often concentrate only on the former. And when they do, they frequently adopt an obsolete positivistic, deterministic stance toward forecasting. A group of us at the University of Hawaii have been attempting to determine what a "quantum" approach to forecasting might be. We think that such is likely to be more satisfying and in accordance with the characteristics of society and of our role as futurists than is the more traditional approach.

Nonetheless, I spend more of my energies in trying to understand and teach what theories of societal design might be than in applied forecasting of things to come on my own. Both of these activities should go together. For this reason I contend that futures studies must embrace normative, value-laden aspects fully and responsibly and should not pretend to be an objective, value-free "science."

What helpful or harmful developments can be plotted as *trends* back and forward in time that can be useful for individual or societal decision making? Who should be responsible for identifying and monitoring these trends, and who should have access to information about them, and in what format?

What *events* ("happenings" that cannot be plotted on a trend line) need to and can be anticipated and planned for? What "events" can be transformed into "trends?" Or are the only things important about the future those unanticipated events that seem to lurch society along and that can only be described retrospectively as "history?"

7. Finally, *the future is too important to be left to the experts.* While it is necessary and possible to have a futures orientation become a normal part of all academic and occupational situations, it is still desirable to encourage futures studies to become an academic/occupational discipline in its own right, and for futures research organizations to exist as separate entities or as parts of other organizations. The products of such futures research must be related to and used by relevant decision-makers as possible and appropriate.

To achieve this is hard enough in the present, but if this were all there were to futures studies, I would not be interested in it. There is a third, vital, and inseparable aspect of futures studies that must be linked to the professional futures researcher and to major decision-makers.

From my discussion of Hawaii 2000 it should be clear what that is. Alvin Toffler long ago identified this as "anticipatory democracy"—a necessary form of popular participation and influence in decision making that is based on a clear and conscious awareness of the future, rather than on a narrow or selfish concern with the present or the past.

Thus professional futurists and ordinary citizens need to spend a great deal of time together enriching each other with their ideas, visions, fears, and hopes for the future. For futures studies to become just another academic discipline or just another job would be a disaster—although it must become both in order to achieve viability.

There remains—there must remain—something about "the future as a way of life" that retains the excitement, uncertainty, lure, and romance that created modern futures studies in the first place. When, and if, it becomes too well established, then it will be time to disestablish it. True, we are a long way from that now, but much of the original excitement of "futurism" that reemerges whenever an individual or group first encounters futures studies even now needs to be a permanent, revitalizing part of all our endeavors at anticipating and shaping things to come.

NOTE

1. The best source of information about citizen-based futures exercises is Clement Bezold, ed., *Anticipatory Democracy*, New York: Vintage Books, 1978.

NINE WAYS FOR COPING WITH FUTURE ANGST: WHAT I LEARNED

The book in which I expressed best my position is *The Active Society*. It set forth a theory of deliberate societal change, propelled by active individuals who shape the society to render it more responsive to their evolving needs. Although it deals with the future, it does not assume a higher capacity to foretell the future; certainly not to predict it in detail. However, it lacked a clear conception of the rules that one might follow in seeking to advance into the future—with relatively little knowledge of the future. Over the years I searched for those rules. After explaining the deeper reasons we require such rules, some are offered.

THE NEED FOR HUMILITY

To forecast the future is a lesson in humility. At issue is the arrogant attitude that individuals are at the center of the universe and can comprehend its dynamics, and control its future (a hyperactive position) vs. the humble notion that individuals must adapt to a world that is largely given, driven by forces they neither control nor understand (a suprapassive position).

Although the terms arrogance and humility have obvious religious overtones, they may be used in this context because they evoke alternate views of the social world. Arrogant approaches contain both scientific assumptions and findings about the power and reach of science, technology, and rational decision making and reflect an orientation to the world that is, in part, normative, prescriptive. Whether consciously or not, arrogant orientations encourage those who subscribe to them to approach their natural and social environment with a hyperactive, rationalistic stance. Cases in point are teachings that guide executives to approach the world by setting goals they individually prefer, establishing which means are most cost-effective, and then proceeding to act on this based on their analysis; in the notion that firms (and other institutions) can be usefully viewed as the products of a rational design; and in the assumption that by enacting laws, societies may change themselves, say, to become more egalitarian. The claims of those who say that they can read the future often contain an element of arrogance.

Similarly, the opposite orientation—that of humility—contains both scientific findings and assumptions about the limits of individual ability to collect and process information, to draw proper conclusions, and the fact that any active agent must start by seeking the consent of others for a joint course of action if one can be found, as well as reflecting an orientation to the world that, whether deliberately or unwittingly, encourages people to accept their fate and station, both in nature and in society. A case in point is medieval church doctrine, which taught people that they were each born into a position in life and were to make the best of it (or seek a more elevated afterlife) rather than attempt to change their status in this world. Psychoanalysis, major segments of the sociology of deviance, and transcendental meditation have each been criticized because they discourage people from seeing fault in the system and attempting to change it. Realization that we are not given the faculty of reading the future is a sign of humility.

The arrogance/humility orientation encompasses many facets. One facet concerns the assumption as to how powerful the actor is. It is arrogant to assume a high concentration of power in a country's elite faced by mindless masses, one chief executive officer faced by rank and file that can be motivated, through properly designed payments and supervision, to fulfill his or her will, and so on. Humble theories deal with the pluralism of actors, interest groups, and veto groups (among which power is distributed) and with coalition and consensus building.

Another facet concerns the assumption about the nature of the *relations* (or bonds) among the actors. The arrogant orientation tends to see each individual as complete unto himself or herself; the humble one tends to see them as deeply intertwined. Here the discussion focuses on the assumptions about the ability of actors to understand the future into which they inject their intervention, their cognitive or *knowledge capabilities*, their ability to know and render proper decisions and, above all, foretell the future. Before this is attempted, we note that more than the desire to know compels people to seek to read in the future.

FUTURE ANGST

Future angst afflicts people, institutions, even nations. It is a sense of advancing without control into unknown time zones, of stumbling in darkness over a terrain never before negotiated. Futures research and forecasting seek to reduce this angst by rational means (for example, providing ranges within which future developments are *likely* to fall) and seek to reassure people (for instance by pointing out that various widely expected catastrophes are quite unlikely). At the same time, false prophets and merchants of modern snake oil reassure people by claiming to *know* the future in detail, to be able to pick the stocks that will soar, to foretell the price of gold by 1990, or to crown the next superpower. Among their earmarks, other than unfounded certainty about their predictions, are the age-old devices of Delphi-like opaque statements. Typical are forecasts that are said to hold in the "longer run," without specifying the time period within which or the conditions under which they will come true. Another case in point are statements such as those by Herman Kahn in his 1982 book *The Coming Boom*, where he asserted that certain future developments were "not implausible," which is quite vague as to the expected probability. Statements by some other futurist writers are tautological: "Unless we do something violently stupid with our future, the externals of hope and love and laughter will still be there," says futurist Gerard K. O'Neill of Princeton University.

The problem is that futures studies today is like medicine in its early stages; its capacity to illuminate is still limited. Reference is made to human, cultural, economic, political—in short, social—forces, not to changes in nature. Radioactive decay, the movement of the planets, and biological aging are much more predictable but not, by themselves, what most decision-makers and policymakers deal with. Once the limitations of *social* forecasting are recognized and deeply accepted, one is open to a major change in orientation.

The greater one's desire or need to know the future, the greater one's future angst. The symptoms of those afflicted include obsessive preoccupation with foretelling the future, rigid belief in forecasting, and deficient reality testing—not learning properly from the experiences of past forecasts. We scoff at some peoples for their belief in rain-making dances, but those of us who bet on a favorite number or buy stock because the zodiac is right are hardly more rational.

An elementary desire to know the future is far from sick; it is an integral part of a wholesome need to learn how to cope. However, we do invite trouble when we forget that the future is sectorialized. Some aspects of the future are predictable. We know, for instance, that lunar eclipses occur in an eighteen-year cycle (every 6,585.32 days, to be exact), that strontium 90 has a half-life of eighteen years, and that about 51.46 percent of all children born in the United States in 1990 will be male. Unfortunately, when it comes to many other matters—the stock market, inflation levels, consumer tastes, crime rates—we move in much less predictable future sectors. Those who need to negotiate these sectors are most prone to future angst.

I particularly remember one encounter with this form of anxiety because it cost me a hefty consulting fee. A major newspaper invited me to consult with its Committee for the Future. The Committee was worried that twenty years hence, with an increase in leisure time and of such activities as watching TV and playing electronic games, there would be few readers left for its momentous reportage. At the time the Committee also had to approve the construction of a large newspaper-processing plant. The cost of the plant had to be amortized over twenty years, and unless one could assume at least a steady sale of newspapers for two decades, the building could not be justified. Hence the desire to *know* sales for the next twenty years.

I explained that it just plain could not be done. The senior chairman of the Committee, with evident agitation, wanted to know why not. He pointed to a pile of newspaper clippings about the future that someone had assembled for him. I pointed out that future sales depend on numerous factors, each of which could be predicted only loosely, and that when one combines several vague assumptions, one is left with poor predictions. I was never invited back. I learned later that someone did deliver the desired prediction, and the plant was built.

REDUCING ANGST

One should not conclude from all this that the future is a mystery that cannot be approached rationally. On the contrary, there are important lessons to be applied by people, institutions, and nations, once they overcome their future angst. These lessons emerge from what I call, somewhat immodestly, "Etzioni's nine rules for stumbling serenely into the future."

1. *Know what future sector you're dealing with and how relatively predictable it is.* Here a rough rule of thumb might help: Matters concerning objects, such as mechanical or chemical developments, are, on average, easier to predict than those concerning bodies, such as biological aging or the course of an illness; those concerning bodies are, on average, more predictable than social-human matters, such as what people will vote for, buy, or believe.

2. *Rarely rely on pinpointed predictions; allow for a margin of error.* For example, the following *U.S. News & World Report* prediction on gasoline costs is too precise: "The price of gasoline now (October 1978) is 64 cents; the price in 1983 should be $1.05." To predict that the price would be more than one dollar and less than two would have been a humbler forecast, more indicative of our capacity, and a more reliable guide for the future.

On the other hand, the U.S. Census Bureau's population projections are a fine example of range forecasting. The Bureau provides four projections for the size of the U.S. population in the year 2000, ranging from a low of 246 million Americans to a high of about 283 million. Different assumptions are built into each projection. Together they remind us that we may know more about the ball park we'll find ourselves in than about our precise seats in it.

3. *Trust shorter-run predictions more than longer-run.* A report published in *Technological Forecasting and Social Change* concludes: "Shorter forecasts are more accurate, . . . for example, five-year petroleum-consumption forecasts have had a median error of about 6 percent and ten-year forecasts

an error of around 13 percent. Motor vehicle registration forecasts have median errors in percentages roughly equal to the forecast lengths in years."

4. *Know thy forecaster. Occasional errors or good calls are not important. A systematic record is the best indicator.* When lawyers or tax accountants advise you, you should know about their previous court cases or tax audits. Often such information is unavailable or does not take specifics into account. For instance, a lawyer may do well in routine matters but not in complex ones, or vice versa.

When the information is available, it should not be overlooked. Thus if you need complex surgery, go to a large hospital. Why? Because its surgical teams get more of a chance to practice and keep up their skills. Death rates are significantly lower in hospitals where 200 or more such procedures are done each year than in those that do but a few score.

5. *Assume you'll have to revise your plan as you proceed.* People who deal in commodity futures have one rule they cherish most: Cut your losses short, let your profits run. Applied to the world at large, that means you should be prepared to run for cover if your expectations turn sour. Use new information that comes your way to change your course of action.

In testimony before Congress, this same principle was applied to the financing of social security by Peter Morrison, director of the Population Research Center at the Rand think tank. In order to keep the fund in balance, contributions must increase if the population tends to age and live longer. The fund got way out of balance not merely because the predictions about life expectancy and aging turned out to have been erroneous, but because changes in trends were ignored for too long. Morrison favors adjusting the contribution rates every few years. In this way a society can cope with the future without assuming its predictions are highly reliable—acting like a driver who constantly adjusts his course as new segments of the road come into sight.

6. *Give preference to reversible steps over those that are difficult or costly to reverse.* Simple illustration: If you plan a vacation and have serious doubts whether you can go, make reservations on flights and with resorts where there is no penalty for cancellation. The same holds for investing your money. Four-year certificates, for instance, pay higher interest rates than shorter-term ones, but you are penalized if you withdraw ahead of time. It is one thing to lower your thermostat to save fuel; it is quite another to tear out your oil burner to replace it with a gas heater—only to find out that coal has become most advantageous.

7. *Never commit all your resources to one course of events. Hedge your bets (diversify). Keep a strategic reserve.* Expect something unexpected to occur. Thus wise investors never put all their money in nonliquid items, such as houses, lest they be without funds in an emergency or be forced to pass up an opportune buy. Similarly, those who invest in several stocks rather than in one, or who make several forms of investment (stocks, bonds,

gold, and real estate) are reported to gain better over the years. The same lesson can be applied to other matters: Better to build up two or three friendships, for instance, than to "invest" all your emotions in one.

8. *Use futures studies for nonpredictive purposes—for enlightenment, broadening the mind, and even entertainment.* In the late 1950s *Life* magazine predicted that in 1975, "the family helicopter will be as attainable as the family convertible is today; air pollution will be eliminated; and steamers will haul passengers to Europe for as little as 50 cents."

If you took such predictions literally—and junked the car, waited for the family helicopter, set aside fifty cents for your European passage—you would have been disappointed. But if you read these as fascinating "what-if" tales, you would be richer for it.

9. *Plan to do things that are good, perhaps even fun, in themselves. Then, if their future use fails, you're still ahead.* A congressional committee found thirty-five projections about the future of energy in the United States. Some have stressed the pivotal role of nuclear energy, others the wisdom of massive use of coal, still others the need to find more oil. Whoever turns out to be right, though, a good case can be made for our relying as much as possible on the "soft" paths—solar, waves, wind. The more we follow these paths, the more we use resources that are clean, safe, and inexhaustible. Thus even if we find more oil than anyone expected or a way to make more kilowatts more cheaply out of nuclear reactors, the side benefits of soft technology would still put us ahead.

The same holds true for driving at slower speeds. We may or may not run out of oil by the year 2020, but we do know that a fifty-five-mile-per-hour speed limit saves not only gas, but also lives. In 1974, the first year of the lower speed limit, there were 4,500 fewer highway deaths.

All these rules can be summarized by the thought that we should approach the future, indeed the world, with greater humility and less arrogance, as people who have much to learn but know *relatively* little. As my experience grew and my research accumulated, I came to the conclusion that individuals who dash forward, putting excessive confidence in their or others' forecasts, will fall flat on their faces while the meek will inherit the future.

Walter A. Hahn   **10**

FUTURES IN POLITICS AND
THE POLITICS OF FUTURES

While engaged in long-range research and development planning at the
National Academy of Sciences in the mid–1950s, I was offered a job at
General Electric as a defense systems "product planner." What's that? I
asked. Peter Schenck, my new boss-to-be, said that the work principally
involved developing "a clear but erroneous picture of the future." Although
"futures" was not to appear in my title or job descriptions for the next two
decades, hindsight shows that I had embarked on a career as a *futurist*.

I have had the good fortune to be a participant-observer in two interacting
tracks of the futures movement since the mid–1960s. One track concerns
the use, misuse, and nonuse of futures concepts and techniques in governmental and political affairs. The other track concerns the initiation, activities, and sometimes demise of voluntary sector futures-oriented associations. I think of the first track as futures in politics and the latter as the
politics of futures. The editors put the question to me directly: What have
you learned?

This essay is, of necessity, partly autobiographical, but the focus is on
what is different now about the way I think and write about the future.
My discontinuous references to people, places, positions, and papers are to
provide context to the answers to the editors' question. Because the answers
change with time, I will summarize my "lessons learned" by decades, starting
with 1965.

A BEGINNER'S BIASES: PRE–1965

Although involved in technological forecasting, policy planning, and operations research-management science activities in both government and

This essay appeared originally in the *Futures Research Quarterly* (Winter 1985). Copyright
1985 by the World Future Society. Reprinted, with changes, by permission of the publisher.

business throughout the 1950s and early 1960s, my first awareness of modern futures concepts came in 1962 from reading Rachel Carson's book *Silent Spring*. But I don't recall being aware of the term futures until I saw its synonyms used in Bertrand de Jouvenel's *The Art of Conjecture* (1964). My frame of reference while reading these and other new books and periodicals was that of a business operations researcher-management scientist in a General Electric defense component. My forward thinking at that time was expressed as follows: "The orientation...is toward problem anticipation, recognition and prevention, and in developing better understanding about the nature of the business."[1] The time horizon was about five years. We were thinking of the business as a whole, but if any of us had used the term holistic, we would have been chided on our spelling. For priority setting we regularly used hierarchical ordering techniques we called "lattices" in our published papers and "spider webs" in the office.[2] They were only a little less refined than today's logic trees. In our business setting we faced the dual problems of competition for resources for our "way out stuff" and choosing a research portfolio acceptable to peer line operating managers. One accepted solution in 1962 was establishing a "bimodal distribution of research payoffs" portfolio.[3] The idea was that, rather than compete with bottom-line managers in looking into the near future (one to two years out), the management scientists both extended their own focus to five or more years ahead and did some consulting for the line managers on current problems. Being simultaneously noncompetitive and helpful seemed to do the trick.

When I returned to government it was possible to apply some of the industrial advances to public sector issues. But particularly in the non-defense agencies, one had to proceed gingerly when dealing with such non-factual or nonprovable areas as technological forecasting. Some serious, almost apologetic words from my 1964 National Aviation Weather Systems Study (NAVWESS) appear a bit amusing today:

Chapter 4.0.0 is rather unique and it is expected to be controversial. Entitled, "FORECAST OF TECHNICAL AND OPERATIONAL CHANGES OCCURRING ANNUALLY THROUGH 1970," it is an attempt...to describe the most likely evolution of the present system *if* present plans and constraints are not drastically changed. The reader should bear in mind that this chapter does *not* describe what *ought* to be done. Nor is it a crystal-ball effort claiming that the prescribed course of events is beyond control and in the hands of Kismet. Policy, resource, personnel and technological changes will occur. This forecast merely attempts to describe a mean course or par value for use by decision-makers in evaluating possible changes.[4]

To summarize, what had that futurist-to-be of the 1950s learned by 1964 that is relevant to the editors' question? Where did I start my futures learning?

Lesson #1	Interdisciplinary teamwork involving mutual respect and trust is required to pursue complex forward-looking, analysis-synthesis efforts and synergistic results.
Lesson #2	For success and survival, a forward-looking study group's time horizon must be at least twice as far out as the short-range horizon of its parallel line managers' *and* it must do something useful for the managers in the present. Stated another way: don't compete on your peers' or your boss's turf; be helpful now and think ahead.
Lesson #3	Labels are important:

	Good Labels	*Bad Labels*
	Applied business research	Planning
	System	Operations research and synthesis

Lesson #4	The qualitative aspects of decision making are often at least as important as the quantitative aspects, and the two can, and must, be considered in parallel.
Lesson #5	There are no current rewards for current actions that pay off in the future, but there are risks.
Lesson #6	Few major decisions affecting society, technology, the economy, the environment, or politics are made solely in either the public or the private sector—the public-private nexus is where the action is.

LEARNING THE TRADE: 1965 TO 1975

At least for me, 1967 appears to be the landmark year for the start of the modern futures movement. I still have two dog-eared volumes from 1967: Kahn and Wiener's *The Year 2000...* and Daniel Bell's *Daedalus* book, *Towards the Year 2000....* I also have aging copies of a new 1967 periodical, *The Futurist*, with which the World Future Society made its debut.

While reading the new stuff of the futurists, I was still speaking the then-current language of U.S. government bureaucrats—PPBS—Planning, Programming, and Budgeting System. I was director of policy planning in the Weather Bureau. The government directives on PPBS had stretched our vision out to five years, and we were required to be explicit about "alternatives" and "inputs."

Those of us in technical agencies also were keenly aware of legislative branch discussions of a new term, technology assessment. It was first used in 1966 by Congressman Emilio Daddario and had been coined in his discussions with congressional staffers Phillip Yeager and Edward Wenk and Capitol Hill visitor Charles Lindbergh. TA (as it was instantly abbreviated) had to do with the long-term, indirect, and heretofore unanticipated consequences of technological initiatives. TA was to answer "What if...?" questions where technology, broadly defined, was the change agent. Adding to the new vogues of thinking further ahead were the social and political consequences of *Silent Spring*. The environmental movement was coming to a peak. President Nixon had created a Cabinet Committee on the Environment and passage of the Environmental Policy Act of 1969 soon followed, with its now-familiar "102–3c" environmental impact statements.

Two of my papers in this middle 1960s period reflect the then-current rational analysis-planning view of the future. In one sense it was almost a reactive view. A budget request required a program analysis. An expenditure of federal funds required an accompanying environmental impact statement. A technological initative under consideration might require an impact assessment. Quantification, analysis in depth, and process were dominant characteristics of those triggered, forward-looking activities.

For example, in 1965 I wrote, with reference to the work of the Weather Bureau's Office of Policy Planning, "much of the work is internal management consulting and management systems design... [for] leading and coordinating the planning process of the Bureau."[5] Process usually had specific organizational connotations. The PPBS analyses and plans were produced by specific staff offices and "signed off" on by the line executives. The technology assessment considerations focused on creation of a new congressional office.

The role of futures thinking in politics accelerated in 1967. Daddario's subcommittee of the Congress had commissioned studies by the National Academies of Science (NAS) and Engineering (NAE). The NAS study concluded that the technology assessment concept was feasible.[6] The NAE study determined that existing methods and techniques, while needing improvement and expansion, were adequate to perform the assessment function.[7] A third massive (521-page) report by the Congressional Research Service (CRS) documented fourteen completed cases of TA-like activity and explicitly introduced two new ideas to the dialogue: (1) in the conflict between the political and technical aspects of a national issue, Congress should give the political aspects priority, and (2) Congress needs an "early warning system."[8] Few scientists and engineers agreed with either of these ideas. The president's science advisor, Lee Dubridge, even testified that TA was really just "technology arrestment."

The politicians at the other end of Pennsylvania Avenue were approaching the future in a different way. President Nixon, on July 13, 1969, created a National Goals Research Staff (NGRS) within the White House. The staff was to lead an effort to enunciate our national goals by the approaching magic bicentennial date of July 4, 1976. Several key ideas reflecting those of then-current futurist writers (e.g., Gabor, Bell, de Jouvenel, Fuller) were wrapped up in one brief sentence of the president's statement, "We have reached a state of technological and social development at which the future nature of our society can increasingly be shaped by our own conscious choices ... [which] require us to pick among alternatives."[9] In contrast to the congressional emphasis on technology, the president emphasized the social aspects. Both explicitly included qualitative as well as quantitative considerations. I was privileged to be appointed to the NGRS, and in 1970 we were able to reinforce the above theme in the title of our first (and last!) report, *Toward Balanced Growth: Quantity with Quality*. Although we did not label it as such, in our "Introduction" we recorded our view of the status of futures thinking as of July 4, 1970:

We must simultaneously attend to what is urgent, and do our best to focus and respond to what is imminent ... Making intelligent policy choices becomes increasingly complex as society itself becomes more complex, and as the consequences of various courses of action become more far reaching and more intricately intertwined. ... We will have to develop better institutional arrangements for the people to relate to the leadership and better mechanisms of policy analysis to serve all parties.[10]

The emphasis on process at this time was demonstrated by a MITRE Corporation report, *A Technology Assessment Methodology*,[11] prepared under contract to the Office of Science and Technology (OST) in the Executive Office of the President. In seven volumes the report defined a sequence of steps to be followed in "the TA process." MITRE senior vice-president, Charles Zraket, said in his introduction to the report: "An expanded national planning process is required ... to support political and operational discussions at all levels of government, in private enterprise and in citizen and community groups."[12] Some of us were roundly criticized for commenting that the OST had spent a quarter of a million dollars to have MITRE reinvent the scientific method. The strains between the analytical Cartesian-reductionists and the emerging systems synthesis and "qual with quan" types were beginning to show.

Many of us involved in the early 1970s with PPBS, policy planning, technology assessment, goals formulation, and the emerging of futures studies were continually preoccupied with how and where to organize the efforts. For example, the legislative branch created a new organization and the executive branch eliminated both an existing one and a proposal for another.

In late 1972 the fifth of a series of bills to create a congressional Office of Technology Assessment (OTA) was passed. Last-minute Senate and House floor changes created an OTA with two rather novel features. First, OTA was to be a 100 percent congressional organization, with no executive branch or civilian appointees in its hierarchy, although an advisory board of citizens and congressional support agency representatives was retained. Second, the congressional board governing OTA was composed of equal numbers of members from each party in each house. At this time I worked for the Congressional Research Service with responsibility to support congressional action on bills for an OTA. In response to "why a new organization in Congress?" we said in the Senate report on the Technology Assessment Act:

The proposition of this report is that the Congress is the proper national forum for deliberating and deciding upon conflicting goals, values, priorities, resource alternatives and the distribution of benefits, rises, and costs, all of which are involved in technology assessment... [and there is a] need by the Congress for new institutional means to serve its unique interests and responsibilities.[13]

Meanwhile, in the executive branch the NGRS had been disbanded by the president after issuing its first annual report (of six planned), and its functions were "absorbed" by the Domestic Council, chaired by John Ehrlichman. There was brief but intense consideration of substituting a "private" (that term was supposed to convey "nonpolitical") Center for National Goals and Alternatives. The effort was spearheaded at various times under varying titles by leaders of The Conference Board and the Aspen Institute, with design suggestions from Anthony Wiener and Willis Harman. President Nixon also assigned Ehrlichman to deal with the private goals center idea, and neither it nor the NGRS functions were ever heard of again. Proposals for *A Technology Assessment System for the Executive Branch*, as a congressionally initiated report from the National Academy of Public Administration in July 1970 was titled, likewise disappeared into the political maw of the Nixon White House staff.[14]

The years 1971 and 1972 were big ones for those of us involved with forward-looking activities. In May 1971 the growing World Future Society attracted a thousand participants to their first general assembly in Washington, D.C.; while on June 21, 1971, a presidential directive put the PPBS system out of its misery. In February 1972 President Nixon and his secretary of commerce, Maurice Stans, sponsored a White House Conference on The Industrial World Ahead: A Look at Business in 1990. A month later the relatively new Club of Rome received its first report, *The Limits to Growth*, launching worldwide debates about "the global problematique" that continue to this day.

In 1973 we saw the creation of the International Society for Technology Assessment (ISTA). As ISTA's first president, I wrote in the premier issue of our journal, *Technology Assessment*:

The Society's founders thought long and hard about the questions, "Why a society?", "Why an international society?", "Why a journal?" and "Why an international congress?" They concluded that this society and its activities were viable activities to meet an emerging class of recognizable problems that demand control and solution and for recognition of a number of opportunities that otherwise would be missed. Problems are interrelated to a degree never before recognized; interdisciplinary in a way that requires the participation of physical, biological and social scientists, engineers and humanists; and international in that the proper treatment of the subject cannot be limited by national boundaries. There is no existing written or face-to-face information exchange that allows a continuing display and discussion of the impact of these problems. More importantly, there is no forum in which the sophisticated analyst-assessor can directly interact and be accessible to (1) his "customers," the decision and policy makers, and (2) the public who are affected by his and his "customers' " thoughts and actions.[15]

ISTA held its first International Congress on Technology Assessment (ICTA) May 27–June 2, 1973, in The Hague. Attending were 225 persons from twenty-one countries. The three honorary chairmen were Dutch futurist Fred L. Polak; American Emilio Daddario, "father of TA" (then with Gulf + Western Corporation); and, from the United Kingdom, the Right Honorable Anthony Wedgewood Benn, MP. Futurist Alvin Toffler, a participant in the founding of ISTA, was also a member of the ICTA program committee.

At The Hague TA congress there were many differences over such matters as terminology, methodology, and institutional form. But the central TA debate echoed the controversies in parallel futures discussions between the reductionists and the holistic-systemic types. I summed this up in my closing address to ICTA:

There are two dominant schools of thought on this question—"sequential" and "participative." The sequentialists argue that the assessment practititoners should perform their functions free from all political, organizational and personal biases and then transmit or present the objective statement of options and impacts to the decision maker. The participants argue that this procedure is neither practical nor desirable. TA is a process that explicitly involves more than objective factual elements. Values, judgments, choices, experience, and political, economic, social and environmental forces are an integral part of TA. Therefore, the power structure, the public, and the practitioner must all interact for viable assessment. What is important is not which of these views should prevail, but how to achieve an acceptable and workable balance between them in conducting real impact studies.[16]

The sequentialist or "scientific" view was best expressed by Congressional Research Service author Franklin Huddle:

The process of Technology Assessment is one of three elements in the management of technology by society. The first is the process of science and technology, producing innovations as solutions to social problems and needs. These may be economically attractive, or may require public funding: either way, they become candidate claimants for politicl decision making. The second element is the assessment of these technologies as solutions. The third element is the political process by which the social benefits and costs are finally judged and appropriate public action decided upon. Technology Assessment, then, is the technological information input to the political decision process.[17]

To the discomfort of the many reductionists present at ICTA, Member of Parliament Tony Benn came down hard on the other side:

We can no more separate technology assessment from the political process than we can separate economics or ecology from politics. All three are intimately connected with man's need to determine his own future according to his own values and preferences, instead of leaving the strong to decide it for him. We shall deceive ourselves if we think that the new and sophisticated techniques of analysis and forecasting which this congress has been discussing will be allowed to grow quietly in an academic atmosphere free from the distracting glamour of public controversy and hot political debate. Those who are developing and refining these methods of assessment should never be allowed to get detached from these arguments, nor presume to adjudicate from their monastic isolation on the mundane conflict between those with power and those who already have been denied it. Their fast growing expertise will not protect them from the need to take sides in that conflict.[18]

Earlier, in January 1973, the House of Representatives had established a ten-member bipartisan Select Committee on Committees to review House Rules X and XI, which define the jurisdiction and procedure of all committees of the House. Several futurists were invited to testify, with particular reference to the general oversight provision. Among them were Victor Ferkiss of Georgetown University, Willis Harman and Charles Williams of SRI International, and Bertram Gross of Hunter College. In my testimony concerning technology forecasting and futures research, I said that Congress should consider

the establishment of a systematic way to conduct futures research (and/or to monitor existing futures research efforts) in a pooled-work component of the legislative branch. It is too expensive to do in small intermittent studies and too informative and important to leave to occasional volunteer efforts by outsiders. Forecast and futures information is of a much looser kind than that based on fact and history. It must be judged and used in different ways and with more caution. But it can furnish implications of both what might happen and what can happen.[19]

After the work of the Committee, House Resolution 988 was adopted on October 8, 1974. Among its provisions was a change in the general oversight provisions of Rule X to include what is now referred to as "the foresight provision": "2(b)(1) Each standing committee (other than the Committee on Appropriations and the Committee on Budget) shall on a continuing basis undertake futures research and forecasting on matters within the jurisdiction of that Committee."[20] While far from clear or in general use, the terms futures research and forecasting were used to connote that which practitioners do, while "foresight" was more associated with the overall function and users or decision-makers.

Again to summarize, by 1975, what additional lessons had I learned?

Lesson #7 | Beyond analysis, forecasting, and planning, futures think quires awareness, synthesis, alternatives, and choice.

Lesson #8 | Preassessment of impacts (or consequences) of proposed is possible and can, but does not necessarily, lead to more informed decision making. (This is a special case of the more generally accepted "rule" that better or more information does not always lead to better or right decisions.)

Lesson #9 | Parties in power should never announce national (or other) goals. Those not in power demand instant fulfillment, which is impossible, and those whose goal was not first or not listed become instant enemies. (Note: This is sometimes called "Moynihan's Law," referring to Daniel P. Moynihan, who pointed this out to the National Goals Research Staff in his role as presidential counsellor.)

Lesson #10 | Technology assessment is not a discipline or a profession.

Lesson #11 | The same arguments used to institutionalize futures research and technology assessment in the legislative branch were used to de-institutionalize them in the executive branch.

Lesson #12 | Scientists, engineers, operations researchers, et al. are threatened by including qualitative, holistic, subjective, political, foresight, social, participative ... aspects in decision making.

Lesson #3 (1975) | Labels are important:

Good labels	Bad labels
Future(s)	Goals
Small is beautiful	Futuristics
Future shock	Futuribles
Technology assessment	Futurology
Club of Rome	Mellontology

ONE PRACTITIONER'S EXPERIENCE: 1975 TO 1985

In the mid–1970s the nation was just recovering from its Watergate hangover as its bicentennial fever grew. Two big futures events of 1975 were the World Future Society's second general assembly and the First Woodlands Conference on Sustained Growth. WFS focused on "The Next 25 Years: Crisis and Opportunity." Woodlands fanned the limits-to-growth debates.

On Capitol Hill the OTA had begun to issue studies low on impact assessment but responsive to congressional requests about technology—a pattern it still follows. A few committees and subcommittees explored futures issues and held foresight hearings, but implementation of the foresight provision was of low priority. The "reform class" of ninety-one freshmen in the 93rd Congress searched for meaningful agendas with first-term (re-election) potential. Of use to them were the biannual (for each new Congress) "emerging issues" lists required of the CRS under the terms of the Legislative Reorganization Act of 1970.

In 1976 approximately thirty members, representing both houses and both parties, formed a Congressional Clearinghouse on the Future (CCF). Through the Clearinghouse members met with futurists and one another to discuss emerging issues and trends. Herman Kahn, Bucky Fuller, Margaret Mead—almost all the futurists—participated in the CCF's "Dialogues" sessions, futures fairs, and other events. For example, congressmen listened to Alvin Toffler's "anticipatory democracy" theme of the times (more consciousness, peripheral vision, futures and more participation) but seemed reluctant to concede that they were the elected *representatives* of the body politic. CCF continues as an active program and still publishes a newsletter, *What's Next?* for circulation on Capitol Hill and beyond.

The CRS, in response to its congressional clients' expanding needs for alerting and "what if...?" information, established an interdisciplinary Futures Research Group (FRG). FRG provided training in futures-related methodologies for CRS and congressional staff. It also designed and implemented a Futures Information Retrieval SysTem (FIRST) as an add-on to the existing research, documentation, and reference information systems of the Library of Congress. The arguments between the tenured, bureaucratic guardians of the tight traditional classification logics and the new futurists' needs for innovation and flexibility were long, hard, and sometimes heated. To the credit of all parties they were ultimately productive. Old Library of Congress records can now be accessed for futures-oriented items, even though they were not entered that way, and new information is being filed with "futures" designators for even better access.

On the association front a variety of events were occurring. In 1976 the ISTA held its Second International Congress (2ICTA) in Ann Arbor, Michigan, with the theme "Technology Assessment: Creative Futures." While successful in information exchange, 2ICTA clearly showed the strains of attempting actually to perform technology assessments. The continuing internal struggle for control of ISTA broke out into the open at the 2ICTA annual business meeting. Those not in control wanted considerably more "democratic" process than the founders and financial backers were willing to accept. But these "management" issues were really surrogates for the deeper differences between (1) those who saw ISTA as a loose forum, open to all, with no functional sections, interest chapters, or national segments, and (2) those who wanted ISTA to be a structured nineteenth-century professional society developing "the discipline" of TA. Curiously, calling TA a discipline was to many a solution to a more pragmatic problem: that interdisciplinary assessors could not get their applied work published in the narrow, traditional refereed disciplinary journals. But ISTA was not up to dealing with any of these issues. It had been seriously weakened in 1973 by a financially ruinous battle with its Dutch services contractor, and again in 1974, when the English publisher of the ISTA journal declared bankruptcy. The follow-on Israeli publisher put out the last issue of ISTA's journal in the winter of 1976. The brave words of my report as chairman of the board at 2ICTA in Michigan were *not* prophetic: "To all those members who have stayed with us during all of these troubles we give our thanks.... I believe [ISTA] can continue to serve as a 'forum for social impact evaluation' as stated on its letterhead."[21] Within a year we quietly terminated ISTA's corporate charter. ISTA "the forum" was no more, but the idea for a society and a journal for recognizing academic assessment contributions was still very much alive. By 1980, at the World Future Society meeting in Toronto, the International Association for Impact Assessment was born. The leaders of what some incorrectly called the born-again ISTA effort were academics from Georgia Tech. An explicit goal was to create an interdisciplinary society with a refereed journal.

While the Congress was focusing on dialogue and the technology assessors on technique, others in the futures movement increased their concern about "the global problematique." The Club of Rome (CoR) held its 1976 meeting in Philadelphia. The most memorable event of the affair was a violent clash of politics with futures. Dinner speaker Vice-president Nelson Rockefeller delivered a major pro-growth address to the limits-to-growth crowd. "What politician could ever be elected on a no-growth platform?" asked Rockefeller, as he described the Republican administration's plans to stimulate growth. Although a bit shaken, CoR leaders Aurelio Peccei, Alexander King, and their colleagues stuck to their agenda. While preaching egalitarianism, the meetings' six levels of colored badges effectively protected the privacy and status of some of the "more-equal" participants and their admittedly elitist CoR hosts. Whatever one's feelings about elitism, its effectiveness in achieving access to money, the powerful, and the press must be acknowledged. To promote those accessibilities and to make everyone on earth aware of the problematique, CoR was encouraging establishment of affiliated national associations. USACoR—the United States Association for the Club of Rome—was created in 1976.

USACoR followed the parent model in being limited to 100 invited members with a central mission of communicating the nature and consequences of the global problematique. One subtle difference in American values was to have a big difference on USACoR years later. USACoR members were carefully chosen to include representatives of the widest range of occupations, intellectual pursuits, wealth, activist interests, employment sectors, ages ... and especially to be balanced between female and male members. A positive result of this was that the internal governance of USACoR provided me, as a board member, with an outstanding example and rewarding experience of male-female respect and cooperation. Differences were plen-

tiful and strong, but gender was never part of them. A significant contribution of USACoR was that approximately thirty of its members cooperated
in writing the book *Making It Happen*,[22] a collection of essays on what
members personally are *doing* or *have done* about the problematique beyond
exhorting others to action.

But USACoR's style and active membership have changed significantly
from its origins. The negative aspect of diverse representation and of the
later decision to triple membership was that eventually differences over
direction, style, programs, and so on overwhelmed the common interests.
Were it not for the continuing patience and generous financial support of
one key benefactor, USACoR might not have survived. One member, elected
in 1982, resigned a year later complaining, frankly, that he had joined to
hobnob with "the biggies and they don't attend the meetings anymore." At
least no one in USACoR tried to make a discipline out of the global problematique! Today a stabler and low-key USACoR network-style association carries on a varity of positive, American-style activities that CoR's
founder, the late Aurelio Peccei, would be proud of.

In 1979 a nonprofit Congressional Institute for the Future (CIF) was set
up in the private sector to parallel the Congressional Clearinghouse on the
Future, which could no longer accept public funds or provide service beyond
the Congress. The CCF and CIF pair coexist today as caucus-like entities,
focusing the activities of approximately 100 members of Congress interested
in foresight and futures.

Two brief examples provide lessons about the ease and difficulties of
conducting futures activities in political settings. When Senator Adlai Ste-
venson was appointed chairman of the newly established Subcommittee on
Science, Technology and Space (STS), he requested "innovative" support
from the CRS in acquiring information useful to setting the subcommittee's
agenda and priorities. In an initial twenty-page briefing paper we first
painted the global setting of the next two to ten years, a national context,
and a "science, technology and space" view. These successively smaller filters
still produced too large a menu of issues and opportunities relevant to the
subcommittee. We then wrote three one-page scenarios (more of the same,
pick your disaster, and cooperative change) of alternative STS futures. This
permitted the senator, subcommittee members, and staff to align their assumptions with those of one of the three pure or mixed scenarios. Issues
common to more than one scenario received special attention as possible
high priority items. The subcommittee expressed considerable amazement
that some issues appeared in all three scenarios and thus represented nearly
"must" items for its attention.

This experience demonstrated that, with a receptive and active client, a
futures (or other) team can use new (to that client) techniques and approaches with ease and effectiveness. We also demonstrated to ourselves
and others that some of this "futures stuff" can be applied to political

decision making. Nor was it a one-shot effort. A more advanced variation on this exercise was incorporated into my two-year-long Joint Economic Committee (JEC) Special Study on Economic Change, *Research and Innovation: Developing a Dynamic Nation (1980)*.[23] In it, we reviewed the past two decades of innovation studies, looked ahead for the next three, and again developed alternative futures scenarios to aid the Congress in selecting suitable policies and actions. But unlike the Senate case, committee leadership and membership changes were made just as the study was completed, so there is no direct evidence of use of the JEC scenarios or foresight.

A second example of forward thinking in political and bureaucratic environments concerns the Five-Year Science and Technology Outlook (5YSTO). At the end of a long series of debates between the executive branch and the Congress, the requirement for a 5YSTO emerged in PL 94–282, the National Science and Technology Policy, Organization, and Priorities Act of 1976. Specifically, the requirement was "to identify and describe situations and conditions which warrant special attention within the next five years, involving 1) current and emerging problems...and 2) opportunities...involving science and technology."[24] The congressional view of what the executive branch should do had prevailed...or had it?

For a long time nothing happened. Then the science and engineering community learned that Frank Press, director of the Office of Science and Technology Policy (OSTP) and science advisor to President Carter, wanted the National Science Foundation (NSF) to prepare the Outlook, not OSTP. The experienced bureaucrats at NSF instantly saw the problems of their producing a "scientific" and objective document that would be reviewed, perhaps altered, and sent to the Congress by the political appointees of the White House as the administration's views. The proposed solution to the dilemma was to have the Outlook prepared under contract by the prestigious National Academies of Science and Engineering (NAS-NAE). But the academies' policies require public release of their normal products, and thus any later changes by the NSF, OSTP, or others would be clearly visible. Over a year was spent in discussion before it was agreed that the academies would make parallel submissions to NSF and for public release.

What is of interest in this context is that these delays and discussions were not over some startling or contentious substantive matter in bioengineering, synthetic materials, or theoretical physics—no forecasts or outlooks had yet been made. The discussions were over advance control of the futures information yet to be developed. Eventually, the law was implemented, and in May 1980 the first 5YSTO came into existence, conveying evidence of continuing wariness. The NAS-NAE material went to NSF and simultaneous commercial publication was authorized. The NSF "official" 5YSTO document contained a six-page signed "Statement of the Director of the National Science Foundation." The completed Outlook was submitted to the Congress by the President as required by law. Three additional Outlooks have been prepared by the NAS-NAE as of 1985. These were completed with less tension, with the NAS-NAE writing the technical chapters, other contractors supplying some policy discussions, numerous contributions from other agencies and departments, and the OSTP and NSF cooperating in the overall process.

Readers should not draw implications of any ill will, ignorance, or illegality on the part of any individual, political party, or administration for this example. Different individuals, of the opposition party, in the following administration, succeeded effectively in abolishing the requirement for a 5YSTO in the Reports Elimination Act of 1982.[25] Resistance to foresight would not seem to stem from personal or party motivations. Either institutional reasons or something about the nature of futures information itself appears a more likely cause.

A very different learning situation in my experience might be titled "the demise of the CRS Futures Research Group." The CRS-FRG had continued to serve a number of congressional clients in the late 1970s and into the 1980s. Among the projects were identification of emerging issues, assistance in developing committee foresight hearings, considerable member and staff consultation, and a variety of activities in support of CCF. A major client over a two-year period was the House Committee on Energy and Commerce. CRS assisted the Committee with several major hearings, an intense foresight workshop, and the preparation of five Committee prints totalling more than 1,400 pages.[26] A new director of CRS, following the one who authorized establishment of FRG, made several administrative changes. The individual FRG staff members were transferred from the Group to the several CRS research and support divisions. Futures work was to be "coordinated" through an interdivisional committee, with all congressional requests for futures studies, issues analysis, information, and so on flowing up and down the normal CRS divisional and management hierarchies. I served as chairman of the committee as the senior specialist in Futures Research, an individual researcher reporting to the director, and, although resident with one division (Science Policy), was not organizationally a part of management or of any division. The division chiefs naturally used the newly acquired ex-FRG analysts on the highest priority divisional assignments, which often were not futures work. Interdivisional negotiations and paperwork for services on specific futures projects drained time from substantive research. The sequential and multiple review processes by the discipline-oriented divisions stretched delivery time, raised hackles, and, at least in the minds of the futures analysts, reduced quality.

In 1981 I left CRS for teaching and research at George Washington University. In 1982 the leader of FRG, Dennis Little, also left CRS for a higher position in an executive agency. The former futures analysts specifically recruited and trained by the FRG expanded their activities within their respective divisions, and other analysts within the divisions were also given futures assignments. The good news was that within CRS, a futures-oriented assignment was no longer treated differently from any other, and the full resources of CRS could be applied. The bad news, from a futurist's viewpoint, was that special skills and close interdisciplinary teamwork of the initial effort were no longer possible. Only the congressional clients and CRS management can determine which way, or in what balance, the diffuse vs. team approach to futures research works best in that particular setting.

Meanwhile, two other foresight-oriented activities in associations were unable to get off the ground, while another blossomed with unusual speed. I had been elected to the National Academy of Public Administration (NAPA) in 1974. At almost every annual spring meeting I would raise the topic of the needs and opportunities for applying foresight, both in public administration practice and to the affairs of NAPA. It came to be known as Hahn's biannual "rain dance." But it never rained. In 1982 NAPA rather reluctantly permitted organization of a few matrix "working groups" across its mainstream, standing-committee structure. One was Foresight. Not much happened in any of these peripheral work groups until a new NAPA president was chosen in 1983. Then the Foresight Working Group was given a spot in a plenary session of the NAPA annual meeting. It was the last session on a Friday afternoon. The handful of determined members in attendance could muster no enthusiasm for an action agenda. This first substantive foresight activity probably was also NAPA's last. The energies to trigger and sustain interest in foresight among these most senior and honored public administrators were beyond what a few foresight evangelists could sustain.

The other sputtered foresight initiative was in the American Society for Public Administration (ASPA). The 1982 ASPA president created a Commission on the Future of ASPA. My task was to prepare a draft paper for the Commission, "Public Administration: A Futures Perspective."[27] Only one of the other forty-one members of the Commission commented on the draft, and the ASPA staff published my *draft*, complete with typos and blanks, as part of the Commission's final report. One line of its lengthy report said, "The Society shall emphasize foresight, and orient public administrators to changes coming in the next decade and beyond."[28] In July 1984 a subsequent ASPA president, admittedly "from Missouri" concerning foresight, generously provided me access to the ASPA Council in my efforts to implement action in ASPA along the lines of the quote above. No action resulted. As in NAPA, the personal energies required to initiate foresight exceeded the supply, and there was no real demand. Despite good intentions, need and practice with respect to foresight in our two leading public administration associations remain far apart.

The blossoming foresight-related association activity was mainly private-sector oriented. On December 4, 1981, Howard Chase (of Howard Chase Enterprises) and Raymond Ewing (Allstate Insurance Co.) met with ten others in New York City's Harvard Club to found the Issues Management Association (IMA). An initial IMA meeting in March 1982 at the Library of Congress was attended by three times the thirty foresight and issues managers expected. This was the first formal linking of the federal government foresight movement and the business-based issues management movement that had been emerging in parallel for at least seven years. As this is being written, IMA has grown to more than 500 members, has held eight major meetings, is the hub of a network of regional networks, has developed an issues management "tutorial" for beginners, has an executive director, publishes a newsletter, and is discussing a journal and electronic communications.

In the main, IMA is an active network of predominantly U.S. and Canadian industrial issues managers, government foresight practitioners, and suppliers, analysts, synthesizers, etc. of environmental awareness information and processes. After the euphoria of its founding, IMA is now maturing. Its ambitions exceed its resources; some strains are developing: neophytes vs. practitioners, U.S. vs. Canadian, East Coast vs. West, industry vs. government, umbrella vs. elitists. But the differences are still within the expected limits for any new association finding itself and its niche. IMA, of course, faces the same dilemma as ORSA, TIMS, WFS, ISTA, IAIA and many other associations: is issues management a discipline/profession, an interdisciplinary activity of many professionals, or something else? Howard Chase argues in his 1984 book that "an issue/policy management science and profession is in the process of being born. It contains within itself origins of the future."[29] As a founder and now chairman of IMA, I stated in the November 1984 IMA *Newsletter* that "I see foresight and issues management as a professional activity of both managers and functional specialists, but not as a discipline or profession per se."[30] Déjà vu?

To summarize one more time, what had I learned by 1985?

Lesson #13	Futures is good politics but may be bad for some politicians and most bureaucrats.
Lesson #14	Doomsday scenarios, erroneous forecasts, and outrageous statements attract the media and conference-goers. In organizational settings the hierarchical urge to "kill" the bad-news messenger and isolate the deviants continues.
Lesson #15	The initiation, pursuit, and success of futures activities seem to be unusually dependent on the presence, personality, and persistence of specific individuals.
Lesson #16	Futures, foresight, and issues management are not disciplines or professions per se, but they can be and are pursued in a professional manner by members of many professions.
Lesson #17	Futures-oriented associations are shaped as much by the needs of financial survival and commonplace internal power struggles as they are by theories, methodologies, information, technologies,

	and societal needs; (internal) politics vitalize associa[...] casionally destroy them.
Lesson #18	Voluntary-sector associations are an inevitable, sy[...] essential factor in establishing and conducting fut[...] activities in government, industry, the voluntary sector, and, especially, academia.
Lesson #3 (1985)	Good labels are essential:

Good labels	*Bad labels*
Foresight	Technology assessment
Issues management	Club of Rome
Global 2000 (in 1980)	Global 2000 (in 1985)
Megatrends	Doomsday

(Note: Is the more general point of Lesson #3 extended that fashions in labels change with locus and time?)

EPILOGUE AND ON TO 1995

For more than two decades I have enjoyed the opportunity to be a participant-observer of futures-oriented activities in the back rooms of politics and in the boardrooms of associations. Like most simple questions, the one posed by the editors of this volume—What have you learned?—turned out to be difficult to answer. It took considerable research and reflection to extract the foregoing eighteen "lessons learned." They are an eclectic lot. In the cold light of hindsight some appear obvious, others trivial, and many will probably be challenged by those who have learned different lessons. A few may be useful to others in their future futures endeavors.

Two general "lessons" come out of this total experience:

Lesson #19	Reductionists resist perceiving or accepting the emerging holistic/qualitative paradigm, in part because they view any change as an *or* (i.e., replacement) rather than as an *and* (i.e., synthesis) situation. Additional resistance comes from their inability to see the emerging new paradigm while trapped inside the existing old one.
Lesson #20	Futures and foresight are rewarding activities, but sometimes they are frustrating and lonely. Pessimism, cultism, and showmanship can be occupational hazards. No one can predict the future, but all of us can discover signals in our environments that (1) give us clues to likely alternative futures and (2) can suggest which of the futures that we want to create for ourselves are probable or possible.

Reviewing these twenty lessons confirms my proposition that futures is an essential aspect of politics (public and private) and that the parallel (internal) politics of futures are equally essential for change and improvement in futures practice. It also strengthens my belief that it is in the mutual and self interests of parties in business, government, academia, and the voluntary sector freely to share foresight and futures information before it becomes proprietary, politicized, or used in position taking.

I have learned some things about myself from this exercise. I now see myself as a pragmatic, social optimist (but not a utopian) futurist. I really believe that all of us, as global citizens, will find ways to survive and live with one another and nature on our fragile spaceship Earth. This will not be easy or trouble-free, and some individuals and groups will suffer great hardships. Wise social management of technology is required and possible. My combined experiences in marketing and as a bureaucrat have left me with a fascination for labels, which I manufacture liberally for new situations: 2ICTA, SYMRO, FIRST, 5YSTO, NAVWESS, F&IM.... Also, once I find someone else's good word, I hang on to it: synthesis, forum, network, voluntary sector.... My research for this paper revealed a phrase of McLuhan origin which, by my constant repetition, must now be a personal futures trademark: "Look out of the windshield instead of the rear-view mirror." Although once a card-carrying reductionist (physicist, operations-researcher), I have resisted all attempts to label or shape any of the family of futures-oriented developments as either a discipline or a profession per se. But I have pushed hard for their performance in a professional manner in ever-changing interdisciplinary formats.

The term futurist has been on my business card for a number of years, so I am often asked the question, "What is a futurist? What is unique?" When the questions are serious—which mostly they are in recent years— my answer is a *futurist* is one whose work or avocation includes *all* of the following five characteristics:

1. a future time orientation;

2. a varying set of eclectic concepts, methods, techniques, sources, styles ... ;

3. a holistic/systemic view, usually emphasizing synthesis over analysis;

4. often the product is the process, and presents conditional alternatives rather than an "answer or solution"; and

5. is (in part) an acknowledged art form involving subjectivity, creativity, insight, innovativeness, and the ability to communicate in multiple media and formats.

To suggest that I have learned twenty lessons in twenty years is simultaneously imprudent and indicative of the novelty, complexity, and difficulty of systematically considering the future as essential in matters of governance, entrepreneurship, research and education, voluntary-sector activities, and personal living. Over this period I also have faced twenty squared, or maybe twenty cubed, unanswered questions. A few samples, focusing on both futures in politics and futures associations, are:

- How do individuals and groups establish and, especially, reestablish trust?
- How can we encourage and reward risk-takers and view their "mistakes" positively as learning experiences for us all? Why can't we all learn to learn?
- How can each of us become more globally, culturally, and linguistically literate, tolerant, and integrative?
- Can networking be promoted, enhanced, perhaps even "managed," without destroying the essence of this promising voluntary process for conducting human affairs?
- Is the familiar product-user model applicable to the futurist-client relationship? Teachers can't "learn" their students, nor can psychoanalysts cure their patients. Learning and mental wellness are achieved by very personal efforts, whatever the external assistance. Is the futurist's role similar in serving as an alerter, options poser, catalyst, socratic synthesizer ... ?
- Is there a paradox about futures information that suggests that some individuals in power would rather be surprised by the future events themselves than by information *about* what is possible or likely to occur? Acknowledging that I have observed only limited cases, is there any significance to the impression that this behavior appears stronger among public executives than in legislative or business executive settings?
- How can futures-oriented associations operate without money? Or, more realistically, why don't foundations, corporations, rich individuals, etc. invest in futures-oriented associations? After all, the future is the only thing we can do anything about.

Answers to these and many other questions are what I hope to have learned by 1995. Good futurists and foresight practitioners avoid singular, flat predictions with hard dates, but I will venture one: my reading of this essay in 1995 will be a sobering experience. In the 1950s I was employed to paint "a clear but erroneous picture of the future." Now, in the 1980s, I am attempting to help others paint fuzzy but useful pictures of alternative futures. In the 1990s I hope to restore the word clear, remove "erroneous," and retain the plural in "futures." Futures and foresight not only signal the emerging paradigm; they are part of it. I am glad I got into all this—futures is fun!

NOTES

1. Walter A. Hahn, "Applied Management Sciences Research in a Decentralized Industrial Firm," *Management Sciences Models and Techniques*, London: Pergamon Press, 1960, 2: 394.

2. Walter A. Hahn, "Applied Business Research," *IRE Transactions on Engineering Management*, March 1962, EM. 9:1:5.

3. Ibid., p. 7.

4. Walter A. Hahn, *National Aviation Weather Systems Study* "(NAVWESS)," Federal Aviation Agency and U.S. Weather Bureau, June 1963–April 1964, p. ii.

5. Walter A. Hahn and H. D. Pickering, "Program Planning in a Science-Based Service Organization," *Research Program Effectiveness*, ed. M. C. Yovits, D. M. Gilford, R. H. Wilcox, E. Staveley, and H. D. Lerner, New York: Gordon and Breach, 1966, p. 72.

6. *Technology: Processes of Assessment and Choice*, National Academy of Sciences, Washington, D.C., July 1969.

7. Committee on Public Engineering Policy, *A Study of Technology Assessment*, National Academy of Engineering, Washington, D.C., July 1969.

8. Congressional Research Service, *Technical Information for Congress*, Report for the House Committee on Science and Astronautics, April 25, 1969, pp. 91–137.

9. National Goals Research Staff, *Toward Balanced Growth: Quantity with Quality*, Report of the National Goals Research Staff, The White House, July 4, 1970, p. 221.

10. Ibid., p. 24.

11. Martin V. Jones, *A Technology Assessment Methodology: Project Summary*, The MITRE Corp., Washington, D.C., June 1971.

12. Ibid., p. v.

13. *Technology Assessment for the Congress*, Staff Study for the Senate Committee on Rules and Administration (92–2), November 1, 1972, p. 4.

14. *A Technology Assessment System for the Executive Branch*, National Academy of Public Administration, Washington, D.C., July 1970.

15. Donald Cunningham and Walter A. Hahn, "The International Society for Technology Assessment," *Technical Assessment*, London: Gordon and Breach, Science Publishers Ltd., 1972, 4:1:6.

16. Walter A. Hahn, "Presidential Address to the First International Congress on Technology Assessment," *Technology Assessment*, London: Gordon and Breach, Science Publishers Ltd., 1973, 2:1:7.

17. Ibid., pp. 7–8.

18. Ibid., p. 8.

19. *Committee Organization in the House*, Panel Discussions before the Select Committee on Committees (92–1), June and July 1973, 2:3:786, 791.

20. *Committee Reform Amendments of 1974: Explanation of H. Res. 988 as Adopted by the House of Representatives*, Staff Report of the Select Committee on Committees (92–2), October 8, 1974.

21. Walter A. Hahn, "A Status Report: International Society for Technology Assessment," *Technology Assessment*, Gordon and Breach, Science Publishers Ltd., August 1973, p. 13.

22. John M. Richardson, ed., *Making It Happen: A Positive Guide to the Future*, Washington, D.C.: U.S. Association of the Club of Rome, 1982.

23. Joint Economic Committee (96–2), *Research and Innovation: Developing a Dynamic Nation*, Special Study on Economic Change, December 29, 1980.

24. *National Science and Technology Policy, Organization, and Priorities Act of 1976*, PL 94–282, May 11, 1976.

25. *Reports Elimination Act of 1982*, PL 97–804.

26. House Committee on Energy and Commerce (97–1), *The Strategic Future:*

Anticipating Tomorrow's Crises, August 1981, Print 97-U; House Committee on Energy and Commerce (97–2), *Congressional Foresight: History, Recent Experience, and Implementation Strategies*, December 1982, Print 97-MM; House Committee on Energy and Commerce (97–2), *Public Issue Early Warning Systems: Legislative and Institutional Alternatives*, October 1982, Print #97–00; and House Committee on Energy and Commerce (98–1), *Foresight in the Private Sector: How Can Government Use It?* Report of the Foresight Task Force, January 1983, Print #98-B.

27. American Society for Public Administration, *Final Report of the Commission on the Future*, April 1983, p. 11.

28. Ibid.

29. W. Howard Chase, *Issue Management: Origins of the Future*, Stamford, Conn.: Issue Action Publications, 1984.

30. Issues Management Association, *The Issues Management Newsletter*, Washington, D.C.: November 1984.

TWENTY YEARS
IN THE FUTURE

For the past six years of a twenty-year career as a working futurist, my primary activity has been the business of my eponymous firm J. F. Coates, Inc. The firm earns its way by selling intellectual services of a specialized sort. We study the future under contract or grant for corporations, public-interest associations, and government agencies. Ancillary tasks connected with the study of the future, such as seminars, workshops, courses, and lectures, are part of our services. This paper presents observations about the study of the future, its practice and practitioners. But before getting into that, some personal history may be of interest because it reveals factors shaping my work style.

As a child of a working-class family, at about the age of ten, I noticed that most household controversies ("so, whatsa tomato?") or disagreements could be settled by checking with the right written source. Two years later, having discovered the public library and having read an encyclopedia, it became clear that one could know everything—you just had to read from wall to wall—an endless joyful enterprise. My first real encounter with near omniscience was the late Professor Henry Finch, Department of Philosophy, Pennsylvania State University. He confirmed my own aspirations in this regard and provided me with the special opportunity to teach a course I had never taken. One lesson: formal training is not always crucial to effective performance and may even deter the breaking of new ground or fresh approaches.

Finch also introduced me to nonrelativistic pragmatism, which is a most solid philosophical base for the study of the future. It is grounded in the history of philosophy and can accommodate a variety of methods for developing knowledge. At the same time it is strongly committed to human progress. My earlier undergraduate training in chemistry, with the associated engineering background, provided a solid basis for appreciating the rational structure of the world and the powerful role of numbers, quantitation, and models in understanding first the physical world and then everything else.

I was particularly fortunate to be an undergraduate at Brooklyn Polytech, a first-class school teeming with returning GIs. They set a pace that, in retrospect, I realize was uncommonly brisk and adult. As a young student, that was just the way things were. The undergraduate thesis demonstrated early in my formal education that one might discover new things that fit a larger human enterprise.

After a decade of work in the laboratory as a bench chemist and researcher, an opportunity came my way to spend a year in Washington at a military think tank, the Institute for Defense Analyses (IDA). It came about because a former boss thought that my catholicity of interests would fit in nicely with a new program of military research and development (R&D) on counterinsurgency. The one-year invitation stretched to almost a decade. Work at IDA presented the exhilarating experience of working every day in an environment where I was average or less than average in ability.

Our military R&D planning was multidisciplinary and strongly futures-oriented, simply because the cycle of development in military application is such that nothing done today is ever likely to reach practical fruition in much less than a decade. So, we were constantly looking 10, 15, and 20 years ahead to anticipate future situations requiring new logistics, new materials, new approaches, and new plans.

Perhaps the one person at that institution who taught me most about how to think was John Kincaid, a man brilliant enough to have taught Plato himself. The work style at IDA brought with it a number of worthwhile lessons. It emphasized the value of different experiences in dealing with a complex situation. It instilled a profound regard for the knowledge and experience that others bring to a situation, and it highlighted the inestimable and perhaps unsurpassed value of the 200-hour conversation.

As a team process, it realistically illustrated what John Brooks later described so well in *The Mythical Man Month* as the essence of effective team research. IDA also developed critical review processes that showed that one can dissect, critique, find strengths and weaknesses in an intellectual product and, at the same time, move forward without bruising egos and demolishing personalities. This experience is one significantly rare in corporate and governmental situations, and almost universally absent in the academic environment, where critique tends to be interpreted as assault, disagreement as attack, and face-to-face open exchange as one-upmanship. Team research does go on at universities, usually in a highly structured and authoritarian mode, in terms of a big physics project, or in the well-elaborated research program of a premier biologist. There is little teamwork, however, among intellectual peers, since the reward system works so aggressively against cooperation. On the other hand, the university no longer has a near monopoly on knowledge-generation. Alternative institutions are coming effectively to compete in many areas, which, of course, will challenge and may slowly modify faculty behavior.

Then came the opportunity to join the National Science Foundation (NSF), in a program then aborning that came to be known as Research Applied to National Needs (RANN). I was deeply impressed with the good auspices of that employment, since I joined the Foundation sight unseen. The job offer was made on the basis of a barroom conversation with a then young physicist bureaucrat, Joel Snow, who, as a mark of his own accomplishments and perspicacity, later received the Fleming Award.

The NSF offered an unbeatable mix of ingredients for the applied intellectual: money to disperse in the public service, the latitude to shape a program of some significance, and the opportunity for what is now vogueishly called "intrapreneurship." Of course, the great secret of government is that it is the last great redoubt of the free enterprise system. With good luck, great encouragement, and scores of willing associates, both within and without the Foundation, I helped to shape several programs that were futures-oriented. One was a program in applied telecommunications policy and another was in technology assessment, the early anticipation of the impacts of technology on society.

With that experience as a base, I was invited to join the congressional Office of Technology Assessment (OTA) as assistant to the director. I later assumed responsibility for exploratory research at OTA. My position was internal advisor, consultant, and critic. In the transition from one director to another, in an organization not then fully immunized against the pathogens of politics, scores were settled and I was out. My choice was to either find another job or attempt to fulfill my decades-long ambition of establishing a micro-miniature think tank. I chose the latter, simply out of fear that further delay might drain the battery on this aspiration.

The experience at NSF and at OTA, first in the role of sponsor and later directly assisting others in doing futures-oriented work, reveals several structural characteristics of American personality and of American institutions. These amount to lessons, insofar as they must be taken into account in attempting to apply any futures paradigm to organizational change. First is the profound effect of fear of change, both personal and imputed to those around us. Fear acts as a powerful brake on the willingness to entertain views of a future substantially different from the present or to promote actions that are at significant odds with current practice. The second lesson is that few ventures succeed, a large number fail, and most are in an indeterminant "mush." The benefits of the mush, put most charitably, include education—we always learn *something*—and the hope that the next effort will build on the first and be more successful.

Any futurist who expects more than a ten percent success rate in promoting visible change in any enterprise he or she is associated with is almost surely jejune or out of his or her mind. By custom, leaders crave the imaginative, the innovative, the bold. But when actually confronted with it, they blanch, squirm, and backtrack—although usually not as far as the starting point.

As a sideline activity along the way, I took an active interest in the World Future Society and hosted a radio interview program on the future. I have also taught courses on the future and on the impacts of technology at both George Washington and American universities. As an adjunct professor teaching graduate courses in the science policy program at George Washington University, it has become pathetically clear how intellectually crippling today's conventional undergraduate education is. Instead of liberating minds, it shackles them to the course mentality, to the right-answer approach, and to an ingrained sense of limited personal mastery, if not frank incompetence. Few graduate students seem to preserve any sense of elan, of intellectual curiosity, or awareness that they can do, think, and understand anything. In the graduate school, where I team-teach with Vary T. Coates, we find that our primary objective is to break the students out of the crust of conventionality and open up to them the tools, techniques, and the mental orientation to effectively think about the future. Our students range from callow youths to jaded bureaucrats, and each brings special knowledge that, in an eclectic course, adds excitement and challenge for everyone.

My various roles as analyst, sponsor, bureaucrat, advisor, teacher, and purveyor of intellectual services concerning the future converge in several themes. I turn now to these lessons learned over the past twenty years.

The following observations are presented more or less randomly, since there is no reason to offer them otherwise. They are high points of observation rather then a systematic, closely knit analysis of the field.

1. Most people in their ordinary activities look to the future as interesting, exciting, amusing, or engaging. On the other hand, for persons in senior level positions in an organization, the future can be intimidating. Such persons may either refuse or be unable to believe that the future can differ significantly from the present. The reason for this is understandable. People in positions of authority got there not by playing out the future, but by building on hard-won lessons of their more youthful past. Thus they perceive any promise of substantial change as an intrinsic, major, calculated threat to their position and their authority. In winning an organization over to the future, one must deal directly with this ego threat and assuage fears by demonstrating—early and often—that the future need not be a disaster for them personally or for the organization. There are usually positive and beneficial alternative actions opened by even the most foreboding of emerging futures.

2. All futurists are optimistic. For some, the journalistic and more explicitly ideological, that optimism is often overlaid by threats and alarms

of imminent dire outcomes, should one fail to heed their call, a call more often moral rather than practical. In the work we do, the effective future is five to fifty years. Intrinsic to the study of the future is the sense and celebration of human competence and capability: when we are informed, we can manage our affairs better, and more safely enrich our lives, than when we are not.

3. The study of the future is an art form, which may draw on the sciences and other organized knowledge. Like the other creative and performing arts, a futures study is the best effort of the craftsman artist, but it must withstand the only test we have—the critic and the user.

4. The study of the future is neither necessarily hard nor easy. The mass market futurist too often trivializes the study of the future or has a facile, partial, doctrinaire, or narrow outlook. The academics, in their own self-serving ways, too often conjure up difficulties that one seldom encounters as a practical matter. Most theoretical problems and academic obstacles never appear. But then scholarship is not one of the "helping" professions.

5. Exploring assumptions is the key to the game. A most important goal in applied futures is to involve people who will be acting to shape the future. Helping them to make explicit their assumptions about the future is near magic in its effect. An explicit assumption almost invariably invites its own questioning. Once one begins to question assumptions, one opens the door to creating alternative futures.

6. In addition to the basic concept of alternative futures, three other widely shared fundamental concepts inform the study of the future.

- We can identify trends and foresee their implications to an extent that is useful for planning.
- We can intervene to a degree significant enough to encourage welcome trends and discourage those less desirable.
- We have a moral obligation to use this capability to anticipate and to intervene.

7. The study of the future is neither value-free nor ideology-free. The choice of techniques for studying the future carries with it implicit beliefs about the role of knowledge in shaping action. Bureaucrats delight in the Delphi technique because it ostensibly depends on expert knowledge, gives quantitative results, and can broadly explore an area. The ideological assumption that those are key factors in bringing about bureaucratic change misses the need for subtlety, for exploration, for exchange of ideas, and the exploratory elements intrinsic to building alternative images of the future. The Delphi carries with it the intrinsic belief that information speaks for itself and that "expert" is a plenary category.

The ideological elements of futurism are most clearly seen in those futurists who argue a central single-factor-driven future: the risks of war, the risks of nuclear power, the new salvation of solar energy, or the impending disasters from uncontrolled population growth. In almost every one of these cases the ideology is a form of secular religion, in which a single action, straightening out of our moral spine, will save the future. Ideology is unavoidable, insofar as it reflects what each of us implicitly or explicitly must have—a world view. Success cannot lie in purging ideology, but rather in attempting to make it explicit. Those who sponsor futures studies, or who use them, should aggressively probe to understand the ideological perspectives underlying a particular work or a particular futurist's approach.

8. Ideology frightens people, so clients and others are best dealt with by clearly describing the intellectual substructure of the methods and techniques and the underlying beliefs in the major schools of contemporary futurism. To put this in consumer terms, futures research calls for more truth in packaging. Or, to use an older slogan, *caveat emptor*. It is difficult for clients to recognize that they buy ideology whenever they engage a futurist. The modeler, for example, usually has as a substrate belief, a scientific approach to problems that assumes one can find relatively fixed relationships that can be conveniently put in the form of a mathematical model, and thereby manipulated to improve understanding, be augmented by better data collection, and used as a mechanism for developing solutions. This is almost a bridge-builder's engineering strategy. This is part of a larger perspective, which would make the study of the future a science, or a discipline. One could argue the merits of that case in detail. The point here is understanding that there is an argument. In my arts model of the study of the future, one can accommodate a concept of schools, of techniques that are teachable, and of the notion that some of us are more adept than others in the pursuit of the art. The arts model, however, ultimately leaves open the prospect that techniques will be superceded, interests, needs, and fashions change, and that there is no fixed, correct, or best way to deal with any futures problem.

9. The field is new enough that, to a large extent, futurists act as independent entities, with little or no attention to the intellectual networks and connections that link them. Ungrateful children that we are, we ignore our intellectual antecedents. Few scenario-builders acknowledge their indebtedness to the late Herman Kahn. Even fewer acknowledge the central position of Daniel Bell, with his concept of the postindustrial society. In my own intellectual development as a futurist, Bell and Kahn hold paramount positions. Yet one does not have to adopt the entire package. Kahn's methodological contributions, the incredible scope of his knowledge of the human enterprise, and his ability to integrate as well as to analyze can be divorced from his addiction to economic conservatism, his too lavish celebration of the market system, and his gun-shy conservatism regarding the personal, individually profound changes implicit in the unfolding future.

10. The key organizational problem that corporations face in coming to grips with their external environment is their inability to comfortably em-

brace the potential for radical change in the face of overwhelming desire to preserve continuity with the past. Also, the acute endemic parochialism of middle- and senior-level executives in most large corporations undercuts their ability to work for positive and necessary change. Parochialism cuts them off from understanding the larger flow of events and the value of insights into the future. Unfortunately for most organizational officials, whether in or out of government, the future is something that will happen *to* them and with which they must cope. It is not generally seen as a still protean situation in which they can become primary actors, creating new shapes, forms, and outcomes.

11. Most people are not cut out to be futurists. Intellectual capabilities have little to do with the qualifications. Many otherwise fine minds lack the strong sense of playfulness and the ability to tolerate an enormous amount of uncertainty that are the primary requirements for futures thinking. So much of our intellectual community is trained to a define-and-document-the-truth mentality, that the contingencies, speculations, and open-endedness of the future drives them away. Ironically, historians have a particularly difficult time thinking about the future.

12. Interest in the future has never been more widespread among public and private organizations, nor more eagerly sought after. In terms of the corporation, the traditional and limited kind of futures work reflected in strategic planning has been severely rocked by what has come to be known as the corporation's external environment; examples include changing social values and foreign competition. The most solid elements of corporate planning, market forecasting, and technological forecasting have now become unmoored. Understanding a corporation's future in terms of the totality of external factors influencing it is high on every chief executive officer's agenda. The ups and downs of corporate, government, and other organizational interests in the future preclude any assurance of continuing prosperity for the study of the future. But at a different level, the field must inevitably prosper. As the awareness of the future, as a subject for human intervention, understanding, management, and control, becomes a more conventional part of our thinking, examination of the future as an explicit and conscious subject must expand. Put differently, what I take to be our genetic proclivity—to seek knowledge and understanding and to control our environment—assures a long-term viability to the study of the future. Only the details are unsure.

13. A second development in organizational strategic planning is an unfortunate foreshortening; a movement from a 20- to a 10-, a 5-, and, in many organizations, a 3-year, long-range or strategic-planning framework. On the other hand, under the pressures of competition and the threats of corporate or business collapse, a countermovement to reinterpret and extend the depth of the long-range future has now begun.

14. Perhaps the most positive futures movement in the corporation is the

opening up of the area known by the jargon term issues management. It is the attempt to anticipate those issues that, when mature, will have a strong effect on the corporation in two to five years. The objective is to gain enough lead time and maneuvering room to frame a more positive response to emerging trouble. This is a sharp turnabout—a highly positive response after twenty years of corporate denial and resistance to challenges from public interest groups and government. Successfully engaging these short-term future issues will almost certainly open the way to embrace the longer-term future issues.

15. Under the rubric "irony of ironies," long-range planning in government has never had a more auspicious environment than under the Reagan administration. While deploring with fear and trembling any prospects of central planning, the current administration waggles its finger at the bureaucracy and asks, "Why don't you behave like the big boys?" (these being the real people out there doing corporate planning). As a result, nearly every agency of the federal government, from the oldest and stodgiest, like the Bureau of Mines, to those with ever-new functions, such as the Internal Revenue Service, is aggressively adapting corporate models of planning to better understand their own future prospects and options.

My personal measure of the maturing role of futurism is that the day has happily passed when people, on learning that I am a futurist, automatically come back with a trite jocularity such as "Where do you buy your crystal ball?" The questions now are "What can you do to help me?" and "How much will it cost?" My answers of course are "Quite a lot" and "Very little."

LESSONS LEARNED FROM FUTURES RESEARCH

Sometimes I am a little hesitant about identifying myself as a futurist, having in the back of my mind the thought that women allegedly able to foretell the future were burned at the stake at Salem and elsewhere. However, I suppose I would need to be much more dramatically successful at it than I am to be labeled a witch; so far, my broomstick has shown little propensity to soar.

My job title, of course, has never been "futurist," and I am sure that the same is true for most futurists. I have usually been categorized as a "policy analyst," and I see futurism as a dimension of that activity, a dimension that I have more and more come to regard as essential.

My interest in futures research emerged at the intersection between technology impact assessment and policy analysis. It has also been an extension of my intense interest in history—especially the history of governance and constitutionalism. Rather than formulate "lessons learned" from being a futurist, as I was asked to do, it comes more naturally to me to recall the many lessons that come from this multiple perspective. There is still another perspective that I was asked to address. When I agreed to write this piece, the editors suggested that I comment especially on the lessons learned from futures research from the perspective of a woman futurist. But I have no idea whether—or rather how much—of my perspective toward the future, or toward the practice of being a futurist, is related to being a woman. Each of us, after all, has a unique perspective derived from all the complex factors and experiences that make up our identity. On the other hand, I must warn that futurists as mothers and fathers run some special occupational risks. For example, one teenaged offspring sidled up to me with the question, "You remember what you said in that talk last week about how sexual mores are changing? Well, how much did you really mean that?"

More seriously, perhaps combining the perspectives of history and futures research helps one as a woman or as a feminist to understand, without despair, the way society has dealt with women through history. One sees it in terms of the long-range trend from savagery to eventual civilization, still to be fully achieved. If this perspective makes it difficult to see history as a gigantic male chauvinist conspiracy, it also keeps one from wasting moral indignation on the past and directs it instead toward more constructive attempts to shape the immediate and long-term future.

A Good Technology Assessor Must Be a Good Futurist

My professional work began in 1969 with technology assessment—that is, the attempt to anticipate and analyze the way in which technological change will bring about social change, and therefore give rise to problems and opportunities that have implications for policymakers. The underlying assumption in "TA"—one that I find inescapable—is that social behavior, institutions, and, ultimately, law and policy change to adjust to and make use of new technological capabilities. These social changes do not occur without some stress and disruptions; some groups gain and others lose by the changes.

Thus technology assessment is, by definition, applied futures research. Yet those involved in the early development of technology assessment often seemed to shy away from explicitly acknowledging this fact. For example, the first major assessment in which I participated was an assessment of STOL (short takeoff and landing) airports in downtown business districts, in about 1970. For nearly a year the government assessment team concentrated on forecasting technological development, the cost of land, and the demand for services, blithely ignoring all questions about what might happen in the next decade to the physical, social, economic, and political dynamics of city life—ignoring the environmental movement and demands for citizen participation in decision making taking shape all around them. Technology assessors came rather painfully to the recognition that during the years in which a technology is being developed, other aspects of society do not stand still, and that economic conditions, political forces, values, and institutions continually evolve. Without some foresight about what social institutions, social behavior, law and policy will be changed over time, one cannot foresee how they might respond to new technological capabilities. Consequently, a good technology assessor must be a futurist.

Futurists Should Avoid the Temptation to Moralize

This orientation perhaps explains a problem I have with the work of some futurists: they appear to treat value change as an independent variable—as a force that somehow independently changes (or perversely refuses to change) over time, thereby causing (or failing to cause) behavior to change. Most such futurists give no satisfactory explanation for the dominance of particular sets of values or for why and when these change. They also have an unfortunate tendency to latch onto some presumably more desirable set of futures values and become preachy, if not dogmatic, ideologues.

I have often observed what I believe is an occuptional hazard for futurists: the temptation to moralize. Some who began as "scientific forecasters" broadened their perspective to become social forecasters, and then, discerning that some possible futures were more desirable than others, became strong advocates for those futures. From one perspective this is as it should be—one can argue that there is little value in developing a capability for conceptualizing alternative futures unless that insight can help society to make effective choices in moving toward a better future. Unfortunately, some of these futurists, in crossing the boundaries between describing what *may* be or what *can* be to what *should* be, fail to make explicit where those boundaries were crossed, and even forget that they have crossed them. We need, I am sure, both futures analysts and dreamers; but I want to know which is which.

I am myself increasingly sure that value change is a dependent variable: the way by which the social organism—the society or the culture—responds to a changed environment. That changed environment is, very often, the result of technological change. While not a thoroughgoing technological determinist, I see the tools that people use to cope with their environment as fundamental and primary factors in the way they behave, the way they interpret their physical and social world, the values they express, and the way they formulate for themselves their individual roles in everyday life, perhaps even their personal identity. To me, therefore, understanding changes in our growing technological capabilities is a central concern in understanding the future, as well as in understanding the present (i.e., policy analysis) and in understanding the past (i.e., history).

The Necessity for Real Interdisciplinarity

There are other strong overlaps between the perspectives of technology assessment, policy analysis, and futures research: the necessity for real interdisciplinarity, the willingness to acknowledge uncertainty and conflicting evidence and still derive useful conclusions, and the need to balance and reconcile competing values and interests. In all three fields, one quickly learns that disciplinary purity, dogmatic expertise, and righteous refusal to compromise are all self-defeating.

I have, over the past sixteen years, moved from involvement in the early experimental, methodological development of technology assessment (at the George Washington University's Program of Policy Studies) to work as a consultant and contractor in direct decision-oriented or policy-oriented assessments, first at the university, later in a federal mission agency, an engineering firm, a futures research business (J. F. Coates, Inc.), and, most recently, in the U.S. Congress' Office of Technology Assessment.

The Value of Combining Political Science and History

It is at this point that I see the value of a combined political science and history background in my present work. If political science is the study of politics as "the art of the possible," history is the study of the effects of improbable events that nevertheless occurred. Political science deals with the space available for short-range maneuvers or tactics to influence the future. In this space, established trends and driving forces are very strong and very limited. The practice of futures thinking accustoms one to identifying such trends and forces and their possible limitations. But the study of history reveals over and over again both the disruptive power of exogenous or random events and the capability that individuals and organized groups have to modify, thwart, or disrupt long-established trends when they are determined to do so.

Freedom Can Sometimes Lead to Irrelevance

In a university there is a valuable freedom to think broadly, but that freedom can sometimes lead to irrelevance. Working directly for a client in business is a lesson in practicality; one is always confronted with the question "so what?"—what implications do alternative future conditions hold for present actions? Which trends can be changed, and which must be recognized and accommodated? In an engineering firm one must work with people whose natural tendency is to ride roughshod over obstacles, scoff at timidity, and solve problems with daring and technical ingenuity. In a government bureaucracy one learns to listen closely to the doubters, the warning signals, and the diverse interests, to hoard one's political capital and expend it selectively. As one works more and more directly for decision-makers, the balance of concern tends to shift from *possible* futures, although these must inevitably provide the context, toward "the most probable future"—more exactly, to those sets of nested probabilities that represent possible paths from here to there. There are obvious traps. Herman Kahn's observation that the most unlikely future is the surprise-free future should be every practical futurists' golden rule.

Bite the Bullet: Suggest Actions

I more and more realize, however, that scenarios of alternative long-range futures are in themselves of little use to desicion-makers whose ability to act is limited, almost always, to specific interventions that must be justified in terms of short-range results. Moreover, the decision-maker, whether bureaucrat or elected official is always assailed by multiple issues, many contending interests, and many demands for his attention and his indignation. The role of the policy analyst as practical futurist calls for interpretation and judgment. What do alternative long-range future outcomes imply for present actions? When is the time ripe for action, and when would present actions foreclose or distort future opportunities, or expose the political decision-maker to unnecessary pressures and attacks that could limit his or her future effectiveness?

The Dangers of Rigorous Quantification

Another lesson I have learned is the danger posed by attempting to make forecasting, as a subgenre of futures research, "scientific" or rigorously quantitative. Quantitative projection of trends is seldom useful to decision-makers without the context and interpretation provided by qualitative analysis. Worse, it is almost always misleading. Psychologically, it is perceived to have a degree of certainty and precision that the forecaster neither intends nor accepts himself. It focuses attention on those factors and forces that can be quantified—often the least critical. Decision-makers' own, usually excellent, sense of human behavior often leads them either consciously or intuitively to discount such forecasts, thereby weakening the credibility of all futurists.

Econometric models have been the worst offenders in this regard, followed closely by technology forecasts. Attitude surveys and polls present another problem, that of repeatedly ignoring the fact that conclusions are nearly predetermined by which questions are asked (and not asked) and the way they are phrased. Almost inevitably, as social scientists persist in struggling to be more "scientific," we will be seeing "sociometric models" purporting to forecast social trends on the basis of social statistics. These are likely to be the most misleading of all.

To be a futurist is inevitably to be confronted with the realization that we are still learning how to ask questions about the future and are a long way from having easy answers. And yet I also know that questioning the future and formulating out of the murky uncertainties and beckoning opportunities some tentative answers is both a great deal of fun and a highly useful enterprise.

THE GODS OF THE COPYBOOK HEADINGS: A CAUTION TO FORECASTERS

The problems of forecasting are captured neatly in an item that appeared in the "24 Years Ago" column of my local paper, the *Sidney Daily News*, for December 27, 1983:

DES MOINES—Within the next 30 years, average annual auto production will total 15 million units; cars will have television sets; auto accidents on the nation's highways will be eliminated by means of electronic controls, and American's cars will be equally at home in the air or on the ground.

These predictions are to be sealed in a time capsule in the new $2 million *Look* magazine building in Des Moines. The time capsule will be opened in January 1987 when *Look* magazine will be 50 years old.

These forecasts seem laughable today. True, we do have portable television sets that will run off the electrical system of a car. Not many cars have them, however, and they certainly shouldn't be used by the driver. On everything else, the "forecast" missed badly. And to top it off, *Look* magazine is no longer around to celebrate the fiftieth anniversary of its founding. For all I know, even the *Look* magazine building may have fallen victim to urban renewal.

In my writings and in my classes I advise people to study the failed forecasts of others in order to learn from their mistakes. Learning from the mistakes of others is a painless way of gaining experience. Unfortunately, too much emphasis on learning from the mistakes of others can lead one to overlook the value of learning from one's own mistakes. And for that matter, from one's own successes. Therefore, in addressing "what I have

This essay appeared originally in the *World Future Society Bulletin* (Nov.-Dec. 1984). Copyright 1984 by the World Future Society. Reprinted, with changes, by permission of the publisher.

learned" I will focus mostly on mistakes I have made, with a few unexpected lessons from my successes thrown in.

THE COPYBOOK HEADINGS

Back in the days when schools still taught penmanship, there was an institution known as the "copybook." At the top of each page was a sentence or phrase in elegant script. The student was supposed to practice penmanship by copying this "heading" on the lines provided, down the length of the page. The "copybook headings" were not mere random sentences, but were selected to provide moral uplift as well: "All that glitters is not gold"; "The wages of sin is death"; and so on.

In 1919 Rudyard Kipling published a poem entitled "The Gods of the Copybook Headings." The gist of the poem was that these trite copybook sayings remain true through the ages. Even though from time to time people come to believe that they can dispense with the wisdom of those sayings, they eventually pay the price for disregarding that wisdom. Kipling's warning was that, every time we forget them, "The Gods of the Copybook Headings with terror and slaughter return."

In a nutshell, that's what I have learned. The lessons were not something new. They were a reminder that the rules had not changed, much as I might have thought they had. The rules applied to me, not just to my students. So while I continue to try to profit from the mistakes of others, the main point of this essay is to help others profit from my mistakes. I am going to give some examples of my successes and failures and try to provide lessons from them.

WHERE IS THE HELICOPTER?

In 1970 I prepared a forecast of helicopter performance and published the forecast in an Air Force report. I later included the same forecast in the first edition of my textbook (Martino, 1972:326). The issue I addressed was the development of vertical takeoff and landing (VTOL) aircraft. If these aircraft were to be competitive with conventional aircraft, I argued, they would require comparable costs per ton-mile of cargo carried and would require comparable productivity (ton-miles per hour) per unit cost. As proxy measures for the cost of a ton-mile and cost of a ton-mile per hour, I used gross takeoff weight and weight empty, respectively. It is generally accepted in the aircraft industry that both capital and operating costs of an aircraft are closely correlated with the weight of the airframe. I examined the historical trends in both helicopters and fixed-wing aircraft through the end of the 1960s. I projected that by the end of the 1970s, the cost per ton-mile for VTOL aircraft would be competitive with that of fixed-wing aircraft (in the same weight class, that is), while the productivity would still be somewhat lower than that of the new fixed-wing aircraft I expected would be introduced during the 1970s. All the historical data I used were for U.S.-built aircraft, and my forecast was the basis for a recommendation that the U.S. armed forces should plan to incorporate VTOL aircraft starting about 1980.

How did things turn out? A heavy-lift helicopter actually was introduced in 1978, which falls just above the productivity trend I projected in 1970, well within the expected error. From the standpoint of projecting helicopter performance, the forecast was a success. However, it contained enough significant errors to make it worthless.

The most significant error dealt with costs. I had expected helicopter costs to come down to a level competitive with fixed-wing aircraft. However, the Mi–26's cost per ton-mile is considerably above that of fixed-wing aircraft. It is even above the cost of helicopters introduced in the 1960s, and is comparable to the cost of U.S. helicopters introduced in the mid–1950s.

IMPORTANT LESSONS

What are the lessons of this forecast-gone-wrong? The most important news are lessons that I already teach my students, but that I disregarded in making the forecast. First, I frequently emphasize the importance of looking at technological developments on a worldwide basis. The United States is not the sole source of technological development. In the case of helicopters, it is particularly important to look at developments outside the United States. The first self-propelled model lifting airscrew was built and demonstrated in Russia in 1754. Several Russians attempted to build practical helicopters over the next 125 years. In particular, in 1871, D. K. Chernov developed the theory of wings and propellers, recognizing that they would produce lift or thrust by deflecting the airstream in accordance with Newton's Third Law of Motion. In 1909 N. Ye. Zhukovsky published his theoretical research on the forces acting on a helicopter rotor. In that same year Igor Sikorsky, not yet twenty, began construction of his first (unsuccessful) helicopter at his home in Kiev. Several other inventors tried to build helicopters over the next two decades but were unsuccessful.

Boris N. Yuriev, one of Zhukovsky's students, was in 1925 put in charge of helicopter research at the Central Aero- and Hydrodynamic Institute. He emphasized both theory and practice and put Russian helicopter development on a sound foundation. Through the 1930s and 1940s various Russians built a series of autogiros and helicopters, which flew after a fashion. The event that provided them with real inspiration, however, was the 1938 demonstration flight of the German Fa–61 helicopter, *inside* Berlin's Deutschlandhalle before an audience of Nazis.

Several Russian helicopter projects were started during World War II, but they did not bear fruit until after the war was over. Since the end of the war, however, Russian helicopter development has been determined and steady. The Mi–26 was not a "freak," or a copy based on "stolen technology." It was the next logical step in a progression of designs that can be traced back to the 1920s. It is worth noting that the pioneer helicopter designer in the United States, who was largely responsible for founding the U.S. helicopter industry, was Igor Sikorsky, who emigrated to the United States after the Russian Revolution.[1]

The point of this description is that all this information on the Russian helicopter history and development was available in 1970. Had I taken the trouble to dig it out, I might have recognized that Russian helicopter development has an even longer history than does U.S. development, and that the original work in the United States was in fact carried out by a Russian émigré. Thus any projections I made regarding helicopters should have taken the Russians into account.

Then there is the question of costs. In my forecast I took it for granted that no one would want a VTOL aircraft unless its ton-mile costs were competitive with those of fixed-wing aircraft. While my basic assumption was valid, my definition of "costs" was too narrow. I looked only at the aircraft itself, not at the infrastructure. A fixed-wing aircraft requires a runway; but a helicopter can operate from any firm, dry launching pad. The relative costs of the two must therefore include the costs of the "airfields" from which they operate.

In the United States, which already has a well-developed system of highways and airfields, the marginal costs, which are the only costs relevant to a decision, are essentially the capital and operating costs of the aircraft. In the Soviet Union, with a primitive system of highways and airfields, the choice between use of fixed-wing aircraft or helicopters must take into account the cost of building runways for the fixed-wing aircraft and, moreover, of first building the highways by which construction equipment can reach the proposed runway sites. Thus the high operating and capital costs of the Mi–26 are not a deterrent to its use in the Soviet Union and in other primitive areas because it is still cheaper than building the infrastructure for fixed-wing aircraft.

Finally, it is worth noting that the United States still has nothing like the Mi–26. It does have an experimental VTOL aircraft, the LTV V–530, which is competitive with fixed-wing aircraft in both cost and productivity. Its payload is one-fourth that of the Mi–26, and its gross takeoff weight is less than half that of the Mi–26. Its range is about four times that of the Mi–26, which is an important part of its competitiveness in cost.

In summary, the lessons relearned are:

1. Technology knows no national boundaries. Look to the whole world, not a single country, for advances.

2. Don't use too narrow a measure of performance. Costs of supporting

and complementary technology are important too, not just the cost of technology itself.

CHEMISTRY BY COMPUTER

One of the "hot" areas of research in chemistry during the 1960s was "chemistry by computer" (Wahl, 1970a, 1970b). The basic idea was simple. The arrangement of the atoms in a molecule is governed by the rules of quantum mechanics. Thus, in principle, it is possible to compute all the properties of a chemical compound on the basis of its composition. The chemist would never need to synthesize the compound and test it; he could compute its properties instead. Or conversely, given a desired set of properties for a compound, the chemist could search alternative formulations and find the one that most closely meets the specifications without ever touching a test tube.

Once quantum theory was developed in the 1920s and 1930s, this possibility existed. However, it was out of reach because the computations necessary were too tedious and lengthy in practice. Moreover, a great many of the empirical values needed for such computations had not yet been measured. With the devlopment of large digital computers, however, the picture seemed to have changed.

During the 1960s a great deal of effort went into writing computer programs to carry out quantum mechanical calculations, allowing "chemistry by computer." There was an encouraging degree of initial success, and by the middle of the 1960s these programs could compute the behavior of ionized helium and of two-atom molecules quite accurately. By 1970 the leading researchers in computer chemistry were optimistic about extending their success to molecules with twenty to twenty-five atoms.

I gathered a consensus forecast of some of the leading researchers and published the results in my textbook (Martino, 1972:387). The forecast stated that by the middle 1970s, the cost of quantum mechanical calculations would be competitive with the costs of actual laboratory chemistry, at least for molecules of moderate size. The forecast also stated that by 1980, most laboratory chemistry would be devoted solely to gathering the empirical data necessary to support quantum mechanical calculations. Actual chemical "design" and analysis of new compounds would be done by computer rather than in the laboratory.

The forecast missed the mark; computer chemistry was nowhere near replacing laboratory chemistry, even by 1984. Was computer chemistry a flash in the pan, then? Did it turn out to be a loser? Not at all. A perusal of any recent issue of *Chemical Abstracts* will turn up several articles describing applications of quantum mechanical calculations to interesting and practical problems. However, chemistry by computer is still only a small part of the whole of chemistry. It has a long way to go before it drives chemists out of the laboratory and to the computer terminal.

When I put my forecast together I was in no position to pass judgment on the technical issues involved. However, this is not unusual. I know little about the details of most technologies that I forecast. In most cases I try to learn only enough about them to find out who are the right people to ask questions of, and what questions I should ask them. Nevertheless, in retrospect, it is clear that I should have been suspicious of the optimistic forecasts I was hearing—not because the people who were giving them to me were technically incompetent in computer chemistry but because they were making judgments about issues distinct from computer chemistry, issues in which they had no particular expertise.

The first issue has to do with the rapidity of diffusion of an innovation. Recent studies have found that a new type of instrument takes five years or more to be adopted by half the experimenters in a particular field (Sanford, 1983). Even back in 1970, when diffusion studies were far less prevalent than they are now, it was already known that scientific fields are not transformed overnight by a new instrument or technique. Hence the problem was not with the idea of chemistry by computer, but with the forecasts of historically unprecedented speed in shifting the way an entire field of science conducted its activities.

A second issue deals with the costs of computer chemistry vs. laboratory chemistry. In 1970 we had already seen a two-decade history of dramatic drops in the cost of computation. Thus it was easy to believe that further drops in the cost of computers would dramatically reduce the cost of doing chemistry by computer. What should have been apparent, however, was that the cost of laboratory chemistry would also decline.

Microprocessor-controlled instruments, to cite just one example, allow laboratory chemists to automate their data collection and analysis. Thus one chemist can do a great deal more chemistry per day with today's instruments than he could have done a decade or two ago. I am not saying that anyone should have specifically forecasted the development of microprocessor-controlled instruments. On the contrary, I advise forecasters that it is not their responsibility to invent what they forecast. But in this case I should have looked at trends in the productivity of chemists and in the costs of doing laboratory chemistry, instead of accepting the implicit assumption that the cost of laboratory chemistry would remain fixed while technology was reducing the cost of a competitive means of performing chemistry. At the very least, the firms that had a stake in laboratory chemistry, such as instrument manufacturers, would have been stimulated to improve their products in order to protect their markets.

Thus there are at least two lessons in this experience, lessons that are not at all new, but that I had to relearn.

1. When you question an expert, make sure the questions you ask fall

in his or her area of expertise. In particular, don't ask an expert in the mechanics of some technology how rapidly that technology is likely to diffuse. Answering the second question requires a completely different kind of expertise.

2. When a competitive techology arrives on the scene, don't assume that the old technology will roll over and play dead. It may well continue to improve at a rate at least as rapid as it showed before the competitor arrived. Indeed, the presence of a competitor may stimulate it to even more rapid advances.

COMMUNICATIONS SATELLITES

In 1978 Ralph Lenz and I prepared a forecast for the National Aeronautics and Space Administration (NASA) that projected widespread use of communications satellites by the year 2000. Specifically we predicted a level of use equivalent to 22,000 TV channels. To give some idea of how much communications capacity that is, if every man, woman, and child in the United States spent four hours a day at a teletype, it would just fill up that many channels. Our forecast was not well received by many in the telecommunications industry. There were three main objections:

1. Satellites in synchronous orbit had to be spaced four degrees apart to avoid mutual interference. Therefore, there was a limit to how many could be operated. At the time we made our forecast, industry spokesmen were already voicing great concern about "crowding of the orbital arc."

2. Frequency allocations for satellite use were made by international agreement. Limits on the number of satellites the United States might operate (because of the spacing problem) and on the number of frequency bands available (by international agreement) would not permit the level of use we had forecasted.

3. In any case, what would anyone ever do to fill up that many channels? Clearly the whole population of the country was not going to spend a fourth of its waking hours at a keyboard.

In making our forecast we were not looking at technological capability per se, but at level of use as well. This is quite common in technological forecasting, since forecasters are often required to estimate the rate at which some new technology will replace an older one, or the rate at which some new technology will occupy an empty market niche. Therefore, we based our projections on the rate at which the level of satellite use was growing and looked for bottlenecks that might hamper growth. We found no bottlenecks in areas such as potential launch rates, lifetime of satellites, or power levels and sizes of satellites themselves. Thus, we stuck to our forecasts despite the objections of many in the industry.

It is still too early yet to tell how our forecasts will look in the year 2000.

Nevertheless, we have made some effort to see how they are tracking reality so far. In terms of numbers of satellites in operation, our forecasts track reality fairly well. Satellite size is increasing just about as we forecasted, although the specific steps in size that we forecasted are not appearing. Moreover, the price of satellite channels is holding up well, and buyers are eager to obtain them at the current market prices. This indicates that there is an economic demand for additional satellite channels.

What about the objections, then? How is satellite use overcoming the problems that were cited as invalidating our forecast at the time it was made? The first problem, satellite spacing, has already gone away. In 1983 the Federal Communications Commission (FCC) reduced the allowable spacing to two degrees, thus at a stroke doubling the capacity of the orbital arc available to the United States. The reduction in allowable spacing came from a combination of two developments: higher satellite power and better ground antennas. Because improvements in these areas are expected to continue, there is already talk of reducing the allowable spacing to one degree. Thus the limit on numbers of satellites from orbital spacing requirements has turned out to be much less stringent than originally expected.

The problem of international frequency allocation has also proved to be more tractable than originally expected. Other countries do not really care what the United States does *inside its own borders*, so long as our use of the spectrum does not interfere with their use of the spectrum inside their borders. At the 1983 international conference that made frequency allocations for satellite use in North and South America, the other nations involved allowed the United States just about all we had asked for. Certain portions of the spectrum that had previously been allocated for other uses were reallocated for satellite broadcast use in the United States. In anticipation of this result, the FCC had already advised people using those bands that they would have to vacate them by 1985 to make them available for satellite broadcasting. The lesson here is that particular uses of frequency bands are the result of human decisions and are not determined by laws of nature. If people make frequency allocations, they can also change them.

Moreover, there are several technologies waiting in the wings that can conserve bandwidth even further. One of these, cross-polarization, was already in limited use in the 1970s. Cross-polarization allows two satellites to use the same channel in the same geographical area by polarizing the signals at right angles to each other. This can double the available channel capacity if needed. Other technologies, known generally as "bandwidth compression," offer the possibility of squeezing the same signal into a narrower channel (for instance, by not retransmitting the part of a TV picture that has not changed since the last frame). These technologies have not yet been adopted because they are not yet needed. But they will be available to expand channel capacity if that is required.

The issue of what will we do with all those channels is also turning out to be far easier to answer than expected. In the early 1970s Comsat Corporation, which operates all U.S. international satellite communications, decided to get into the direct broadcast satellite (or DBS) business, that is, direct broadcast of programs from satellite to household. Comsat had a number of bureaucratic obstacles to overcome, but by the end of the 1970s the FCC invited applications for "construction permits" for satellites in the DBS service. More than a dozen applicants came forward asking for permits. In 1982 the FCC granted permits to eight of the applicants, including Comsat's DBS subsidiary, Satellite Television Corporation (STC). STC had originally proposed to begin service in 1985. However, in early 1983 the FCC granted additional permits to the rest of the applicants. Some of these later applicants proposed to use existing satellites instead of building their own, and thereby to begin service in 1984. STC immediately met the competitive threat by advancing its own plans so as to begin operation in 1984 as well. By April 1984 two competing DBS operators were already providing programming to the Midwest, and other DBS operators were providing programming in New York, New England, and eastern Pennsylvania. If all the applicants actually provide service, they will require more channel capacity than is currently allocated to DBS. At this point it would be risky to forecast that the channel capacity will not be made available. Historical precedent indicates that if the service appears commercially viable, channels will be preempted from other uses and allocated for DBS.

DBS will of course not fill up all the channels we forecast would be used. Even if all the present applicants for DBS permits are granted channels, they would not require that much channel space. Nevertheless, with sixteen years to go on our forecast, there is time for additional services to come into existence, just as DBS grew from nothing to a major user of channels in less than ten years.

What lessons can be drawn from this success story? Again, the lessons are well known, and I teach them to my students.

1. Make certain that any suggested limits to progress are genuine technical limits, not administrative, political, or economic limits. Limits based on human decisions can be overcome if people want to overcome them. This is what happened in the case of limited channel allocations.

2. Make certain that any suggested technical limits are fundamental limits, set by laws of nature, and not merely limits set by a particular technical approach. If they are the latter, normal technological progress is likely to bypass them. This is what happened in the case of the satellite spacing limitation.

3. Do not give too much weight to the objection "What will we do with all that capability?" In a sense, this is a mirror image of the "limits to growth" argument. Obviously, these two positions cannot both be correct. If there are external limits to growth, then humans will use all the capability that becomes available. If they do not use all the existing capabilities, then

growth is self-limiting and externally imposed limits to growth are irrelevant. Historically, neither objection has been well founded. Generally, humans have used all the capability they could get and then devised ways to get more.

4. Do not be too specific about events, particularly when specificity is not important. Whether the next step in satellite design is an increase in weight of precisely 2,000 kilograms is not nearly as relevant, from the standpoint of the designer or the user, as the fact that increases in weight will occur, and that satellite weights will have passed certain levels by particular times. That is, if the main point is continued growth in some variable, a forecast of specific values is not really of much help to the forecast user.

THE RETURN OF THE GODS

The "lessons" I have cited here may seem trite and unexciting—but that is precisely my point. Every forecaster is supposed to have learned them early in his or her career. The problem, just as Kipling described, is that these words of wisdom from the Gods of the Copybook Headings sound so dull and dreary that there is a temptation to desert them for the Gods of the Marketplace, who promise results without effort or discipline.

Thus the specific lessons described above are not really my central theme. They merely illustrate my central theme—the rules of good practice in forecasting still apply, no matter how trite they sound. Although following them does not guarantee that a forecast will be correct, failure to follow them always leads to trouble sooner or later, and usually sooner.

This is "What I have learned," which I should never have forgotten. If others can benefit from these mistakes, they will not represent a total loss.

REFERENCES

Everett-Heath, John. *Soviet Helicopters*. London: Jane's, 1983.

Martino, Joseph P. *Technological Forecasting for Decision Making*. New York: Elsevier-North Holland, 1972.

Sanford, Thomas W. L. "Trends in Experimental High-Energy Physics." *Technological Forecasting and Social Change* 23 (1983): 25–40.

Wahl, A. C. "Chemistry by Computer." *Industrial Research*, February 1970, pp. 46–49.

Wahl, A. C. "Chemistry by Computer." *Scientific American* 222 (April 1970): 54–70.

Harold A. Linstone   **14**

WHAT I HAVE LEARNED:
THE NEED FOR MULTIPLE
PERSPECTIVES

LOOKING BACK: RECOGNIZING THE LIMITATIONS

My career in California's aerospace industry began in 1947. During my years in the Theoretical Aerodynamics Group under Dr. Allen Puckett at Hughes Aircraft Company, I completed my doctorate in mathematics at the University of Southern California. At that point I was asked to start an Operations Analysis Group, and this activity, in turn, led to my first corporate planning task: a forecasting study in 1959. My team created the acronym MIRAGE 70, for Military Requirements Analysis—Generation 1970. Unclassified excerpts from the 1960 report were published in Linstone (1962). The results of this privately funded study were of such interest to the potential customer that I was invited to brief the secretary of the army, the director of the Bureau of the Budget, and the head of the State Department Policy Planning Staff. The top management at Hughes requested a briefing only after learning of the active interest exhibited in Washington. I suspect that one reason for the government reaction was the fact that the study was independently done, that is, with private funding. We see here a confirmation of the biblical adage "A prophet is not without honor except in his own house."

The horizon of MIRAGE 70 was 1970 and the focus encompassed the 1965–1970 period. Both total war and limited war were considered. A total war was defined as one involving a nuclear attack on the United States. Four American objectives were examined in the total war area:

This essay appeared originally in the *Futures Research Quarterly* (Spring 1985). Copyright 1985 by the World Future Society. Reprinted, with changes, by permission of the publisher.

a) deterrence of an attack on this country;

b) defense of the continental United States if deterrence fails;

c) "winning the war" if deterrence fails;

d) deterrence of undesirable actions beyond the United States (for example, deterrence of a Soviet attack on Western Europe by threat, possibly escalating to attack on the United States).

The conclusion reached in the study was that (a), deterrence of an attack on the United States, is

a realistic goal but by no means automatically attainable. It is especially sensitive to Soviet technological innovations, less sensitive to Soviet offensive-force size! Soviet achievements in offensive systems (e.g., very accurate ICBMs) force U.S. shifts in procurement with little increase in spending, whereas Soviet defensive achievements (e.g., effective ballistic missile defense) may require major U.S. budget increases. It is most important for the United States to maintain flexibility in its deterrent weapon systems. Duplication of existing systems, large build-ups of a single system, and insistence on quantitative parity do not seem warranted; anticipatory R&D of new deterrent weapon concepts is vital (Linstone, 1962:130).

The other three objectives were found to require not merely a retaliatory force, but a ballistic missile defense capability increasing in effectiveness from (b) to (d). Because the difficulty of a truly effective defense was found to be extreme, (d) was judged "hopeless." Today, a quarter of a century later, these conclusions are still considered valid by "rational" analysts but challenged as academic by those who see even (a), equivalent to mutual assured destruction (aptly labeled MAD), as irrational.

The sensitivity of the limited-war portion of the U.S. military budget to Communist activity in 1965–1970 was clearly recognized. A trend away from formal limited wars to unconventional conflicts was also stressed. Direct participation with specialized forces designed primarily for small conflicts in areas such as Laos and Cambodia was considered "most likely" if deterrent steps (alliances, shows of force) failed (Linstone, 1962:116–117). A major rethinking of the limited-war force structure was envisioned. This (1959–1960) study found that "a listing [of good R&D risks] derived on this basis differs somewhat from the selection of items prepared by more usual means, although considerable overlap is evident" (Linstone, 1962:133). There is an important point here to which we shall return.

In 1963 I joined Lockheed Aircraft Corporation as associate director of corporate planning—systems analysis. After the success of MIRAGE 70 I directed three more national security "needs analyses" there (MIRAGE 75, 80, and 85).

One important rule we invoked was to do each study differently. As noted in the introduction to MIRAGE 85 (Linstone et al., 1970:1):

1. A meaningful ten- to fifteen-year technological forecasting study does not lose its value as a basis for R&D planning in four years. A new study should extend the horizon and focus on significant changes.

2. Iteration of the same type of analysis with the same group of people tends to settle into a self-justifying or routine pattern—a deadly threat to successful forecasting.

The final study looked from 1970, the horizon of the first study, toward a 1985 horizon. The study pointed to three *misconceptions* that were driving the defense-planning process:

1. *The United States today has an effective across-the-board capability, varying from total war to informal or guerrilla conflicts.*
   Clearly, the rethinking of the approach to unconventional conflicts urged in 1959–1960 had not gone far by 1970.

2. *The U.S. military establishment is flexible in strategic or long-range planning. The process thus achieves consistency between the changing conflict environment and the development of needs.*
   Actually, the size and age of the defense establishment militate against responsiveness. Changing environments are seldom translated into innovations in mission and operational concept needs. The basic motto is still "more of the same," but with higher performance and more sophistication.

3. *Technology can provide the answer to all problems in the next ten years.*
   This unbounded faith is reflected in consistently overoptimistic weapon effectiveness and cost estimates. Peck and Scherer (1962) analyzed 12 programs and calculated an average cost overrun factor of 3.2 and a development overrun factor of 1.36. Another study examined 13 major missile and aircraft programs involving sophisticated electronics and found that only 4 were performing electronically at more than 75% of their specifications (*Washington Post*, January 26, 1969, A–1; Linstone et al., 1970:101–103). It was also noted that lessons from the past were often ignored.

Example 1. Deep interdiction not directly in support of a battle (e.g., strategic bombing), is not very effective. The futility of strategic bombing of German and British industry in World War II is well documented—from the Air Force's Strategic Bombing Survey at the end of the war to Albert Speer's writing in Spandau Prison. Unless annihilation is brought about, deep aerial bombing attacks serve primarily to stiffen and unify the enemy's resistance. The lesson was relearned in Korea and again in Vietnam. Before the interdiction raids began in 1965, there were no North Vietnamese military formations identified in South Vietnam and the Viet Cong were equipped with captured weapons. When the raids stopped in 1968, the Viet Cong had been reequipped with Communist bloc weapons of current production and five or six North Vietnamese divisions were maneuvering in

South Vietnam with several thousand men supplied within fifty miles of Saigon (Broughton, 1969).

Example 2. The Maginot Line was conceived as a barrier to run along the entire eastern border of France to the English Channel. The French parliament refused to fund the originally planned line. The Germans, being mobile, bypassed the Maginot Line rather than penetrating it. In Vietnam the hastily conceived "McNamara Line" also failed to extend along the entire land boundary of South Vietnam—and was also unsuccessful (Linstone et al., 1970:114).

The most significant implication drawn in MIRAGE 85 is that

we buy what we like and believe we can build rather than what we need. The typical American prefers to buy a new car every 3 years, each time with more luxury options and horsepower, and modest style changes. He can drive it at speeds he will never be able to use and its size is far in excess of his space needs. He adds STP to his engine although it has no recognizable value. He thus spends far more than he needs to in both original investment and maintenance. But he is a satisfied customer and even urban congestion and smog do not normally divert him to public transportation when it is available.

The same applies to the military, and this is most significant for our study. The evolving conflict environment as well as current weaknesses suggest major qualitative and quantitative changes in U.S. military forces. *These often involve tactics, training, organization, test and evaluation, and motivation—thus casting new technology in a secondary role. But there is little expectation that such changes will, in fact, take place. The gap between what is needed and what is marketable means that a "needs analysis" is, in fact, a mirage* [Linstone et al. 1970:115–116; emphasis in original].

Over the decade covered by the four MIRAGE studies we had learned valuable lessons; we had been stripped of our innocence, our assumption of objective analysis as a determinant of national security needs. The systems analysis approach or technical perspective on defense planning was simply inadequate.

This experience was the beginning of the realization that other perspectives were vital if the gap between analysis and action was to be bridged.

There were, of course, other clues. Elting Morison (1966) provides an interesting illustration of a technological innovation in the U.S. Navy a century earlier.[1]

The *USS Wampanoag* was a 4,200-ton "advanced technology" destroyer built for the Navy and commissioned in 1868. She had sails and a steam engine, was fast (over 17 knots), and the sea trials proved her to be a magnificent technical achievement—ahead of ships in any navy at that time.

In 1869 all naval steamships were scrutinized by a board of naval officers. The mood of the board is documented. The steam vessel, said the board, was not a school of seamanship for officers or men:

Lounging through the watches of a steamer, or acting as firemen and coal heavers, will not produce in a seaman that combination of boldness, strength, and skill which characterized the American sailor of an elder day; and the habitual exercise by an officer of a command, the execution of which is not under his own eye, is a poor substitute for the school of observation, promptness and command found only on the deck of a sailing vessel [Morison, 1966:114].

The board examined the *Wampanoag* and developed a bill of particulars leading to the conclusion that the ship was "a sad and signal failure" and could not be made acceptable. They were in a state of peace and opposed building ironclads needed in war to avoid giving unnecesssary alarm. There was a large supply of timber in the navy yards "which the interests of economy demand should be utilized." They noted the familiarity of the workmen with wooden-ship building and their dependence on it for a livelihood.

The ship was laid up for a year and soon sold by the Navy. Morison ponders this strange turn of events:

Now it must be obvious that the members of this Naval Board were stupid. They had, on its technical merits, a bad case, and they made it worse by the way they tried to argue it.... [But after a time] I began to be aware of a growing sense of dis-ease.... Could it be that these stupid officers were right? I recalled the sagacious judgment of Sherlock Holmes. The great detective, you will remember, withheld the facts in the incident of the lighthouse and the trained cormorant because, as he said, it was a case for which the world was not yet fully prepared. Was this also the case with the *Wampanoag*?

What these officers were saying was that the *Wampanoag* was a destructive energy in their society. Setting the extraordinary force of her engines against the weight of their way of life, they had a sudden insight into the nature of machinery. They perceived that a machine, any machine, if left to itself, tends to establish its own conditions, to create its own environment and draw men into it. Since a machine, any machine, is designed to do only a part of what a whole man can do, it tends to wear down those parts of a man that are not included in the design....

I don't happen to admire their solution, but I respect their awareness that they had a problem.... [It] is not primarily engineering or scientific in character. It's simply human [116–122].

In these passages Morison shifts perspectives. A decision that appeared "stupid" when viewed from one perspective suddenly became reasonable when seen from the other. Thus a new technological system was held back for reasons that would be exceedingly difficult to uncover with a conventional analyst's perspective. His technical/rational worldview has proved dazzlingly successful in dealing with the well-structured problems of science and technology. Its paradigms include the following characteristics:

a) The definition of "problems" abstracted from the world around us and the implicit assumption that problems can be solved

b) Optimization, or the search for a best solution

c) Reductionism, that is, study of a system in terms of a limited number of elements (or variables) and the interactions among them

d) Reliance on data and models, and combinations thereof, as modes of inquiry

e) Quantification of information

f) Objectivity, the assumption that the scientist is an unbiased observer outside of the system he or she is studying, that truth is observer-invariant

g) Ignoring or avoiding the individual, a consequence of reductionism and quantification (for example, use of averages) as well as objectivity

h) A view of time movement as linear, i.e., at a universally accepted pace reckoned by precise physical measurement with no consideration of differential time perceptions, planning horizons, and discount rates

The Club of Rome's *The Limits to Growth* study and its offspring constitute an almost perfect example of the abstraction, reductionism, data and model orientation, and linear movement of time. Forrester (1971:18) insists that "all systems that change through time can be represented by using only levels and rates. The two kinds of variables are necessary but at the same time sufficient for representing any system."

Berlinski (1976:83, 85) sees this unconditional statement as the prevailing pedagogical maxim: "Pile up an imposingly complex system of equations and then subject them to an analysis of ineffable innocence.... Power and scope are often inversely related.... In *World Dynamics* and *The Limits to Growth* ... the scope is unbounded but the insights are slight."

Forrester and Meadows carried their model runs out to 2100; a German team inbued with Teutonic thoroughness, examined time spans of 1,000 and 10,000 years (Hugger and Maier, 1973)!

Systems analysis is now described as the application of "the logical quantitative and structural tools of modern science and technology" to complex sociotechnical problems (Quade and Miser, 1984). To Herbert Simon (Miser, 1980:146) it is a "celebration of human rationality ... the challenge is to enlarge this celebration to include the rational management of all society's systems and their problems." The disappointments and criticisms of futures research are rooted, in large measure, in this captivating illusion.

LOOKING FORWARD: OVERCOMING THE LIMITATIONS

Two books, by Allison (1971) and Churchman (1971), both published soon after completion of MIRAGE 85, provided the signposts that showed a way out of the dilemma. Allison used three models or perspectives in studying a decision process: the rational actor model, the organizational process model, and the bureaucratic politics model. Churchman brought forward the Singerian inquiring system, a pragmatic meta-inquiring system that includes application of other inquiring systems (such as data-based, model-based, dialectic, and intuitive) as needed.

Our institutions' concern in futures research and long-range planning is invariably with ill-structured sociotechnical systems. What does the multiple perspective concept (Linstone, 1984) offer? Table 1 indicates the nature of the needed perspectives: the technical/analytical (T), the organizational/societal (O), and the personal/individual (P).

It is common practice to divide technological forecasting into two complementary types: (1) exploratory or capability forecasts and (2) normative or needs forecasts (Martino, 1972:287). The former focus on what can be done in the future, based on the past and present technological capability; the latter focus on what *ought* to be done in the future. Not surprisingly, exploratory forecasts almost always have a dominant T orientation. They involve extrapolations of technology trends as well as analytical models of growth and substitution. In theory, the long planning horizon or low discount rate[2] associated with the T perspective should be of direct benefit to such forecasts. While analysts do use a low discount rate for the future, we observe that they are sometimes inclined to apply a considerably higher discount rate to the past. For example, they may pay excessive attention to short-term trends, extrapolating on the basis of recent historical data only and thus missing the more meaningful, less distorted longer-term trend, that is, the "envelope curve".

The O and P perspectives may insinuate themselves quite subtly into exploratory forecasts. The analyst's tool kit does not force his attention on assumptions and professional biases. These may be based on years of personal involvement in a narrow aspect of technology and communication with peers who think of the future in terms of the same descriptors of capability (Martino, 1972:566–571).

On the other hand, dominance of the T perspective on the part of the technological forecaster also has important consequences. It tends to drive him inexorably toward greater technological sophistication in addressing future needs. This reminds us of the third misconception noted in MIRAGE 85.

Uncertainty is treated in the T perspective by seeking analytic ways that appear to reduce it, rather than by increasing the capability of adjusting to changes that cannot be anticipated.

A priority needs list for the military based solely on a T perspective (as was done in the early MIRAGE studies) looks very different from one based on, say, T *and* O perspectives. The T perspective makes sure that the list includes unglamorous items, such as changes in training and maintenance procedures or in communications equipment. However, a list based on both T and O perspectives features the more prestigious items in the firepower

Table 1
Multiple Perspectives

	Technical (T)	Organizational (O)	Personal (P)
World View	Science-technology	Social infrastructure: Hierarchical (caste) ... Egalitarian (sect)	Individuation—the self
Ethical basis	Rationality	Justice/fairness*	Morality
Goal	Problem solving / Product (study, design, explanation)	Stability and continuity* / Process / Action and implementation	Power, influence, prestige / Status maintenance or improvement
Modes of inquiry	Abstraction and modeling / Data and analysis	Dialectic/adversary / Negotiated reality/consensual	Intuition, persona, individual reality / Experience, learning
Time concept	Technological time	Social time	Personal time
Planning horizon	Far / Often little breadth	Intermediate distance / Intermediate breadth	Short distance / Variable breadth
Discount rate	Minimal	Moderate	High (with rare exceptions)
Constraints	Problem simplification by limiting variables, relations / Cause and effect / Need for validation, replicability (or "audit trail")	Fractionating/factoring problems / Problem delegation to others or avoidance if possible / Agenda ("problem of the moment")* / Bureaucracy often pervasive / Political sensitivity and expediency* / Loyalties, credentials / Restricted access by outsiders (caste) or recruits members (sect) / Reasonableness, common advantage / Recognition of partial unpredictability / Long-range planning often ritualized / Satisficing (first acceptable, rather than best, solution)* / Incremental change, slow adaptation / Parochial priorities	Hierarchy of individual needs (security, acceptance, self-fulfillment) / Challenge and response / Each construes attributes of others / Inner world (subjectivity)
Characteristics	Objectivity emphasized / Prediction / Optimization (best solution) / Feedback loops recognized / Quantification / Use of averages, probabilities / Trade-offs / Uncertainties noted: many caveats ("on one hand . . .")	Standard operating procedures / Compromise and bargaining / Monitoring and correction / Uncertainties avoided* / Fear of error*	Need for certainty, beliefs / Creativity and vision of the few / Cope with few alternatives or variables only / Filter out images inconsistent with past experience / Game playing ("homo ludens") / Focus on simplistic hypotheses rather than scanning many / Leaders and followers, mystique / Fear of change and unknown
Communication	Technical report, briefing	Directive, conference, interview / Private language with insiders / Hortatory language with public	Narrative (story), discussion, speech / Importance of personality

* Usually applies to hierarchical structures only

Source: Linstone (1984:64–65). Copyright 1984 by Elsevier Publishing Co., Inc. Reprinted by permission.

Table 2
An O Perspective on Oil Reserve Forecasts

	When prices are high	When prices are low
Industrialists favor	High forecasts "Major new supplies can be found if prices are high."	Low forecasts "Higher prices are needed to bring on more supplies."
Consumers favor	Low forecasts "Oil is no longer the solution."	High forecasts "No need to raise prices."
Conservationists favor	Low forecasts "High prices encourage overproduction."	Low forecasts "Low prices encourage overconsumption."

Source: Wildavsky and Tenenbaum (1981:300). Reprinted by permission.

and vehicle areas—glamorous aircraft, ships, and weaponry.[3] As Representative J. P. Addabbo (D-N.Y.) recently observed, "the Pentagon doesn't like anything that's small" (*Sunday Oregonian*, April 10, 1983:A–14).

In the nonmilitary area an example of the O perspective determining "needs" is found in the electric utility industry, the largest single sector of the U.S. economy, with net assets of about 250 billion dollars. Their claim that healthy industry growth requires an increase of at least three percent annually in electrical demand implies a total capital investment of about one trillion dollars by the year 2000 (Lovins and Lovins, 1982:156). In the eyes of Wall Street, there is increasing danger that utilities are overspending themselves into insolvency. Their ingrained O perspective prevents many of them from recognizing that they should view themselves as purveyors, not of electricity, but of energy services (or the financial means of acquiring them). Such a shift could brighten their futures dramatically.

The dialectic approach often seen in the O perspective is beautifully illustrated by the history of energy resource forecasts in the United States. As Wildavsky and Tenenbaum (1981) have shown, the deep division between industrial interests and conservationists on oil and gas resources was already apparent in the early 1900s. Each side seized on the 1908 U.S. Geological Survey (USGS) estimates to confirm its policy stand.[4] Many forecasts have been made since then. Except for the World War I and II periods, each faction habitually accuses the other of manipulating these forecasts for its own selfish purposes. Table 2 suggests the different views on resource forecasts. It becomes clear that the forecasts are the servants of policies already determined or preferred rather than being prerequisites for policy formulation. The T perspective quests for more accurate forecasts in this area are thus rather irrelevant.

In cases where a forecast is done by organization A for client B and few constraints are imposed by B, the biases of A may be decisive for the forecast.

Table 3
Scenario Typology

	Probable	Preferable	Possible
Criterion	Analytical (reproducible)	Value (explicative)	Image (plausible)
Orientation	Exploratory (extrapolative)	Normative	Visionary
Mode	Structural	Participatory	Perceptual
Creator	Think-tank teams	Stakeholders	Individuals

If A is experienced in a certain forecasting technique, it is likely to prefer its use in responding to B—whether or not it is most suitable. A may also be subconsciously influenced by the possibility of future grants or contracts from B and avoid forecasts that may alarm B.

Thus the organizational perspective explains constraints and core assumptions that affect the forecasts (Ascher, 1978:199). Standard operating procedures, morale needs, as well as incrementalism and tradition determine the forecasts in important ways. And the personal perspective also merits recognition. In a thoughtful essay on "Why Forecasters Flubbed the '70s," *Time* (January 21, 1980) recognized a paradox: (1) Forecasters remain human beings and, as such, have optimistic or pessimistic biases; and (2) Forecasters are "triumphantly rationalistic" and exaggerate this aspect in human behavior. (One often wishes that forecasters would exhibit such awareness of the "self.")

Roy Amara (1980) and Uno Svedin (1980) have suggested that scenarios may be usefully classified into three types as shown in table 3. It is striking that these three types can be related to the three perspectives:

Probable (think tank teams)   T perspective
Preferable (stakeholders)   O perspective
Possible (individuals)   P perspective

It is reasonable to expect a T perspective scenario to be analytic and judged on its reproducibility. The O scenario is the product of organizational planning, hence participatory and prescriptive. The P scenario is significant only if it is imaginative or visionary, e.g., Hitler's *Thousand Year Reich*, More's *Utopia*. It contrasts with corporate planners' projections (O) and econometrics (T).

Finally, let us consider the problem of long-range planning in corporate and governmental organizations. Table 1 shows that the T, O, and P perspectives tend to have different planning horizons or discount rates. We might illustrate the interaction of these multiple perspectives by comparing them to beams of light directed at a problem. We would find that each beam has a different illuminating distance (like high and low headlights in an automobile). So we arrive at the catch: (1) Multiple perspectives are critical in developing insights on complex sociotechnological problems; and (2) The differential horizons of the three perspectives make it hard to develop an action orientation or link between analyst and decision-maker.

At this stage of their development, multiple perspectives appear promising. At the very least they bring to the surface vital core assumptions and minimize self-delusion; at the very best they stimulate ideas that can be converted to actions facilitating our journey into the future.

From a personal point of view, I have been able to shed most of the frustrations—the quixotic quest for more comprehensive mathematical models, the unending parade of pedantic methodological refinements, the apparent irrationality of real-world decision-makers and the difficulties of implementation.

Hegel suggested that "the mature individual is the individual who can hold conflicting world views together at the same time and act, and live, and that his or her life is enriched by that capability—not weakened by it" (Churchman, 1977:90). This is what I have learned and what makes me more at ease with complexity.

NOTES

1. The following discussion is excerpted from Linstone (1984).

2. It is useful to introduce the concept of discount rate here. We discount future problems or opportunities the same way an economist discounts future dollars. A long planning horizon is then equivalent to a low discount rate; a short horizon, to a high discount rate (Linstone, 1973).

3. Examples: Although close air support of ground forces is an important air mission of maneuver warfare, the Air Force prefers strategic bombing and is traditionally unenthusiastic about the subservient and unglamorous mission to assist tactical Army operations. It prefers the faster F–16 fighter to the slower A–10, even though slow speed may be vital in this task. Similarly, the glamorous new Bradley infantry fighting vehicle (nearly two million dollars each) is preferred by the Army to its 1960 M–113 armored personnel carrier (eighty thousand dollars each) despite the former's severe operational handicaps (Time, March 7, 1983:14).

4. At that time, USGS forecasted total U.S. oil resources between 10 and 24.5 billion barrels and indicated that we would run out of oil between 1935 and 1943. In 1974 USGS (Vincent McKelvey) estimated a range between 200 and 400 billion barrels.

REFERENCES

Allison, G. (1971) Essence of Decision: Explaining the Cuban Missile Crisis. Boston: Little, Brown and Co.

Amara, R. (1980) The Futures Field. Menlo Park, Calif.: Institute for the Future.

Ascher, W. (1978) Forecasting: An Appraisal for Policy-Makers and Planners. Baltimore: The Johns Hopkins University Press.

Berlinski, D. (1976) *On Systems Analysis: An Essay Concerning the Limitations of Some Mathematical Methods in the Social, Political, and Biological Sciences.* Cambridge, Mass.: MIT Press.

Broughton, J. (1969) *Third Ridge.* Philadelphia: J. B. Lippincott Co.

Churchman, C. W. (1971) *The Design of Inquiring Systems.* New York: Basic Books.

Churchman, C. W. (1977) "A Philosophy for Complexity," in H. A. Linstone and W. H. C. Simmonds, *Futures Research: New Directions.* Reading, Mass.: Addison-Wesley Publishing Co.

Forrester, J. W. (1971) *World Dynamics.* Cambridge, Mass.: Wright-Allen Press.

Hugger, W., and H. Maier. (1973) "Finding Invariant Structures in Forrester's World Dynamics—an Analysis by Simulation." *Technological Forecasting and Social Change 5,* 349–378.

Linstone, H. A. (1962) "An Approach to Long Range Planning," in J. A. Stockfisch, ed., *Planning and Forecasting in the Defense Industries.* Belmont, Calif.: Wadsworth Publishing Co.

Linstone, H. A. (1973) "On Discounting the Future." *Technological Forecasting and Social Change 4,* 335–338.

Linstone, H. A. (1984) *Multiple Perspectives for Decision Making.* New York: North-Holland.

Linstone, H. A., et al. (1970) MIRAGE 85, vol. III. Burbank, Calif.: Lockheed Aircraft Corp.

Lovins, A. B., and L. H. Lovins (1982) "Electric Utilities: Key to Capitalizing the Energy Transition." *Technological Forecasting and Social Change* 22:2, Oct. 1982, 188–200.

Martino, J. P. (1972) *Technological Forecasting for Decisionmaking.* New York: American Elsevier Publishing Co.

Miser, H. J. (1980) "Operations Research and Systems Analysis." *Science* 209 (4452), 139–146.

Morison, E. E. (1966) *Men, Machines, and Modern Times.* Cambridge, Mass.: MIT Press.

Peck, M. J., and F. M. Scherer (1962) *The Weapon Acquisition Process—An Economic Analysis.* Cambridge, Mass.: Graduate School of Business Administration, Harvard University.

Quade, E. S., and J. H. Miser (1984) *Handbook of Systems Analysis.* New York: North-Holland.

Svedin, U. (1980) "Scenarios, Technology and Development." Paper presented at the Conference on Natural Resources and Regional Development, the Semi-Arid Case, Cocoyoc, Mexico, October 8, 1980.

Wildavsky, A., and E. Tenenbaum (1981) *The Politics of Mistrust.* Beverly Hills, Calif.: Sage Publications.

PART III
Reflections on Learning

ADVENTURES IN LEARNING

> Freedom is an ideal which throughout human evolution has inspired the most sublime philosophies and creeds.
> —Bronislaw Malinowski, *Freedom and Civilization*

> All human beings are born free and equal in dignity and rights.
> —Universal Declaration of Human Rights, 1948

At birth, nobody knows about the freedom he or she is supposed to have been born with.

A little later one learns how to fight for future freedom. To eat what and when one chooses, dress as one desires, go to bed late, and keep up with peers, a child struggles for liberation from parental control. In adolescence this struggle becomes sharper.

With adulthood, views change. Adults have more power—at least over children. They learn to relish even slight control over others. They invent more sophisticated defenses against control over themselves. With minds and bodies changing, they often cling to unchanged modes of behavior and thought. In other words, they learn how to stop learning. Their future may be a replay of their past.

We, too, let us confess, have often stopped learning. Again and again we have been so enmeshed in habitual routines that any changes in knowledge, skills, or values have been minor.

Yet like many others, we have often been jolted out of routines by national calamities, social movements, personal misfortunes, and windfalls of good luck. More than most, we have experienced the shock of moving from one culture to another and passing in quick succession through entirely different ways of earning a living. As teachers, our latest roles, we have had the privilege of confronting hundreds of younger people with radically different outlooks on past, present, and future.

We used to think that our biggest spurt of learning started in 1960—for that was when we first met. Actually, we have learned a lot more since then—particularly since the 1970s. Indeed, our biggest burst of learning has been taking place since 1980. Only recently have we realized that under the rubric of freedom we might bring together the most important things we have learned since infancy and adolescence.

Long ago we lost or found so many kinds of freedom that we became confused by the semantic chaos. We saw that for some the "free market," while never an existing reality, appeared to be a sublime creed. Recently, we have become uneasy with liberals, progressives, and radicals who seem to have deserted—or have in fact opposed—the cause of more freedom in the future. The glorious but illusory "freedom now" rhetoric of an earlier civil rights movement seems to have been displaced by attachments to illusory programs, technological fixes, and foundation grants.

We are now more clear about those freedoms whose enlargement we favor as contrasted with others we think should be diminished. Yet we also feel that despite unavoidable interest conflicts, *all* people have some common interest in *all* freedoms—present and future.

In these pages we reflect on the kind of confrontations we have had in the past—and will probably face again and again—with:

- different meanings of the word "freedom,"
- male and female efforts to win freedom from illusion,
- liberation from bad labeling,
- the controls required by *any* form of freedom,
- planning as a road to freedom or serfdom, and
- freedom as the poetry of the future.

Long ago Mohandas Gandhi prefaced his life story with the words "I simply want to tell the story of my experiments with truth." In that spirit we try to tell here the truth about some of our own experiments with freedom—experiments that are continuously changing our view of the future.

"A woman's mind," wrote Oliver Herford in typical male chauvinist style, "is cleaner than a man's. She changes it more often." In that sense, the male member of this partnership is very much a woman. Together, we have been changing ideas and skills continuously.

Many Kinds of Freedom

Plainly the sheep and the wolf are not agreed on the definition of the word "liberty."
—Abraham Lincoln, 1864

"When I use a word," Humpty Dumpty said, in a rather scornful tone, "it means just what I choose it to mean—neither more nor less."

—Lewis Carroll, *Alice in Wonderland*

It takes a long time for anyone to win freedom from the tyranny of emotion-laden connotations hovering over a word like freedom.

Some win this freedom by learning the simple truths of semantics: that the meaning of a word is what it symbolizes in a person's mind, that most words have different meanings to different persons, and that any one meaning usually appears in many forms and dimensions.

But most people suffer confusion before reaching a truth. Thus it has been with our discovering that "freedom" means whatever people choose it to mean. If there are misunderstandings, the fault, dear reader, is not in the stars or the symbol, but in us and how we fail to signal our meanings.

Freedom from Illusion: The Man

We are such stuff / As dreams are made on...

—William Shakespeare, *The Tempest*

Civilization is hooped together.... by manifold illusion.

—William Butler Yeats, *Supernatural Songs*

To enjoy a play or movie, one willingly suspends disbelief. For a magical hour or so, images of struggle, love, hate, or death become reality.

In life's drama, illusions can last a lifetime. We need them. We love them. We ignore people who try to unmask them. And the same person who exults in revealing the mote in another's eye may himself refuse to consider the beam in his own eye and overlook his own failure to distinguish between appearance and reality.

Bert's first immersion in the world of illusion occurred when, as an unemployed college graduate, he came up with the idea of earning some money as a professional wrestler. The excruciating punishment that the professionals obviously endured, he reasoned, was much less than the pain of being jobless. After a long, sweaty summer of daily workouts, he developed a more imposing physique and an even more imposing (but totally mythical) experience record. He then bluffed his way into a contract for a South American tour and bluffed his relatives into thinking he was off to teach English in Argentina. On arrival in Buenos Aires, he received a pleasant shock: all the agonies endured in professional wrestling were make-believe. Pressure was simulated, never applied. The spectator's eyes saw many happenings that never happened. Punches were artfully "pulled," designed to create noise without pain. Bert had to learn bluffing on the job.

Directions from the promoter, Stanislas Zybysco, made things easier. Before every match, Zybysco stage-directed the final outcome—with attention also (as in Aristotle's theory of the drama) to beginning and middle. One wrestler, preferably both heavy and ugly, would play a Villain who breaks all the "rules." Weighing only about 210 pounds at the time, Bert was always a Hero, relying on skill alone, until, after reluctantly losing his patience, he resorted to some "dirty tricks" himself. One scene of unbelievable brutality followed another. Success in having the audience suspend disbelief required friendly cooperation between pretended adversaries. Both Villain and Hero took special care to see that his partner was never hurt. Bert will never forget the villainous Cowboy Jack Russell, who, when lifting him high in the air for a thunderous (but painless) body slam, whispered in his ear, "Gentle as a feather." Publicly, he would then provide comic relief by running away from an "enraged" Hero. In turn, the Hero would become the center of illusory tragedy by being beaten to a presumed pulp. After one such "beating" Bert remembers being carried on a stretcher to the dressing room. On such occasions the spectators would groan out loud in a gut-wrenching Bacchic orgy of pity and fear. This gave them the *catharsis* that, for Aristotle, was the essence of tragedy. It also confirmed—and helped them accept—a tragic principle in their own lives: "Good guys finish last," or "Anything goes."

Later, Bert entered the higher realms of bureaucratic and political illusion. At the U.S. Housing Authority (1938–1941) he found that a brilliant lawyer, Leon Keyserling, had devised a public housing financial plan that made a subsidy of 100 percent appear to be only 30 percent. He learned that neither Nathan Strauss, the agency's administrator, nor other top officials really understood the program they were administering. On Keyserling's recommendation he became a "ghostwriter," preparing speeches that justified the agency's well-meant but stultifying "party line."

Relief from such bureaucratic boredom came only from behind-the-scenes action. Under assumed names Bert wrote a housing article for *Harper's* magazine, a housing column for the *CIO News*, and a brochure for the Philadelphia Tenants' Association. Behind the scenes, he sketched a new-style housing program for Richard Gilbert, a top New Deal economist, who passed it on to Roosevelt's right-hand man, Harry Hopkins. These activities eventually got him into trouble. When cuts came in the USHA budget, Strauss pressured Keyserling into finding a good excuse to terminate Bert's services.

By this time emergency defense preparations were under way. For a few months Bert worked in Richard Gilbert's Research Division in the Office of Price Administration and Civilian Supply. There, he was energized by Gilbert's high-charged brain-trusting on the entire panorama of economic puzzles then confronting America. He received his first statistical shock when he uncovered defects in the way the Bureau of Labor Statistics (BLS) collected price data. A second came when Gilbert pressured him to cease and desist. Why? Not because Bert's findings were wrong, but because the BLS commissioner was indignant at being caught off base. Besides, the defective data was used in the division's macroeconomic projections. Any critique of the data would undermine the division's credibility. So Bert was switched to the less dangerous task of preparing testimony for presentation before hostile congressional committees. This task brought him in to work at the office on the first Sunday of December 1941. He remembers a loud and incredulous exclamation from Gilbert's office: "*How* did the Japanese get there?"

In the ensuing frenzy of war mobilization, without quite knowing how *he* got there, Bert was soon working for Senate committees. He helped to grill executive branch officials, investigate the war effort, and stage-manage congressional hearings. He polished senatorial egos, ghosted senators' speeches, and wrote committee reports. With help from Robert Bowie, then on the secretary of war's legal staff, he learned the mysterious arts of bill drafting. To get bills enacted into law, he built up a friendship network among reporters, lobbyists, and agency officials. He organized a staff of professionals and secretaries (assigned to him and paid by executive agencies) to work around the clock in the rough-and-tumble politics of pressure and persuasion. This experience led him to the Council of Economic Advisers, where he became an informal member of President Truman's White House staff.

There, in addition to helping to organize the Council and its statistical publications, he also worked on the president's legislative program. With the help of Arthur Bentley, he began to understand certain basic similarities between legislative and executive processes:

1. policy statements, like ideological declarations, do as much to hide—as to guide—actual behavior;
2. both branches of government are clusters of struggling interest and pressure groups, each of which are targets and allies of nongovernment interest and pressure groups;
3. to survive, one has to "keep a poker face" and never voice what one really thinks; and
4. the best way to get results is to work anonymously behind the scenes and pass the credit (along with the risk of blame) to others.

He also reflected on the similarities between illusion in professional wrestling and in public policymaking. The actors in both had to be inventive in creating images. In both, things went on behind the scenes that ordinary spectators might suspect but could seldom document.

The differences also became clear. Professional wrestlers were never fooled by the illusions they created. Not so with government. Any small success was sufficient to give an elected official (particularly a senator), cabinet member, agency head, or minor bureaucrat delusions of grandeur.

If a wrestler got hurt, it was a rare accident. In bureaucratic and legislative politics, many people always got hurt—even if only through unintended consequences. If unorganized, they might not even know what hit them.

Armed with this knowledge, Bert set out on a long voyage to dispel popular illusions hiding the realities of power. In a series of books published over many years, he tried to show how laws are *really* made, how the money system *really* operates, how managers *really* manage, how planners *really* plan, how statistics can *really* mislead, how the "great Society" was *really* a will-o'-the-wisp, and how a strong democracy, even America's, could *really* be subverted by a slow drift toward a repressive corporate state. Although some of this work had overtones of journalistic muckraking, Bert did his best to develop theories and models with general relevance.

For a while he believed that once reality had been revealed in print or lecture, other people's eyes would be opened. It didn't work out that way. In time, he opened his own eyes a little more. This led him to the conclusion that perhaps the sheer excitement of learning was justification for his efforts.

It was not until Kusum and he started writing together that Bert *really* began to question his own view of *reality*. In open dialogue with Kusum he voiced for the first time certain perceptions of reality that had long been in the "back of his mind" but were fully suppressed in both writing and speech.

He also began to free himself from the *illusion of thinking himself free from illusion.* With her help, he brought to the surface at least three half-conscious assumptions that had long shaped his conscious life. First, as an advocate of economic rights, he had long excluded from attention those economic rights already enshrined fully in law—particularly individual rights to personal property, managerial rights, and corporate rights. He had also closed his mind to the idea, usually voiced by conservatives, that the rights of labor (and the unemployed) should be held to imply certain duties or obligations.

Second, along with other former technocrats, he had long labored under the illusion that religion and nationalism would both decline in a world of greater dependence on science and technology. He slowly came to see that these tendencies themselves seemed to drive people into religious and nationalist commitments.

Third, he had long presumed that world progress toward true democracy was, in the long run, inevitable, thus failing to come to grips with the powerful antidemocratic forces in every society. Over a ten-year period he tried to dissect the tendencies toward new forms of repressive corporatism ("friendly fascism") in countries of constitutional capitalism, and particularly in the United States. It has taken until now to apply this approach to other parts of the world as well.

Freedom from Illusion: The Woman

Woman may be said to be an inferior man.

—Aristotle, *Poetics*

If a Hindoo principality is strongly, vigilantly, and economically governed; if order is preserved without oppression; if cultivation is extending, and the people prosperous; in three cases out of four that principality is under a woman's rule.

—John Stuart Mill, *On the Subjection of Women*

No woman needs Aristotle to remind her that women have long been thought inferior. The word "feminine" connotes frailty of body and softness of heart, in contrast with masculine brawn and brain. What is flexibility in a "him" is derided as "caprice" or instability in a "her."

Kusum won partial freedom from this illusion during her early years in India. As a child (like other children in her country's feudal aristocracy) she probably knew more about the Rani of Jhansi and other women rulers than did John Stuart Mill as a mature scholar. Besides, one of her role models was a distant ancestress, the Rajput poetess Mirabai of Udaipur. Against enormous pressure from her family, Mirabai left the ancestral home, sitar in hand, to spend her life singing devotional songs to Krishna. Similar devotion, with ample brains, was shown by the nuns who were her teachers at the convent of Jesus and Mary in Mhow and Queen Mary's high school in Delhi.

At home, when a child asked for some dispensation, Kusum's mother would always reply "I'll have to ask your papa." But the children soon caught on: it was Mama, not Papa, who decided. The mother had provided another example of partial liberation by writing romantic novels and becoming a radio commentator. Her widowed mother-in-law, indignant at the insensitivity of her stepson who became ruler after her husband's death, had fled the family palace at Masuda, sold her jewelry, and set up house for herself in Ajmer. Her elder sister, after living in *Purdah* (the women's quarters) from her day of marriage at age fourteen, had torn tradition aside, gone into business, and become a top executive of the Oberoi intercontinental hotel chain.

Other examples were provided by her friend, Lakshmi Menon, deputy minister of foreign affairs, and by Nehru's daughter, Indira Gandhi. Kusum herself followed in their footsteps and plunged into the man-dominated world of affairs. As a program producer at All-India Radio she found many men who needed women to lean on for both stability and ideas. She learned again "what every women knows" (as J. M. Barrie put it in his play by that name): "Every man who is high up loves to think that he has done it all himself; and the wife smiles and lets it go at that." With great glee, she joined the cast of Aristophanes' *Lysistrata* at Edinburgh. Under the direction of Joan Littlewood, she played the scene in which Myrrhina, an Athenian woman, refused to have sex with her husband "unless you men negotiate a truce and make an end of war."

But while escaping the illusion that she was congenitally inferior, Kusum often got trapped by new illusions. For quite a while she boasted about the large number of Indian women—in contrast with American women—in high-ranking government positions. Eventually, however, she came to realize that all the women she was then proud of were members of the well-to-do Indian elite and that most of them came from upper caste Brahmin or Kshatriya families. It was painful to admit to herself—and it is still painful to openly state—that the vast majority of Indian women, particularly those among the lower castes, the outcasts (harijans), and tribals, are still subjected to vicious discrimination and exploitation in family, school, business, and government.

In 1973, eleven years after getting her B.S. at Syracuse, Kusum was thrilled by certain changes she found on returning to America. During her absence the civil rights and feminist movements had left their mark. The progress made by many blacks and women was undeniable. Most of her white, male teachers either tacitly assumed or proudly boasted that racism and sexism were things of the past. When she or her daughter were treated badly, her first reaction was to ignore what was happening or think it her own fault. Then at the University of Pennsylvania and three other colleges she began to see how black or female teachers were denied respect, tenure, or promotion. As a "two-for" (both colored *and* female) she learned how it felt to be used as a showcase coverup for racist machismo. At first she thought that the fault lay with conservatives or reactionaries in the faculty and administration. The rudest awakening came when she saw liberals and radicals combine antiracist and antisexist rhetoric with the unconscious practice of both racism and sexism.

During the 1960s Kusum was entranced by the charismatic spell cast by Jawaharlal Nehru in India and John F. Kennedy in the United States. Nehru's spell was embodied in the new Indian constitution, the five-year plans, and Nehru's remarkable oratory. It was not until the mid–1970s that she consciously realized the formalistic nature of the constitutional commitment to a democratic, socialist, and secular society. In practice, the five-year plans favored a tiny minority of Indian elites who, under the banner of socialism, were building oligarchic capitalism. Secular government officials continued the British tradition of subsidizing religious sects in a way that distracted attention from exploitation and had the effect of encouraging bloody communal conflict between Hindus and Muslims.

By the same time Kennedy became in her eyes not so much a "God that failed," but rather a master illusionist. In his election campaign he had outdone Richard Nixon in cold-war hyperbole. In his inaugural address he had achieved quasimilitaristic hyperbole in his trumpeting "We shall pay any price, bear any burden, meet any hardship" in defense of an undefined freedom. Later, with the help of many masters of conceit, he created the triple image of a "Camelot," in which "the best and the brightest" would lead America toward a "New Frontier." His oratory was not as intellectual as Nehru's, but it concealed much more. The tragedy of his life was his assassination just as he was beginning to move from image-making to a politics of reality.

For many years Kusum tended to place Great Men (and Great Women) on pedestals in her mind. Like her colleagues in both countries, she saw charismatic leaders as the hope for changing the world for the better. With Bert, she lamented the passing of the superhuman heroes of a previous era: Franklin Roosevelt, Eleanor Roosevelt, Mohandas Gandhi, Martin Luther King, Jr., and even Mao, Churchill, and De Gaulle. In her doctoral dissertation she researched the life of two of those figures, Gandhi and Mao, asking the question "How did they each achieve mass communication without the support of any mass media?" To her surprise she found that during the thirty years before their movements won power, the strength of Gandhi and Mao was that each was "of the earth earthy." Each had a "common touch" that was real, not manufactured. Millions of illiterate peasants could identify with them becaue each was truly one of the people, not a messiah from heaven. Each was superordinary, not superhuman. Their followers had the feeling that in cooperation with others, they could do things for themselves rather than rely on leaders for salvation. That was the meaning of Gandhi's *swaraj*, a Sanskrit word meaning both freedom and self-reliance. Neither Gandhi nor Mao was charismatic in the sense of having some divine gift of grace that might foster their followers' dependency. It was only after Gandhi's death in 1948 that charisma was conferred on him by India's post-British establishment. It was only after the Chinese Communists came to power that Mao contributed to his own deification as a way of consolidating elite party power.

Liberation from Bad Labeling

Pin labels on cans, not on me.
—Bess Myerson, Consumer Affairs Commissioner, New York City

In every human soul there is a socialist and an individualist, an authoritarian and a fanatic for liberty, as in each there is a Catholic and a Protestant.
—Richard Tawney, *Religion and the Rise of Capitalism*, 1926

In 1789 the nobles in the French national assembly sat on the king's right, and his capitalist opponents sat on his left. A few years later, as it separated heads from almost any body, the guillotine ignored this distinction.

But the one-dimensional distinction has survived for two centuries. Pollsters still use it in labeling people by their position on a single ideological spectrum. As defined by William Maddox and Stuart Lilie in a study for the Cato Institute (*Beyond Liberal and Conservative*), this spectrum is "the extent to which government should or should not intervene in economic affairs." Without challenging the spectrum's validity, many people object to being labeled. Like some politicians, they want to appear conservative to one group and liberal to another. Besides, a "wrong" label can endanger one's status, job, or possibilities of promotion. In Washington, during the Dies-McCarthy era (1938–1954) and at some colleges many years later, Bert learned that calling someone a radical or a left-winger was a deadly form of attack. In self-protection, many radicals distinguished themselves as liberals. During the 1960s in India, Kusum witnessed the exact opposite. As she demonstrated in her master's thesis, conservatives and liberals posed as socialist revolutionaries. Calling for "total revolution" became a favorite moderate position. The label "right-winger," "capitalist," or "pro-American" could be a libel.

In trying to answer questions on how we should be labeled, we reject Bess Myerson's flippant objection to being labeled. The former Miss America was probably avoiding any serious grade labeling of herself. We prefer our own flippancy: "My heart's on the left, I write and throw with the right hand, try to use both eyes and both lobes of the brain, and my mouth (like some other vital organs) is in the middle."

More seriously, we favor good labeling for people as well as products. One cannot cope with the complexities of either without labels as guides. But labels that offer serious information! When we were very young, all one could find on a can of tomatoes was a picture and a brand name. That was before consumer movements led by people like Bess Myerson interfered with the canners' freedom to say as little as they wanted (or even to lie) about contents. Today, a typical tomato can will offer a three-dimensional list: (1) vegetable and chemical contents, (2) the relative proportions of proteins, carbohydrates, and fat, and (3) the vitamin components. Reading *Consumer Reports* to help understand the differences among automobiles, one discovers dozens of variables—each with many more than three dimensions. The human soul is infinitely more complex. We agree with Tawney's comment, quoted earlier, because we find in most people (in varying proportions) "a socialist and an individualist, an authoritarian and a fanatic for liberty." We each can say with Gandhi, "I am a Hindu, a Muslim, and a Christian." But also, we add, a Jew and a Buddhist.

"How are we to understand the nature of ourselves," asks Douglas Hofstadter (*Science Digest*, May 1985), "when we are composed of so many parts?" He then compares his internal conflicts to "a battle between opposing armies of neurally coded memories, residual atavistic fears, and ancient biological realities." We have a better metaphor. We see the human soul as a legislature in which conflicting interests—some open, many subconscious—struggle for influence. On one issue after another decisions are

made by coalitions among strange bedfellows. "Words alone," to quote
Hofstadter again, "are never rich enough to explain the subtlety of a difficult
choice." The words of the Left-Right continuum may be enough to begin
with, but they seldom take us far enough.

It has been a delight to find libertarian David Boaz of the Cato Institute
arguing that *"American ideologies are too complex to be forced into the
Procrustean bed of the liberal-conservative dichotomy."* He therefore applauds William Maddox and Stuart Lilie for adding a second dimension:
"the extent to which government should or should not regulate individual
behavior in matters of morality and conscience" (*Beyond Liberal and Conservative*), matters often described as "social issues." He also applauds James
Sundquist for adding a third dimension: foreign and military (*Dynamics of
the Party System*). Michael Marien adds a fourth axis—from centralization
to decentralization. William Irwin Thompson tries to escape the lockstep
of Western linear thought by drawing a complex circle: liberals-conserva-
tives-radicals-liberals (*The Edge of History*). Liberals and conservatives
share an interest in technology; conservatives and reactionaries, an industrial
culture; and liberals and radicals, the informational culture. Radicals and
reactionaries, finally, share "a belief in force."

These are all helpful steps on the path toward liberation from bad labeling.
Yet they can still lead to misleading oversimplifications.

In the meantime any effort at liberation from bad labeling is complicated
by changes over time. Even the best label from the past may be out of date
in the present. Many people assume that a man over seventy or a woman
over fifty, like the proverbial dog, can never learn new tricks. This is like
classifying Ronald Reagan as a liberal on domestic economic policy because
(like Bert) he voted for Roosevelt and Truman and belonged to the Americans for Democratic Action.

But for better or worse, people—unlike leopards—*do* change their spots.
Bert grew up in a Republican family, stole cookies as a child, and became
a radical, a New Dealer, a Fair Dealer, a war planner in World War II, a
"cold warrior," and a believer in détente and nonviolence. None of this
properly describes his present orientations. On economic policy his views
are far from what they were when he drafted the Full Employment Bill of
1945 or served with the Truman Council of Economic Advisers. They are
not the same as when he prepared the earlier version of the Full Employment
and Balanced Growth Act of 1978. In fact, he is now uneasy with the
concept of "full employment"—often defined by conservatives as the largest
level of politically tolerable unemployment and by liberals as the maximizing
of resource use without enough emphasis on reduced working time and
fuller opportunities for voluntary leisure. In his preface to the paperback
edition of *Friendly Fascism* (1982), he clarified a theme not properly dealt
with in the hardcover edition two years earlier: the interweaving of dominant

trends toward a manipulative and repressive corporatism ("The New Bill of Frights") with more liberating, but still subordinate, trends toward "true democracy."

Kusum's changes have been more dramatic. As a child she learned how to be a benevolent feudal aristocrat, kind to servants and proud of her accomplishments in Indian dance and music. In Edinburgh, Dublin, and London she became a Westernized Easterner. In the 1960s she started the process of becoming Americanized. In the 1970s this took the form of plunging into the formalities of "content analysis." It was not until the 1980s that she learned how to cope with the limits of what she learned about social science methodology. Coming to a Catholic liberal arts college in 1982, she was, for the first time, able to bring into the open her awareness of the importance of religion in the modern world. Only in 1984, in her "Greek Thought" seminar, did she come face to face for the first time with Homer, Thucydides, Aeschylus, Sophocles, Heraclitus, Plato, Aristotle, and Euclid. Beginning to see the Eastern roots of these "Western" giants, she began to question the traditional hard distinctions between East and West. Together with Bert, she has freed herself from superficial identification of the West with rationality and the East with mysticism. We now find the two blended together in the United States, India, and ourselves.

Today, we use the East-West dichotomy with considerable reservation. After all, these terms date back to the days of the huge European empires, when far-off places were defined in terms of how one got there from London. We are even less enamored with the American-centered use of "West" to refer to the trilateral world of the United States (with Canada), Western Europe, and Japan, and "East" to refer to the Soviet Union, its East European allies, China and other "Marxist-Leninist" countries, or both. In this process we have become American patriots. We enjoy the future orientation that has been part of this country from the birth of the republic. We love the ceaseless creativity that pushes up, like wildflowers, through the crevices of governmental, corporate, labor union, and foundation bureaucracies. We are proud of the common sense of most Americans, who often reject the snobbish elitism of top-down planners.

But our patriotism is not exclusive. With Mohandas Gandhi (whom one of us met in early childhood), we affirm that "our patriotism is inclusive and admits of no enmity or ill will." We would not hurt Russians, Cubans, Iranians, or Japanese to serve Americans. In the words of Mary Parker Follett, one of the many women whose recorded wisdom has long been ignored, "we are truly patriotic only when we are working also that American may take her place worthily and helpfully in the world of nations."

No Freedom Without Control

Freedom defeats itself if it is unlimited.

—Karl Popper, "The Paradoxes of Sovereignty"

Regulation is the connective tissue of a civilized society . . . Society needs more protection, not less.
—Susan and Martin Tolchin, *Dismantling America, The Rush to Deregulate*

Adolescents usually see freedom and control as opposites. Later, if they become parents themselves and find their freedom constrained by children, they will probably continue thinking the same way. It is only natural, then, that as mature adults facing moral, political, or economic choices, they see freedom and liberty on the happy side of a continuum. On the other: the unpleasantness of controls, regulations, tyranny, despotism, or even slavery.

Coming to maturity in India during the last days of the liberation movement, Kusum accepted this dichotomy as natural. Growing up in a family of conservative Jewry, Bert learned that "we, too, were slaves in the land of Egypt" and celebrated the Exodus from bondage to freedom.

Liberation *from* this dichotomy took much longer. In Karl Popper's seminar Kusum first heard about "the paradox of sovereignty": that freedom can *be* freedom only if it is limited. Otherwise, the freedom of a powerful few would undermine the freedom of everybody else. Back in India, she welcomed the Nehru government's actions to limit the freedoms of India's royalty—despite the consequences suffered by her family.

As a New Deal and Fair Deal activist Bert came to a similar conclusion. He saw various government controls as necessry to free the "common man" from being ripped off by "Economic Bourbons." During World War II he saw the control of profiteering as essential to winning the war against fascist tyranny. In other words, no freedom without control. In studying organizational behavior he learned that centralized controls can only be effective when there are enough decentralized freedoms. He found that when decentralized field offices enjoyed more freedom from central control, they could exercise more control over their own subordinates. Similarly, overcentralized controls, as in Stalin-type planning, could have the unanticipated result of promoting random, free-for-all activity—even to the point of chaos—in the implementation of plans. In other words, no control without resistance and unpredictable outcomes.

Still later, the two of us dropped the dichotomy itself. Our first step was to use, instead, the image of a triangle (or trichotomy). This was prompted by researchers who classified small-group leaders as one of three "ideal types":

- authoritarians, would-be tyrants who give little or no freedom to subordinates, or
- democrats, who encourage participation and spontaneity but exercise authority in a responsible and accountable fashion, or
- laissez-faire leaders, who refrain from exercising authority and allow people to do as they please.

In her researches on political leadership by Gandhi and Mao, Kusum found this ideal-type schema helpful as a starter. But it proved ridiculous to place either of those two leaders in one of the three boxes. It made more sense to think of authoritarian, democratic, and laissez-faire styles of leadership as elements that combine in varying proportions. Thus at any one time a leader may bring all three qualities together in a unique synthesis. At different times the structure of this synthesis must change. Thus, to free himself from certain responsibilities of Congress party leadership, Gandhi would become more laissez-faire. To draw reluctant peasants or intellectuals into the Communist party, Mao would become more democratic. Is not the task of analysis, then, similar to that of a chemist? Since leadership is a synthesis of many factors, why not find out what they are? And then try to estimate their relative proportions?

Thus, with first letters used as symbols, we could get this:

$$\text{Gandhi: } D_4A_2L_2$$

$$\text{Mao: } D_2A_5L_1$$

Thinking of elements that combine in varying proportions has many advantages (although nobody can exactly identify, let alone measure, the elements of human behavior). Thus, although water (H_2O) and peroxide (H_2O_2) are both composed of hydrogen and oxygen, the difference between them is vast. One is well advised not to drink the latter. This helps to explain how the similarities between Gandhi and Mao in some respects are fully consistent with their more obvious differences in other respects.

Liberation from dichotomies and ideal types also helps to solve this semantic paradox: *One is free to the extent that one has power to control one's destiny.* Any person's freedom requires controls placed on others, whether by law or by custom. More than this! Freedom is embedded in control. To put it another way, freedom is part of a complex compound that includes elements of both control and the more unpredictable (sometimes chaotic) actions associated with laissez-faire.

Planning under Freedom

The ability to foresee and plan ahead . . . is the first essential prerequisite of freedom.
—Bronislaw Malinowski, *Freedom and Civilization*

If we wish freedom to be safeguarded, then we must demand that the policy of unlimited economic freedom be replaced by the planned economic intervention of the state.

—Karl Popper, "The Paradoxes of Sovereignty"

Toward the end of World War II a fierce debate erupted on freedom and postwar planning. National planning for full employment, thundered the

Austrian free-market economist Friedrich Hayek in *The Road to Serfdom*, would lead to fascism. Herman Finer counterattacked with the charge that Hayek's advice would lead Western democracies down "The Road to Reaction." In *Freedom under Planning* Barbara Wootton argued this way: "There is nothing in the conscious planning of domestic priorities which is inherently incompatible with the freedoms which mean most to the contemporary Englishman or American. . . . A happy and fruitful marriage between freedom and planning can, in short, be arranged." "Planning for freedom," she argued, would guarantee the marriage's success.

Hayek responded skeptically: "We have 'planners for freedom' who promise us . . . not the freedom of the members of society but the unlimited freedom of the planner to do with society what he pleases." Planning for freedom, he argued, would serve all members of society only if it were planning *for*, not *against*, competition.

For twenty years or so we responded to this debate in We-They terms. Wootton and Finer were members of the angelic We who supported Roosevelt and Nehru in their efforts to remedy the injustices of uncontrolled competition and market anarchy. Hayek was the *guru* of the devilish They who were upholding the unlimited freedom of powerful business planners (in India, the "monopoly houses"; in the United States, the "Economic Bourbons") to do with society what they pleased.

More recently, we have found some good among the devils and evil among the angels. We see cogency in Hayek's views (despite his extremist formulations) on the merits of market competition. Like him, we now see serious dangers in centralized government planning.

While still admiring Wootton's lucidity and Finer's passion, we find them both guilty of too much trust in "brain trusts." We cannot accept Finer's bland reliance on formal democratic machinery to protect constitutional capitalism against dictatorial tendencies by statist planners. When Wootton defines freedom as the capacity to do what one wants, we find that childish. It is also dangerous.

With Hayek, we now favor national economic planning for market competition. But we do not see planning and competition as either-ors. To compete successfully, individuals and companies must plan for themselves. They have to rely on government planning of social, monetary, fiscal, and military policies. And to plan for competition, government planners must not only protect nongovernment planning. They must establish firm controls against the excesses of economic competition.

With Wootton and Finer, we favor planning for freedom. This means many constraints over the freedom "to do what one wants." But we dislike "freedom under planning." Instead, we favor *planning under freedom*— planning subordinated to having political and economic freedoms more widely available.

The Most Sublime Ideal

For your information, let me ask you a question.

—Sam Goldwyn

> What art thou, Freedom?
> For the labourer thou art bread...
> To the rich thou art a check...
> Thou art Justice...Thou art Wisdom...
> Thou art Peace...Thou art Love...
> Science, Poetry and Thought
> Are thy lamps...
>
> —Percy Bysshe Shelley, "The Mask of Anarchy"

"Why?" asks the child. "Because," answers the impatient parent. "Why because?" the child responds. "Because I say so!" "Why do you say so?" So it goes...until, with "maturity," the questioning is turned off, or people learn not to question authority.

"Why should I do battle with my blood kin?" Arjuna asks Krishna. Kusum remembers her mother in daily prayers reciting this opening verse from the Geeta. More recently, she learned the essence of Krishna's answer: the main struggle between Good and Evil takes place within opposing tendencies in one's own soul and family.

Bert remembers asking at Passover, "How does this night differ from all other nights?" He learned that there was something more to answer than remembering the Exodus from slavery in Egypt: getting the *torah*, the LAW.

Later, we learned to question the motives of those who used "freedom" or "liberty" as coverups for tyranny or anarchy. We cannot forget the Nazi's bloody efforts to free Germany from "Marxism" and make the world *Judenrein*—"Free of Jews." We observed the struggles of private and public employers (including college administrators) to get a *union-free* environment. We found some of our best friends thinking of freedom as atomistic individualism. We saw people insert after the words "freedom to" almost *any* verb in the dictionary and after "freedom from" almost any noun.

Only in the past year have we come to appreciate the wisdom in Malinowski's vision of freedom as an "ideal which throughout the history of civilization has inspired the most sublime philosophies and creeds." We now seek a vision for our time. Having long seen poetic vision in Popper's philosophic prose, we now see philosophical vision in Shelley's poetry. Shelley's expansive vision—freedom as Justice, Wisdom, Peace, and Love, lit by Science and Poetry and Thought—is one way to start answering our questions. His glowing abstractions also come down to earthy issues found in few other poems. In addition to advocating controls in the name of Justice (his "check" to the rich meant control, not a bank draft), Shelley speaks out on behalf of parliamentary reform, law, and—long before Mohandas Gandhi—the self-control of nonviolence in militant resistance to tyranny.

We have found another dimension (or element) in Cicero's ancient words "Freedom is participation in power." This links the two great ideals of freedom and democracy. It helps us to relate democratic freedom to the structure of power in a family, organization, neighborhood, or nation. In any of these groups, as later observed by Malinowski, "democracy is freedom in action."

Malinowski broadens our view still further. He characterizes security as "freedom from fear," prosperity as "freedom from want," justice as "the balancing and portioning out of freedoms," and the pursuit of happiness as "freedom in terms of human needs and their satisfactions." He emphasizes freedom of conscience, religion, speech, teaching, persuasion, research, cultural creativity, cultural enjoyment, and even free time (leisure) and free association. He then brings it all together by observing that his kind of freedom is nourished by "those cultural conditions under which individuals and groups mature their purposes, execute them efficiently and reap the benefits of their labors." To this, he adds that "the concept of freedom must always be referred to the increase in range, diversity and power in human planning."

Too much? Indeed, for those whose gaze into the future is narrowed by one- or two-dimensional thinking. And far too much for the many futurists who abstract themselves from the moral values of freedom, justice, wisdom, and love. But much too little for us.

We want to add a vision of our own. Suddenly, Cicero, Shelley, Malinowski, and Popper appear in our study. After arguing for a while about freedom, they come to a general agreement; their kind of freedom requires *a seamless web of mutually constraining rights and responsibilities*. Then each gives his own interpretation.

"If I enjoy rights or privileges," Cicero begins, "then I must accept some responsibilities or duties—and one of these is to respect the rights of others." Shelley urges that the web of rights and responsibilities be concretized in "righteous laws." "Yes, planning under freedom," he asserts, "but *freedom under law*." For Malinowski, righteous law is enforceable only to the extent that "ethical values and norms are woven into the web of culture." That web is fragile, warns Popper. "It will be ripped to pieces unless we learn to care more for each other." He quotes Hillel the Elder: "If I am only for myself, who am I?" and "What is hateful to you, do not unto your neighbor."

These are fine responses to questions seldom asked. In these final frenetic years of a technocratic century, few people stop to propound Shelley's old query. If they ask it, they may not stay for an answer. If an answer comes, they may be too busy to listen. If they listen, they may not understand. If they understand, they may accept it too meekly. . . .

For us, "What art thou, Freedom?" is a question that deserves to be asked anew every year and in every generation. It could be a stimulating challenge to futurists willing to escape technocratic traps and engage in the adventure of continuous learning.

Learning, of course, means change—change in ideas, in skills, or in values. As we continue our own adventures in learning, we often wonder who we shall be by the year 2000. Although we both intend to be here at that time, we are sure of only one thing—that we shall not be the same people who wrote these words.

PECOS RIVER MEDITATION

When I was asked to contribute to this anthology, I doubted that I could make the necessary effort to consult my deepest self to produce anything that would do justice to the question "What have I learned?" Later, I realized that the following piece of "not-prose," written after communing deeply with dear friends in New Mexico, was about the best answer I could give at this stage of my life.

Lovers of learning
And all life
Ponder meaning, over steaming cappuccino
Wafting cinnamon
And smooth cream.
Chill snow
Dusting the bright spring morning
In ancient pueblo country
Heart of the Land
Of the Eagle.

What high purpose
Gives deepest meaning to their lives?
Teacher? Learner? Enabler?
Just helping others along?
Lover! Why not say it plain!
Perhaps such candor might offend,
Misconstrued by those in cultures
Which blind people
To their own divinity.

All life is sacred.
Truth that loses its meaning
In a welter of high-tech toys,
Trendy tricks and

Counterfeit spirituality.
Yet each one of us is sacred still,
Holy children of Gaia's love
And teeming plenitude.
How deep, deep we now much reach
To find our
Inner glory.

Blest are those who find special ones
With whom to share the search.
Even as we see the love in
Every one we meet
In every stone and flower
Of the great creation
Still the warmth and comfort
Of each other,
Communing together
In awe and celebration,
Loving the magic, the dreams, the faith,
Is pure benediction.

How best to communicate these meanings?
And the essence of the journey?
"The Hero's Journey," we are told.
Sounds a pompous note?
Separating us from mother's blood,
Soil, trees,
Pots and blankets,
Toys, and
Sacred babies' diapers.

"The Lover's Journey"
Feels better for life's daily round
Of Holiness,
Each task performed
With mindfulness
Each encounter with friend, lover,
Vendor, passer-by,
A pious opportunity.
This loving impulse,
Born anew each day, each generation,
Is the sacred core
Of all sects and cults.
The Golden Rule, Mythic wisdom.
Cultural DNA encoding all our learning,
Distilling all our prayers.

Life's Lovers
Glean the images of history
For universal themes.

Archetypes that can symbolize
The sacred understandings in
Friendly garb and metaphor.
What deeply-known roles
Can the players don
To help reduce the strife,
Re-weave the patterns that bind us all
Within the wheel of life?

Trader, builder, host,
Juggler, jester, scribe,
Artist, musician, hunter,
Poet, farmer, weaver, or gypsy-nomad,
Bearer of strange treasures from afar?
All can bring messages of light
More palatable than those in haughty masks.
King, guru, sage,
Orator, emperor, warrior chief
In horns and antlers
All lead by power and fear,
Dimming each soul's sacred flame,
Creating only dependency and shame.

Lovers lead gently, by attraction
No longer to capture females or DNA,
No longer to give birth to many young,
But to nurture each other,
To make a difference with their sacred lives,
To weigh in on evolution's side.
No longer impaled on sad crosses
Of guilt,
But singing and dancing the songs within
Their souls
And celebrating art!

Lovers always recognize each other
And all who share such meanings.
Beyond all roles, garbs, and many-hued
Disguises.
Lovers with high purposes
May also choose kingly roles,
Accepting karmic risks of leadership.
Some pure souls may don the mask of "success."
Others prefer to flit as butterflies,
Tuning, blending, sharing energies.
All keeping faith mid unlikely scenes,
Honeycombed industrial hives,
Corporate ranches mushrooming
In holy-snow-capped wilderness.

When all remember they are lovers
Then all places are sacred once again,
Each red pepper drying in the sun,
Each seed of corn,
Sweet-smelling cedars flanking
The peaceful stream.
The spirit of all things is in the brisk, chill wind,
The untidy, boisterous dogs,
The winter-coated, sweating horses.

Sacredness is everywhere.
From the lonely pueblo ruins,
To mysterious dugouts, black pots
Lost on sandy isles,
Amid tangled seagrape and diving waterbirds.
Neither is sacredness the province
Of antiquity, or any age.
Each time and culture offers us its gems
Even our own "post-industrial era."
It is for us to seek the treasure,
Even here and now,
To see the beauty in this too,
Amid the strutting "information age,"
The nuclear nightmare.

Lovers always seek and find the grail
Anew in every time and place
To show the truth that art is everywhere.
In beads and shells,
Weavings, pots and purses,
In all the subtle rituals and little things,
In healthy meals,
In warm-fleshed human intimacy,
The highs and lows of daily lives.
No rose without the sacred shit
On which it thrives,
The chaos out of which
All forms are born.

The grail is in ourselves.
Verbs are truth,
Nouns sometimes mislead.
If all things are sacred,
Then, at last,
Each lover's inner light
And reverence
Shine forth.

—Pecos River Conference Center,
Santa Fe, New Mexico, March 1985

SELECTED BIBLIOGRAPHY

This listing of books includes the major works, then and now, of the *What I Have Learned* authors and the modern "classics" of futures thinking recommended by the authors and the editors.

Anshen, Ruth Nanda (ed.). *Beyond Victory*. New York: Harcourt, Brace, 1943.

Ayres, Robert U. *Technological Forecasting and Long-range Planning*. New York: McGraw-Hill, 1969.

Baier, Kurt, and Nicholas Rescher (eds.). *Values and the Future*. New York: Free Press, 1969.

Barnet, Richard J. *The Lean Years: Politics in the Age of Scarcity*. New York: Simon & Schuster, 1980.

Barney, Gerald O. *The Global 2000 Report to the President: Entering the Twenty-First Century*, 3 vols. Elmsford, N.Y.: Pergamon Press, 1980.

Bell, Daniel (ed.). *Toward the Year 2000: Work in Progress*. Boston: Houghton Mifflin, 1968. (Report of the Commission on the Year 2000, first published in *Daedalus*, Summer 1967.)

———. *The Coming of Post-industrial Society: A Venture in Social Forecasting*. New York: Basic Books, 1973.

———. *The Cultural Contradictions of Capitalism*. New York: Basic Books, 1976.

Boucher, Wayne I. (ed.). *The Study of the Future: An Agenda for Research*. Washington, D.C.: National Science Foundation, 1977.

Boulding, Kenneth E. *The Image: Knowledge in Life and Society*. Ann Arbor: University of Michigan Press, 1956.

———. *The Meaning of the Twentieth Century: The Great Transition*. New York: Harper & Row, 1964.

———. *Ecodynamics: A New Theory of Societal Evolution*. Beverly Hills, Calif.: Sage Publications, 1978.

———. *Stable Peace*. Austin: University of Texas Press, 1978.

———. *Human Betterment*. Beverly Hills, Calif.: Sage Publications, 1985.

———. *The World as a Total System*. Beverly Hills, Calif.: Sage Publications, 1985.

Brown, Harrison. *The Challenge of Man's Future*. New York: Viking Press, 1954.

Brown, Harrison, James Bonner, and John Wier. *The Next Hundred Years*. New York: Viking Press, 1957.

Brown, Lester R. *World Without Borders*. New York: Random House, 1972.

———. *Building a Sustainable Society*. New York: W. W. Norton, 1981.

Brown, Lester R. et al. *State of the World 1984: A Worldwatch Institute Report on Progress Toward a Sustainable Society*. New York: W. W. Norton, 1984. (First of an annual series.)

Brzezinski, Zbigniew. *Between Two Ages: America's Role in the Technetronic Era*. New York: Viking Press, 1970.

Chase, Stuart. *The Tragedy of Waste*. New York: Macmillan, 1925.

———. *A New Deal*. New York: Macmillan, 1932.

———. *The Most Probable World*. New York: Harper & Row, 1968.

Clarke, Arthur C. *Profiles of the Future*. New York: Harper & Row, 1962; 1973 (revised); Holt, Rinehart and Winston, 1984.

Coates, Vary T. *Technology Assessment in Federal Agencies*. Washington, D.C.: National Science Foundation, 1972.

Coates, Vary T., and Bernard Finn. *A Retrospective Technology Assessment: Submarine Telegraphy and the Trans-Atlantic Cable of 1866*. San Francisco: San Francisco Press, 1982.

Cornish, Edward. *The Study of the Future: An Introduction to the Art and Science of Understanding and Shaping Tomorrow's World*. Bethesda, Md.: World Future Society, 1977.

Dator, James A. "Neither There Nor Then: A Eutopian Alternative to the Development Model of Future Society," in *Human Futures: Needs, Societies, Technologies*. Guildford, Surrey, U.K.: IPC Science and Technology Press, 1974, pp. 87–140.

Dator, James A., and Clement Bezold (eds.). *Judging the Future*. Honolulu: University of Hawaii, Social Science Research Institute, 1981.

Dator, James A., and Magoroh Maruyama (eds.). *Human Futuristics*. Honolulu: University of Hawaii, Social Science Research Institute, 1972.

de Jouvenel, Bertrand. *The Art of Conjecture*. New York: Basic Books, 1967.

Dror, Yehezkel. *Public Policymaking Reexamined*. San Francisco: Chandler Publishing Co., 1968; New Brunswick, N.J.: Transaction Books, 1983 (with new introduction).

———. *Policymaking Under Adversity*. New Brunswick, N.J.: Transaction Books, 1986.

Drucker, Peter F. *America's Next Twenty Years*. New York: Harper & Bros., 1955.

———. *The Age of Discontinuity: Guidelines to Our Changing Society*. New York: Harper & Row, 1969.

Ellul, Jacques. *The Technological Society*. New York: Alfred A. Knopf, 1964.

Etzioni, Amitai. *The Active Society: A Theory of Societal and Political Processes*. New York: Free Press, 1968.

———. *An Immodest Agenda: Rebuilding America Before the 21st Century*. New York: McGraw-Hill, 1982.

Falk, Richard A. *A Study of Future Worlds*. New York: Free Press, 1975.

Ferkiss, Victor. *Technological Man: The Myth and the Reality*. New York: George Braziller, 1969.

———. *The Future of Technological Civilization*. New York: George Braziller, 1974.

————. *Futurology: Promise, Performance, Prospects.* The Washington Papers, No. 50. Beverly Hills, Calif.: Sage Publications, 1977.

Fowles, Jib (ed.) *Handbook of Futures Research.* Westport, Conn.: Greenwood Press, 1978.

Francoeur, Robert T. *Evolving World, Converging Man.* New York: Holt, Rinehart & Winston, 1970.

————. *Utopian Motherhood: New Trends in Human Reproduction.* New York: Doubleday, 1970; Cranbury, N.J.: A. S. Barnes, 2nd ed. 1974; 3rd ed. 1975.

————. *Eve's New Rib: 20 Faces of Sex, Marriage and Family.* New York: Harcourt Brace Jovanovich, 1972.

————. *Biomedical Ethics: A Guide to Decision Making.* New York: John Wiley & Sons, 1983.

Francoeur, Robert T., and Anna K. Francoeur. *Hot and Cool Sex: Cultures in Conflict.* New York: Harcourt Brace Jovanovich, 1974.

Gabor, Dennis. *Inventing the Future.* New York: Alfred A. Knopf, 1964.

Galtung, Johan. *The True Worlds: A Transnational Perspective.* New York: Free Press, 1980.

Gershuny, Jonathan. *After Industrial Society?* Atlantic Highlands, N.J.: Humanities Press, 1978.

Gordon, Theodore J. *The Future.* New York: St. Martin's Press, 1965.

Gross, Bertram. *The Managing of Organizations,* 2 vols. New York: Free Press, 1964.

————. *The State of the Nation: Social Systems Accounting.* London: Tavistock Publications, 1966.

————. *Friendly Fascism: The New Face of Power in America.* New York: M. Evans, 1980; Boston: South End Press, 1982.

————. (ed.). *A Great Society?* New York: Basic Books, 1968.

————. (ed.). *Political Intelligence for America's Future.* Boston: Allyn & Bacon, 1970.

Harman, Willis W. *An Incomplete Guide to the Future.* New York: W. W. Norton, 1979.

Hawken, Paul, James Ogilvy, and Peter Schwartz. *Seven Tomorrows: Toward a Voluntary History.* New York: Bantam Books, 1982.

Heilbroner, Robert L. *The Future as History.* New York: Harper & Bros., 1960.

————. *An Inquiry into the Human Prospect.* New York: W. W. Norton, 1974; 1980 (updated edition).

Helmer, Olaf. *Social Technology.* New York: Basic Books, 1966.

————. *Looking Forward: A Guide to Futures Research.* Beverly Hills, Calif.: Sage Publications, 1983.

Henderson, Hazel. *Creating Alternative Futures: The End of Economics.* New York: Berkeley Publishing Corp., 1978.

————. *The Politics of the Solar Age: Alternatives to Economics.* Garden City, N.Y.: Anchor Press/Doubleday, 1981.

Hoos, Ida R. *Systems Analysis in Public Policy: A Critique.* Berkeley: University of California Press, 1972; 1983 (with new introduction).

Hughes, Barry B. *World Futures: A Critical Analysis of Alternatives.* Baltimore, Md.: The Johns Hopkins University Press, 1985.

Jungk, Robert, and Johan Galtung (eds.). *Mankind 2000.* London: Allen & Unwin, 1971.

Kahn, Herman. *The Coming Boom: Economic, Political, and Social.* New York: Simon & Schuster, 1982.

Kahn, Herman, William Brown, and Leon Martel. *The Next 200 Years: A Scenario For America and the World.* New York: William Morrow, 1976.

Kahn, Herman, and B. Bruce-Briggs. *Things to Come: Thinking about the Seventies and Eighties.* New York: Macmillan, 1972.

Kahn, Herman, and Anthony J. Wiener. *The Year 2000: A Framework for Speculation on the Next Thirty-three Years.* New York: Macmillan, 1967.

Laszlo, Ervin. *Goals for Mankind: A Report to the Club of Rome.* New York: E. P. Dutton, 1977.

Laszlo, Ervin, and Jong Youl Yoo (eds.). *The World Encyclopedia of Peace.* Elmsford, N.Y.: Pergamon Press, 1986.

Linstone, Harold A. *Multiple Perspectives for Decision-Making: Bridging the Gap between Analysis and Action.* New York: North Holland/Elsevier, 1984.

Linstone, Harold A., and Devendra Sahal (eds.). *Technological Substitution: Forecasting Techniques and Applications.* New York: American Elsevier, 1976.

Linstone, Harold A., and W. H. Clive Simmonds (eds.). *Futures Research: New Directions.* Reading, Mass.: Addison-Wesley, 1977.

Linstone, Harold A., and Murray Turoff (eds.). *The Delphi Method: Techniques and Applications.* Reading, Mass.: Addison-Wesley, 1975.

McHale, John. *The Future of the Future.* New York: George Braziller, 1969.

———. *The Ecological Context.* New York: George Braziller, 1970.

———. *World Facts and Trends.* New York: Collier Books, 1972.

———. *The Changing Information Environment.* Boulder, Colo.: Westview, 1976.

McHale, John, and Magda Cordell McHale. *Basic Human Needs: A Framework for Action.* New Brunswick, N.J.: Transaction Books, 1978.

Marien, Michael. *Alternative Futures for Learning: An Annotated Bibliography of Trends, Forecasts, and Proposals.* Syracuse, N.Y.: Educational Policy Research Center, 1971.

———. *Societal Directions and Alternatives: A Critical Guide to the Literature.* LaFayette, N.Y.: Information for Policy Design, 1976.

———. *Future Survey Annual 1979: A Guide to the Recent Literature of Trends, Forecasts, and Policy Proposals.* Bethesda, Md.: World Future Society, 1980. (Other editions in this series published 1982, 1983, 1984, 1985, 1986.)

Markley, O. W., and Willis W. Harman (eds.). *Changing Images of Man.* Elmsford, N.Y.: Pergamon Press, 1982.

Martino, Joseph P. *Technological Forecasting for Decision Making.* New York: Elsevier/North Holland, 1972; 2nd ed., 1983.

———. (ed.). *An Introduction to Technological Forecasting.* The Futurist Library, Vol. 1. New York: Gordon & Breach Science Publishers, 1972.

Mead, Margaret. *Continuities in Cultural Evolution.* The Terry Lectures. New Haven, Conn.: Yale University Press, 1964.

———. *Culture and Commitment: A Study of the Generation Gap.* New York: Doubleday/Natural History Press, 1970.

———. *World Enough: Rethinking the Future.* Boston: Little, Brown, 1975.

Meadows, Donella H., Dennis L. Meadows, Jorgen Randers, and William W. Behrens III. *The Limits to Growth.* New York: Universe Books, 1972.

Meadows, Donella H., John Richardson, and Gerhart Bruckmann. *Groping in the*

Dark: The First Decade of Global Modelling. New York: John Wiley & Sons, 1982.

Meadows, Donella H., and J. M. Robinson. *The Electronic Oracle: Computer Models and Social Decisions.* New York: John Wiley & Sons, 1985.

Michael, Donald N. *Proposed Studies on the Implications of Peaceful Space Activities for Human Affairs.* Washington, D.C.: The Brookings Institution, 1961.

———. *Cybernation: The Silent Conquest.* Santa Barbara, Calif.: Center for the Study of Democratic Institutions, 1962.

———. *The Next Generation: The Prospects Ahead for the Youth of Today and Tomorrow.* New York: Random House, 1965.

———. *The Unprepared Society: Planning for a Precarious Future.* New York: Basic Books, 1968; Harper & Row Colophon, 1970.

———. *On Learning to Plan—and Planning to Learn: The Social Psychology of Changing Toward Future-Responsive Societal Learning.* San Francisco: Jossey-Bass, 1973.

Muller, Herbert J. *The Children of Frankenstein: A Primer on Modern Technology and Human Values.* Bloomington: Indiana University Press, 1970.

———. *Uses of the Future.* Bloomington: Indiana University Press, 1974.

Platt, John. *The Step to Man.* New York: John Wiley & Sons, 1966.

Polak, Fred L. *The Image of the Future,* 2 vols. New York: Oceana Publications, 1961; San Francisco: Jossey-Bass/Elsevier, 1973 (abridged and translated by Elise Boulding).

———. *Prognostics: A Science in the Making Surveys and Creates the Future.* Amsterdam: Elsevier, 1971.

President's Research Committee on Social Trends. *Recent Social Trends in the United States,* 2 vols. New York: McGraw-Hill, 1933.

Schumacher, E. F. *Small Is Beautiful: Economics as If People Mattered.* New York: Harper & Row, 1973.

Schwarz, Brita, Uno Svedin, and Bjorn Wittrock. *Methods in Future Studies: Problems and Applications.* Boulder, Colo.: Westview, 1982.

Simon, Julian L., and Herman Kahn (eds.). *The Resourceful Earth: A Response to Global 2000.* New York: Basil Blackwell, 1984.

Taviss (Thomson), Irene (ed.). *The Computer Impact.* Englewood Cliffs, N.J.: Prentice-Hall, 1970.

Taviss (Thomson), Irene, Everett Mendelsohn, and Judith Swazey (eds.). *Human Aspects of Biomedical Innovation.* Cambridge, Mass.: Harvard University Press, 1971.

Taviss (Thomson), Irene (ed.). *Our Tool-Making Society.* Englewood Cliffs, N.J.: Prentice-Hall, 1972.

Theobald, Robert. *Habit and Habitat.* Englewood Cliffs, N.J.: Prentice-Hall, 1972.

———. *Avoiding 1984: Moving Toward Interdependence.* Athens, Ohio: Swallow Press/Ohio University Press, 1982.

———. (ed.). *The Guaranteed Income.* Garden City, N.Y.: Doubleday, 1966.

———. (ed.). *Futures Conditional.* Indianapolis: Bobbs-Merrill, 1972.

Toffler, Alvin. *Future Shock.* New York: Random House, 1970.

———. *The Eco-Spasm Report.* New York: Bantam Books, 1975.

———. *The Third Wave.* New York: William Morrow, 1980.

———. *Previews and Premises.* New York: William Morrow, 1983.

————. (ed.). *The Futurists*. New York: Random House, 1972.

————. (ed.). *Learning for Tomorrow: The Role of the Future in Education*. New York: Random House, 1974.

Vickers, Geoffrey. *Value Systems and Social Process*. New York: Basic Books, 1968.

————. *Freedom in a Rocking Boat: Changing Values in an Unstable Society*. London: Allen Lane, 1970; Pelican, 1972.

Wagar, W. Warren. *H. G. Wells and the World State*. New Haven, Conn.: Yale University Press, 1961.

————. *The City of Man: Prophecies of a World Civilization in 20th-Century Thought*. Boston: Houghton Mifflin, 1963; Baltimore: Penguin Books, 1967.

————. *Building the City of Man: Outlines of a World Civilization*. New York: Grossman, 1971; San Francisco: W. H. Freeman, 1972.

————. *Good Tidings: The Belief in Progress from Darwin to Marcuse*. Bloomington: Indiana University Press, 1972.

————. *Terminal Visions: The Literature of Last Things*. Bloomington: Indiana University Press, 1982.

INDEX

ABOUT THE CONTRIBUTORS

KENNETH E. BOULDING is Distinguished Professor of Economics at the University of Colorado's Institute of Behavioral Science and recently served as President of the American Association for the Advancement of Science.

JOSEPH F. COATES is President of J. F. Coates, Inc., in Washington, D.C., a policy research organization specializing in the future. For the past ten years he has been an adjunct professor at the George Washington University, teaching a series of graduate courses on technology and the future. He was formerly Assistant to the Director and Head of Exploratory Research at the U.S. Congress' Office of Technology Assessment, and a program manager for the National Science Foundation's Program of Research Applied to National Needs (RANN). He is the author of more than 100 articles, papers, and publications and holds nineteen patents.

VARY T. COATES is currently a senior analyst and project director at the U.S. Congress' Office of Technology Assessment and a vice-president of J. F. Coates, Inc. She is the author of numerous papers and articles, including "The Organization and Management of Technology Assessment" (1975); "The Potential Effect of Robotics" (1983); and "Technology Assessment in Europe and Japan" (1984).

JIM DATOR is Professor of Political Science at the University of Hawaii and was a member of the Organizing Committee of the Hawaiian Governor's Conference on the Year 2000, which first met in 1969. He has long been active in the World Futures Studies Federation and was recently named Secretary-General of that organization.

AMITAI ETZIONI is University Professor of Government at George Washington University in Washington, D.C. His books include *Genetic Fix: The*

Next Technological Revolution (1973) and *An Immodest Agenda: Rebuilding America before the Twenty-First Century* (1982).

VICTOR FERKISS is Professor of Government at Georgetown University and the author of such books as *Technological Man* (1969) and *The Future of Technological Civilization* (1974).

ROBERT T. FRANCOEUR is the author of seventeen books on embryology, theology, human evolution, reproductive technologies, and the past, present, and future of human sexual relations. Since 1965 he has taught at Fairleigh Dickinson University in Madison, New Jersey, where he is currently a full professor.

BERTRAM GROSS is Distinguished Professor Emeritus, Hunter College, City University of New York, Professor of Government and Economics at St. Mary's College of California, and Visiting Professor at the University of California, Berkeley. He has visited many countries as a United Nations consultant on planning, development, management, social indicators, and budgeting. He was Executive Secretary of President Truman's Council of Economic Advisors and is currently a consultant to members of the Congressional Black Caucus. His books include *Friendly Fascism* (1980), *The State of the Nation: Social Systems Accounting* (1966), and *Political Intelligence for America's Future* (1970).

WALTER A. HAHN is Futurist-in-Residence at the George Washington University School of Government and Business Administration and former Specialist in Science, Technology, and Futures Research with the Congressional Research Service. He was the founding president of the International Society for Technology Assessment and was a founder and is currently the president of the Issues Management Association. He is the author of more than fifty books, articles, and reports.

WILLIS W. HARMAN is Associate Director of the Center for the Study of Social Policy at SRI International and was formerly Director of the now-defunct Education Policy Research Center at Stanford University. His numerous publications include *An Incomplete Guide to the Future* (1979).

HAZEL HENDERSON is the author of *Creating Alternative Futures* (1978) and *The Politics of the Solar Age: Alternatives to Economics* (1981), as well as numerous articles exploring cultural and social change in industrial societies. A frequent guest lecturer at universities, corporate executive seminars, and national organizations, she has also been active as a community organizer and public sector entrepreneur.

LANE JENNINGS is Director of Research for SAI Productions in Annapolis, Maryland, an independent television production company that specializes in futures-related documentary programming. He was Research Director of the World Future Society from 1976 to 1985 and edited *The WFS Bulletin* for seven years. He is still Production Editor for the Society's monthly abstract journal *Future Survey*.

HAROLD A. LINSTONE is University Professor and Director of the Futures Research Institute at Portland State University. He is coauthor of *The Delphi Method* (1975) and coeditor of *Futures Research: New Directions* (1977). He has edited the journal *Technological Forecasting and Social Change* since its founding in 1969.

MICHAEL MARIEN is the founder and editor of *Future Survey* and *Future Survey Annual*. He compiled *Societal Directions and Alternatives: A Critical Guide to the Literature* (1976). He has been a frequent speaker at conferences and has contributed many articles to anthologies and futures journals on topics ranging from "The Two Visions of Post-Industrial Society" (1976) to "The Transformation as Sandbox Syndrome" (1983).

JOSEPH P. MARTINO is Senior Research Scientist at the University of Dayton Research Institute and the author of *Technological Forecasting for Decisionmaking* (1972; revised 2d edition, 1983).

DONALD N. MICHAEL is Professor Emeritus of Public Policy at the University of Michigan and author of *Cybernation: The Silent Conquest* (1962), *The Next Generation* (1965), *The Unprepared Society* (1968), and *On Learning to Plan—and Planning to Learn* (1973).

KUSUM SINGH is Professor of Communications at Saint Mary's College of California and a consulting and contributing editor to the *Journal of Communication*. She was a program planner and producer for five years at All-India Radio and later a faculty member at the Administrative Staff College of India at Hyderbad. Her publications deal with the communication styles of leaders, the communication failures of planners, and policy issues in international communication. She is also joint author (with Bertram Gross) of "Democratic Planning: The Bottom-Sideways Approach," in Alan Gartner et al. (eds.), *Beyond Reagan: Alternatives for the '80s* (1984).

IRENE TAVISS THOMSON is Associate Professor of Sociology at Fairleigh Dickinson University in Madison, New Jersey. Writing as Irene Taviss, her publications include *Our Tool-Making Society* (1972). She was the editor of *The Computer Impact* (1970).

W. WARREN WAGAR is Professor of History at the State University of New York, Binghamton, and the author of such books as *The City of Man: Prophecies of a World Civilization in Twentieth-century Thought* (1963), *Building the City of Man* (1971), *Good Tidings: The Belief in Progress from Darwin to Marcuse* (1972), and *Terminal Visions: The Literature of Last Things* (1982).